God, Education, and Modern Metaphysics

The Western tradition has long held the view that while it is possible to know *that* God exists, it nevertheless remains impossible to know *what* God is. The ineffability of the monotheistic God extends to each of the Abrahamic faiths. In this volume, Tubbs considers Aristotle's logic of mastery and questions the assumptions upon which God's ineffability rests. Part I explores the tensions between the philosophical definition of the One as "thought thinking itself" (the Aristotelian concept of *noesis noeseos*) and the educational vocation of the individual as "know thyself" (*gnōthi seauton*). Identifying vulnerabilities in the logic of mastery, Tubbs puts forth an original logic of education, which he calls modern metaphysics, or a logic of learning and education. Part II explores this new educational logic of the divine as a "logic of tears," as a "dreadful religious teacher," and as a way to cohere the three Abrahamic faiths in an educational concept of monotheism.

Nigel Tubbs is professor of philosophical and educational thought at the University of Winchester, UK.

Routledge Research in Religion and Education

Series Editor:
Michael D. Waggoner,
University of Northern Iowa, USA

God, Education, and Modern Metaphysics

Metaphysics

The Logic of "Know Thyself"

Nigel Tubbs

Routledge
Taylor & Francis Group

LONDON AND NEW YORK

First published 2017 by Routledge

2 Park Square, Milton Park, Abingdon, Oxfordshire OX14 4RN
52 Vanderbilt Avenue, New York, NY 10017

Routledge is an imprint of the Taylor & Francis Group, an informa business

First issued in paperback 2018

Library of Congress Cataloguing-in-Publication Data
A catalog record for this book has been requested

ISBN: 978-0-415-74612-0 (hbk)
ISBN: 978-0-367-19427-7 (pbk)

Typeset in Sabon
by Apex CoVantage, LLC

Contents

Foreword

The opening years of the 21st century brought increased attention to religion as an important dimension of world culture and politics. The dramatic attacks of September 11, 2001, came as a jolting reminder of the potential for violent action that can have bases in religious motivations. Over the same period, we came to see an increase in religious group activity in politics. In the US we see this as an evolution from the Moral Majority movement led by televangelist Jerry Falwell that emerged as a force in the late 1970s as the beginning of the New Religious Right. On further reflection, however, we can see the involvement of religion extending much further back as a fundamental part of our social organization rather than a new or emerging phenomenon. We need only recall the religious wars of early modern Europe through to the contentious development of US church and state relations as evidence of the longstanding role religion has played as a source of competing values and beliefs. That said, there has been a significant upturn in research and scholarship across many disciplines relative to the study of religion in the last twenty-five years. This is particularly the case in the area of the interrelationships of education and religion.

While religious education—study *toward formation* in a particular faith tradition—has been with us for millennia, study *about* religion as an academic subject apart from theology is more recent. Whereas theology departments proceeded from religious assumptions aiming to promulgate a faith tradition, the religious studies field emerged as a discipline like history or sociology that sought to bring a more disinterested social scientific approach to the study of religion. The origins of this approach date back to the European research centers that influenced US scholars beginning in the 18th century. The formalization of this trend, however, is a fairly recent phenomenon as illustrated by the 1949 formation of Society for the Scientific Study of Religion with its own scholarly journal and the uptick in creation of religious studies departments across the US in the wake of the US Supreme Court decision in 1963 that encouraged teaching *about* religion (rather than *for*) in public education institutions. It was also in 1949 that the American Academy of Religion was born out of a group of scholars that had since 1909 been meeting under the various names related to biblical study.

It is out of this relatively recent increase in scholarly attention to the academic study of religion and education that this book series came to be. Routledge Publishers have long been an important presence in the respective fields of religion and of education. It seemed like a natural step to introduce a book series focused particularly on *Research in Religion and Education*. My appreciation extends to Max Novick for guiding this series into being and now to Karen Adler for continuing Routledge's oversight.

God, Education, and Modern Metaphysics is the sixth book in this series. Author Nigel Tubbs aptly situates his offering in the intent of the series noting that "The Journal [*Religion & Education*] and the Series are committed to exploring things that can happen when religious beliefs and religious cultures come in contact with educational ideas" (p. xv, in acknowledgements). His innovative contribution to the burgeoning literature of religion and education here is to argue "that God, seen in the Western tradition as *thought thinking itself* (νοησις νοησεως, *noesis noeseos*) [hereafter NN] is experienced by the individual as the educational necessity to *know thyself* (γνῶθι σεαυτόν, *gnōthi seauton*) [hereafter KT]" (p. 1). He posits that the truth of God in the Western tradition, as reflected in the ancient metaphysics of Aristotle, is grounded in a logic of mastery. That mastery is vulnerable to its own difficulties of logic. (After introducing Kierkegaard's concept of difficulties, Tubbs substitutes *aporias* as a less familiar placeholder term to assist us in detaching preconceptions from the use of difficulties as the argument moves forward.)

> In the vulnerability of mastery to its own difficulties or *aporias* of logic, there is a negation and preservation of truth which expresses itself as a logic of education. In turn, this is a logic of know thyself, and has its actuality in learning or in culture, including in religion.
>
> Clearly this asks a great deal of education, as much perhaps as was asked of it as *paideia* in Ancient Greece or as *humanism* in the European Renaissance. It asks education not only to bear the burden of retrieving God from the logic of mastery, but also to express its learning of God here as the truth of the retrieval. It asks education to find and then to speak in its own voice with its own logic and its own truth. We will come to see that this educational logic is, as Kierkegaard calls it, a new kind of contradiction. In our study of God and education, within this new contradiction and its modern metaphysics, we are commended to ask if God is not in fact to be found in education, and more challenging still, to ask if God *is* education.
>
> (p. 1)

Organized in two parts, the first part traces the ancient metaphysics of "know thyself." Part two introduces a modern metaphysics of this idea.

Professor Tubbs's work is ground breaking—a unique and provocative vision. He demands much of the reader, but the work is well rewarded. These ideas should inspire discussion and debate in classrooms and conference venues.

Michael D. Waggoner
Professor and Series Editor, *Research in Religion and Education*
Editor, *Religion & Education*

Preface

Why is the modern self-reflective mind so often offended by the idea of the religious? For Kierkegaard it was because the religion of his time was not *difficult* enough. In the age of reflective struggle, he believed Christianity had too little of both reflection and struggle. 'The problem is not to understand Christianity', he said, 'but to understand that it cannot be understood' (2004, 146). Is he right? Is such increased difficulty likely to bring the religious and the secular together in powerful new ways, especially if it disturbs some of the most fundamental assumptions carried on both sides?

There is talk of a post-secular society. But is this also a post-rational society? The reflective element of the modern mind houses the authority of reason and rejects any authority that is not grounded on Kant's challenge to think for oneself. To subject all authority to the rational thought of each individual is the cornerstone of modern freedom. Skepticism regarding all other claims to authority extends to sacred texts, to the priesthood, to revelation, and to prayer. Remarkably, perhaps, Kierkegaard saw such skepticism not as secular, but instead as the modern ground upon which religion could find a new form and relevance in the world.

The following study takes up a similar challenge. Its question is, can religion—referring specifically to the logic of God shared by the three Abrahamic faiths—be retrieved in the modern rational and reflective mind by the notion of *modern metaphysics*?[1] Can this modern metaphysics reform the concept of the religious for a modern reflective, critical, and skeptical age? Might it be able to retrieve the religious character of skepticism in an age where spirit is both religious and political, or is both God and freedom? Can modern metaphysics reform the idea of religion so that it comes to know itself in the rational spirit of modernity, and to know the truth of this as *education*?

Reason and revelation have never sat comfortably together. But Kierkegaard draws attention to their dialectical relation, saying, 'How an Apostle understands himself in having been called by a revelation and in having immediate certainty which cannot in any way be dialectical, I do not understand' (2004, 143). Kierkegaard comprehends the individual relation to God

'Socratically' (2004, 143) as the difficulty of knowing that one does not know. He is aware of the dangers and the opportunities here.

> It has constantly been maintained that reflection inevitably destroys Christianity and is its natural enemy . . . The divine authority of the Bible and all that belongs to it has been done away with; it looks as though one had only to wait for the last stage of reflection in order to have done with the whole thing. But behold, reflection performs the opposite service by once more bringing the springs of Christianity into play, and in such a way that it can stand up—against reflection . . . The struggle is a different one; up to the present it has been between reflection and simple, immediate Christianity; now it will be between reflection and simplicity armed with reflection. (2004, 146)

Simplicity, armed with reflection upon itself, is one of the ways in which the modern metaphysics of religion expresses itself. As if this is not difficult enough, in 1848 Kierkegaard calls for a hero who will retrieve Christianity by forbidding people to read the Bible. It has, he says, become necessary for Christianity to preach 'against Christianity' (2004, 150).

But modern metaphysics goes further than the Socratic (as indeed does Kierkegaard) by holding revelation and reason, simplicity and reflection, and immediacy and mediation, together *in the difficulty of their difference*. In modern metaphysics *learning* is the truth of which this difference and its difficulty speaks. If revelation is immediacy and reason is mediation of immediacy, then modern metaphysics finds here an *educational logic* which is religious and secular. When this opposition is treated as something to be overcome, as a battle to be fought and won by one side or the other, skeptics in good faith are faced with the converted, also in good faith, and each, in good faith, resists advances by the other. But modern metaphysics does not rest with this logic of overcoming. Its rationality is not offended by its religious significance, and its religiosity is not offended at the logic and rationality that express it. Immediacy and mediation are of each other in modern metaphysics. If this is absurd, then we are once again close to Kierkegaard. But if it is absurd within the ancient logic of overcoming or mastery, it is so different from the way it is absurd in the modern logic of education. In the latter, the absurd is not offensive. It is educational.

Kierkegaard notes two shapes of the reflective life. One is a childhood of immediacy, carried on into later life, with only a certain degree of reflection coming before death. The other is a childhood of dialectics, reflection, and melancholy until in old age there comes the faith that is 'immediateness after reflection' (2004, 140). Whilst Kierkegaard's own life is the second of these shapes, in the end both lives are those of individuals who are in a difficult relation to themselves while at the same time being in a difficult relation to truth. The first relation here is of the individual reflecting upon itself as its own object. This is the ancient Delphic maxim of *know thyself*. The second relation is this self-knowing measured against a notion of truth that is transcendental and ineffable, leaving the first relation of know thyself as error in relation to the perfect. For modern metaphysics, this double relation has its own logic, an educational logic, a *logic of know thyself*. It is the difficulties of such relations that Kierkegaard believed could reinvigorate both Christianity and Christendom. It is the difficulties of such relations that also constitute modern metaphysics.

Also central to Kierkegaard is the difficulty of *communicating* difficulty in ways that do not sell it short or relieve difficulty in the communicating of it. A direct method of communication does not preserve the difficulty, for it is, as it were, merely shot from a pistol. An indirect method of communicating, for example by maieutic or pseudonym, is better at creating difficulty, by making one aware of one's delusions. But Kierkegaard believes that the maieutic, or the indirect communication of the Socratic method, is still not enough. It creates difficulty but is unable to preserve this difficulty as its own truth. As such, says Kierkegaard, the communication of religion's difficulties requires that its communicators bear witness to such difficulty. Kierkegaard's own writing is a record of him trying to do this, to bear witness to the difficulties of self-relation and its relation to truth, both of which, appearing to be Socratic, are also divine. The challenge, as always for Kierkegaard, is 'to understand himself in existence' (Kierkegaard, 1992, 351) and at the same time to live in the struggle of 'existing in what one understands' (1992, 274).

Even more difficult than the question of how to communicate difficulty—a question relevant to all teachers—is the question of how to begin with difficulty. It is more difficult because this question is also difficult and appears prior to any knowledge of how to work with difficulty or how to communicate difficulty. In fact, what the question reveals is that difficulty already begins with difficulty, or with itself. This offers the strange idea that difficulty appears by presupposing itself, or (to borrow another of Kierkegaard's expressions that will feature again in Part 2) that difficulty so comes into the world that by the fact that it is, it is already presupposed. The presupposition of difficulty *is* difficulty.

If we can go so far as to call this both a logic of presupposition as difficulty, and a logic of difficulty as presupposition, then we might say that the components of this logic are first, that difficulty undermines/negates everything else that presupposes itself to be true; second, that difficulty also undermines/negates any presupposition that difficulty is true, and third, that by undermining/negating itself difficulty also preserves itself. Can this be a logic of difficulty as negation and preservation? If so, can it be the truth not just of how difficulty begins, but also the truth of how everything begins, i.e., within difficulty? The religious significance of this is its relation to the question of creation, or of *the* beginning. Is the answer to the question 'How is the universe created?' that it is created in the logic of the difficulty of its own presupposition, that is, created in the preservation of its negation? If so, the universe is not created as a fact, but as a question, and as its own difficulty.

Modern metaphysics has the vocation to work with this strange logic of difficulty and presupposition, and with its component parts, negation and preservation. But modern metaphysics understands this logic in a very specific way. It sees negation and preservation as the *logic of education*, as the process or culture of learning, and as the template of self-knowing or *know thyself*. This is explored now in the following pages. As we suggested, it is only a short step from here to the idea that the creation of the universe is known to us as the difficulty of the question of its beginning, suggesting a universe created in and as education and learning. In addition, might such education and learning be the truth not just of creation but also of a creator? Is God known, and known absolutely, in and as the difficulty and the love of learning?

Kierkegaard is close to us again here. The dilemma for the individual, he says, is that 'between God and man there is a struggle' (2004, 152). Faced with this struggle, the individual can choose either obedience to God and against man, such that one loves man in God, or choose man against God, humanizing God and finding God in man. Both decisions eschew the difficulty of the beginning. It always seems as if 'one had first of all to have [either] doctrine in perfect form before one could begin to live—that is to say, one never begins' (2004, 150).

Living the truth of such difficulty requires space to be made in areas that are already completely filled up by presuppositions of doctrines that resolve the question of beginnings. As we saw above, 'The problem is not to understand Christianity but to understand that it cannot be understood' (2004, 146). In this sentence, Kierkegaard employs two logics at the same time.[2] The first 'understand' and the final 'understood' are of the logic of direct communication, or of mastery, or of the logic in which understanding is the overcoming of difficulty. The middle 'understand' is the logic of absurdity, of creating and preserving the difficulty by knowing it in such a way as to not overcome it or resolve it. For modern metaphysics, this is a logic of education, a logic of know thyself, and is the modern metaphysical notion of God and freedom.

There is one further difficulty here that commends itself as a beginning. Just how much difficulty does one have to be in to write a logic of difficulty? Even if the logic holds, is this author not compromised by one simple fact? I have not sold all I have and given the money to the poor. This issue remains a difficulty within difficulty, much like the observation that the poor will be with us always . . .

Notes

1. The logic of God in Islam and Judaism are directly discussed in chapters 3 and 8 below.
2. Kierkegaard differentiates 'understanding' in *The Sickness unto Death* (see Kierkegaard, 1954, 221–7).

Acknowledgments

My thanks go primarily to my editor, Mike Waggoner. Mike received a paper from me in 2012 for the journal *Religion and Education*. He saw something in it which he suggested might be suitable for further and deeper development and offered the opportunity to write a book for the series *Routledge Research in Religion and Education*. I hope that my attempt to explore religion and education within modern metaphysics does justice to the faith he has shown in me and in the project. The journal, and the series, are committed to exploring things that can happen when religious beliefs and religious cultures come in contact with educational ideas. Within this brief I have tried to explore what happens when religion and education can be seen to be one shared truth. But I am aware that my writing is often seen as 'difficult'. Where this is to do justice to the nature of the ideas being expressed I try to serve this difficulty as best I can. Where the difficulties are due to my weaknesses as a writer and an educator, then the faults are my own.

I also wish to thank those people who sustain mind and body through long spells of work and the isolation it brings: Derek, Jess, Tom, and Elina in the Modern Liberal Arts team at Winchester; Rowan, whose support for our project at Winchester means so much to me, to the tutors, and to the students; Howard, as always; Hazel, Denise, and Victoria, the wise women of the village who understand the point of health; and Simon and Christina for food and hospitality of the very best kind on the blue island. But above all, I have to thank Rebekah who, often at great cost, offers unstinting support to me and to the larger vision of the work. It is to her that I dedicate this book. Her 'faith in education' is an inspiration.

Finally, *in memoriam* Mike Harcourt-Brown, my good neighbour; *rest in peace, Mike.*

1 Introduction

The idea being tested in *God, Education and Modern Metaphysics* is that God, seen in the Western tradition as *thought thinking itself* (νοησις νοησεως, *noesis noeseos*) [hereafter NN], is experienced by the individual as the educational necessity to *know thyself* (γνῶθι σεαυτόν, *gnōthi seauton*) [hereafter KT]. In exploring God and education, we will not be taking either of them for granted. Instead, it is the very question of their presupposition that concerns us, and which we rehearse briefly now.

The truth of NN in the Western tradition is grounded in a logic of mastery. This mastery is the logic of the One, or of monotheism. The One is the most simple form to which the explanation of the cause of everything can be reduced. Everything derivative of the One is deemed to be imperfect by comparison, ensuring that to the individual mind, the perfection of the One remains ineffable. This means that the individual mind, expressing its imperfections in relation to the perfect mastery of the One, knows itself as the *question* of its own origin, its own beginning, or its own creation, not least in its awe and wonder at the existence of life in the universe. Our aim in what follows is to challenge this logic of mastery with a logic of education that exposes the vulnerability of mastery to its own logic. But it also goes further than this. It suggests that this educational logic constitutes a modern metaphysics that knows truth and God in a different way to that made possible solely within the logic of mastery. In the vulnerability of mastery to its own difficulties or *aporias* of logic, there is a negation and preservation of truth that expresses itself as a logic of education. In turn, this is a logic of know thyself and has its actuality in learning or in culture, including in religion.

Clearly this asks a great deal of education, as much perhaps as was asked of it as *paideia* in Ancient Greece or as *humanism* in the European Renaissance. It asks education not only to bear the burden of retrieving God from the logic of mastery, but also to express its learning of God here as the truth of the retrieval. It asks education to find and then to speak in its own voice with its own logic and its own truth. We will come to see that this educational logic is, as Kierkegaard calls it, a new kind of contradiction. In our study of God and education, within this new contradiction and its modern metaphysics, we are commended to ask if God is not in fact to be found in education, and more challenging still, to ask if God *is* education.

Νοησισ Νοησεωσ, *Noesis Noeseos*, Thought Thinking Itself

In *Metaphysics* XII.7. Aristotle employs the logic of mastery to demonstrate that a prime mover is a logical necessity. There are two presuppositions here. The first is that since the creatures did not create their own universe, the universe stands in need of a creator. The second is that the creator must not suffer from this same imperfection or privation as the creatures. It must be the condition of the possibility of everything including itself, and it must not relate to itself as a question requiring an answer. Without this mastery or perfection or independence, infinite regression in the chain of causality from the compound back to the most simple never comes to an end. For Aristotle, given that the universe does exist, this end and the prime mover have to be presupposed.

Both presuppositions are grounded in a logic of mastery. The logic of mastery presupposes mastery as independence, independence as truth, truth as the One, and the One as the first principle. The prime mover is all of these and masters infinite regression because it alone is able to stand as its own first principle. As such, the prime mover is the One both logically and necessarily, for here logic and necessity are the same—the One. It is unchangeable in itself because it is not dependent upon anything heteronomous. It enjoys its mastery as its own logic and its logic as its own mastery. The mastery is logical because the logic is of mastery. The tautology here is essential, for it has to be self-referential. To not be self-referential would be a contradiction and would need to be mastered again by the logic of mastery and the One.

This reciprocity between the logic of the One and independence as mastery suggests that the ideas of God and freedom are the same idea. The truth of logic and non-contradiction are defined in accordance with the political definition of the master in the ancient Greek world. Both master and truth are free because independent of and unchangeable by another, and true in themselves because they master the chaos of infinite regression, each being a principle in-itself. In the ancient political world, this infinite regression, which has no principle of its own, is the barbarian or the slave whose life is dependent upon its master. Logic, truth, first principle, God, prime mover, and the free individual all express the same thing: independence in and through the logic of mastery.

For Aristotle, it is thought and desire that have this logic of independence and mastery as a metaphysical truth. Thought and desire, thinking and desiring, are the *good*, for it is moved by and for itself. It retains its independence and mastery because thought, desiring of its own truth, thinks itself as its own object. This is the first principle of NN. As we will see, KT registers that the individual is unable to do this. It does not have this process immanently because individual thinking and desiring are moved by their objects and changed in being so moved. In political terms KT in relation to NN is the slave in relation to the master. In strictly logical terms, the master is an identity in-itself and unlike the slave is not compromised by being merely for-another. In this distinction, God and the individual, truth and error, independence and dependence, free master and barbarian slave, are rent asunder. Religion is one cultural reproduction of this broken life.

However, this mastery is not immune to judgment from within the tenets of its own logic. Employed as the answer to the question of creation or of the beginning, the logic of mastery yields unavoidable difficulties. If God, as master, created or decided to create the universe from nothing, then the decision implies a time before the decision and therefore a changeable God. If God created the universe from pre-existing matter, then God was less a master of creation and more a demiurge. Finally, if God is eternal and unchangeable, and infinitely self-realizing, then contrary to the scriptures, perhaps there is no act of creation at all. As the history of the monotheistic faiths shows, these difficulties or aporias of authority gave rise to fierce doctrinal disputes. Each side was compromised by such aporias, and each side struggled for mastery over these aporias to gain an advantage over the other faiths. But in doing so, they employed the same logic of mastery that produced the difficulties. We will explore this below in Part 1.

Modern metaphysics looks at this the other way round. Perhaps it is the aporias and not their masters that are necessarily presupposed in having the universe exist as a question for those within it. Perhaps the aporia of mastery and not the mastery of aporia is the condition of the possibility for knowing both the universe and its first principles. Perhaps the aporia has a logic of its own, different to that of the logic of mastery. In our study of God and education, we will now try to explore what happens when the aporia of mastery is granted its own logic of presupposition within a logic of education.

Γνῶθι σεαυτόν, *Gnōthi Seauton*, Know Thyself

If we are to explore the differences between a logic of mastery and a logic of the aporia of mastery, it is perhaps inevitable that we look at the actuality of this relationship as it works within the mind, that is, as it is *experienced*, or as a process of individual education and learning. However, we must not simply accept at face value the tools of education that are available to us. Education also divides into the logic of mastery and the aporia of the logic of mastery. For example, the logic of mastery presupposes the mastery of the teacher. The child cannot create education for itself, and so education posits the teacher as the necessary condition for the possibility of education. Within the logic of mastery, the teacher enjoys the same logical status as the prime mover, as a necessary beginning.

But this logic of mastery of the teacher also mirrors the same difficulties or aporias of authority and of beginning that accompany the mastery of the prime mover. If a teacher is to teach a preexisting core curriculum of universally true values and knowledge, then the pedagogy must complement their unchangeable nature. This form of mastery and authority is rote learning and memorization, with the teacher's mastery upheld and grounded in the truth of the material. Alternatively, if the teacher and student create the curriculum for themselves, 'freely' and *ex nihilo,* as it were, then education is never the universal or the unchangeable, and only ever contingent, time-bound, and relative. In the former case, the teacher protects against the learning of skills without content. In the latter case, the teacher promotes the learning of skills without the mastery of content. The dualisms of traditional and progressive pedagogy, and of didactic and experiential pedagogy, rehearse this question of mastery in education.

But *both* sides here are opposed by the logic of mastery that they presuppose. Each is opposed by its presupposition of being the beginning of education. On the one hand, the teacher's presupposition of being the beginning of education is opposed by the students, who demand to be their own beginning, or free individuals. They demand for themselves the right to be the master of education in-itself, and not to be its slave. On the other hand, the progressive teacher's presupposition of not being the beginning of education, and instead, of beginning with freedom, is a mere dissemblance of freedom. The teacher has made his freedom here surrogate for the freedom of the students. Both examples expose presuppositions of beginning, and of authority, and neither are immune to the aporia that this logic of mastery inflicts upon itself.

Modern shapes of the logic of mastery in education are found in various imperialisms. Some work to control opportunity according to race, color, gender, and class, and some to control knowledge by defining and authorizing legitimate curriculum content. One aspect of the latter, less commented upon but no less powerful, is that of the mastery belonging to academic subject disciplines. Since the European Renaissance, the disciplines have become increasingly masterful by professionalizing themselves, defining their own internal discipline in terms of methodology, and defining their borders by claims to ownership of content. It was the disciplines, rather than education, which became ends in themselves here.

Less visible still is the way in which the logic of mastery determines what is to count as 'education'. It shapes reason and rationality as mastery and does so by defining in its own image what counts as an 'explanation' of something and an 'understanding' of something. At the centre of this is the way the logic of mastery has colonized the relationship between the question and the answer. The question is seen to have no mastery of its own, no independent status, and of not being a principle in-itself. The question here is presupposed by the logic of mastery to be imperfect, just as the questioner, the creature for whom the universe exists as a question, is judged imperfect in relation to the answer to the question, that is, to God. The answer is defined as mastery of the question. Questions without answers are merely the chaos of infinite regression. The answer, as mastery, brings this chaos to an end. This is how the prime mover and the teacher are seen as the answer to the question of the beginning of the universe and of education respectively.

Most significant here is the way the logic of mastery defines the accomplishment of education as *overcoming*, specifically, the overcoming of the question by the answer. This form of mastery in education is ubiquitous. The answer overcomes the question, as the in-itself overcomes the for-another, or as the master overcomes the slave. Overcoming is served by explanation, understanding and rationality which are the tools of its mastery. In the logic of mastery overcoming is the very definition of what counts as something being learned. It is how one knows one has been educated.

But here too, mastery as question and answer is not immune from the logical difficulties it causes itself. At its most simple and direct, the sovereignty of the answer is threatened when another question is asked of it, and the answer collapses into mere tautology when asked to 'explain' its own authority. The logic of mastery knows and vindicates only one way of reacting to its own logical aporias, and that is to overcome them, to explain them away using its own definition of an explanation. But there is within this aporia another logic, a logic that expresses its truth in and as *difficulty*.

As with the question of the beginning of the universe, so with the question of the beginning of education, modern metaphysics looks at this from the other way around. Perhaps it is the aporia of mastery in education, and not the logic of overcoming, that is necessarily presupposed in the existence of education, or in the universe existing for consciousness as a question. Perhaps the aporia of mastery, and not the mastery or overcoming of it, is the condition of the possibility of education. If so, perhaps the question of the beginning or of creation is really beginning or creation *as* the question, and as the education it commends. Perhaps this beholds a different logic to that of mastery.

For modern metaphysics, this different logic is the logic of education. Its truth is in the movement of learning, learning about itself in learning about its other or its object. This logic is not one of overcoming. It is one of *negation and preservation*. It is of the nature of learning that it undermines what has been learned by what is now being learned, and that it preserve this loss, this negation, as the truth of learning. Where the logic of mastery experiences its own logical difficulties as errors to be overcome, the logic of education has its truth in preserving this experience as learning. To the logic of mastery this merely opens up learning as an infinite regression without end. It looks like nothing ever gets learned. But in the logic of education, this is learning as its own end, redefining 'end' as not being something final, exhausted, or completed, not as a problem mastered or overcome, but as something that must repeatedly return to itself changed by the experience, something whose end in-itself is just such an education.

What follows now, in Parts 1 and 2, is an attempt to illustrate how the logic of mastery yields an educational logic. This is modern metaphysics negating and preserving ancient metaphysics. It still concerns the relation between the Western mind and the thinking of truth. It is still held by the same question of how to explain the universe and human existence within it. It is still rooted in life experiencing itself as the question of itself, and it is still therefore the question of God and religion. But now it adds to this a logic in which the question understands itself as a presupposition; not a presupposition in which the infinite regression of a question has to be overcome by being mastered by an answer, but as a logic of its own, a logic inherent to presupposition. Modern metaphysics asks that the presupposition of the question should come to understand itself. In this sense, we will reread the Delphic injunction to KT as holding within it the educational logic of modern metaphysics. We will find that modern metaphysics and the logic of education are also the *logic of know thyself*.

This educational logic challenges the individual, society, humanity, and the universe to KT. The logic of this education requires that one KT in relation to oneself as one's own other, and that this self-relation also KT in relation to others (to other similar self-relations). But we must be clear. This is not a resolution of differences. The relationship (the logic) lasts only while learning lasts, and as a way of life this means being consistently different to oneself—negation—and consistently the same as oneself—preserved as learning. As we will now seek to demonstrate, KT as it has been lived within the tradition, has seen itself as the work required to know truth, or to know God, or at least to try to mirror the unity of God as thought thinking itself. For centuries this meant trying to find the truth of oneself in the intellectual substance of NN by becoming more like the divine and less like the human. If religion is the cultural expression of the relation between God and the individual, then KT is the struggle and the work of that culture.

* * * *

Giving education the chance to speak in its own modern voice here perhaps asks *even more* of education than was asked of it by ancient *paideia* or Renaissance humanism. There its logic of mastery as freedom was uncontested. In modern times this notion of freedom is no longer fit for purpose. Instead, freedom is to be found in the logic of its own education, where freedom is to learn.[1] If this freedom, this education, knows truth differently to truth within the logic of mastery, and if it reforms the very idea of what a question is, and what an answer is, then this is clearly a challenge to all thinking that is based in a logic of mastery, and that means pretty much everything.

As such, educational logic is as dangerous for the imperialisms of the logic of mastery as it is for the critiques of this imperialism. Opposition to mastery—be it prejudice, or inequality, or discrimination, or injustice, or elitism, or power—is seduced into using the same logic of mastery to overcome imperialism that sustains imperialism. The ambition of *God, Education, and Modern Metaphysics* is that the reader, should he or she wish to make a quantitative critique of its imperialisms and non-inclusions (of which there are many), might at the same time accept the qualitative challenge that the logic of education beholds. This asks that those who would seek to overcome exclusion only in terms of numbers might also seek the logic of education, which lives suppressed in this kind of mastery, and accept therein the qualitative challenge of learning to turn the tyrannies of masterful opposition into educative self-critique. Or more simply, also to work with a different conception of question and answer.

Nevertheless, the logic of mastery continues to define the shape and content of Western culture, both its reactionary and its radical elements. One mastery opposes another, and one set of faces replaces another at the top table—but still this does not feed the world. All-too-rarely is the repetition of mastery understood educationally, or negated and preserved differently, and rarely is education understood as the truth of religious, political, and cultural struggles. If Part 2 below has any merit in this regard, then it might be that it has within it ways to challenge prejudice and injustice not just at the level of quantity (the critique of which remains important nonetheless) but also more deeply at the level of the logic that is presupposed in sustaining and in opposing prejudice and injustice. However, Part 2 will read strangely to eyes looking through the lens of the logic of mastery. Its work will not make sense to the mind for whom oppositions and contradictions are merely canon-fodder for being mastered and overcome.

Part 1 joins NN and KT as they travel alongside each other on a journey from ancient Greece to the European Enlightenment. The journey is characterized by aporia. This aporia holds within it the educational logic that will come to know itself as modern metaphysics. This is outlined in the *Intermezzo*. Here Kant's Copernican revolution takes the logic of mastery beyond that which it can control, and Hegel redefines this lack of control as the error of its fear of being error. This redefines logic, and with it notions of truth and the divine, reversing the presupposition that God is unknowable. The three chapters in Part 2 find this new notion of the divine in a *logic of tears*, in the *dreadful religious teacher*, and most ambitiously (perhaps wildly ambitiously) in holding together the three Abrahamic faiths in an educational concept of monotheism.

In a very important sense, *God, Education, and Modern Metaphysics* keeps in mind throughout Hegel's most profoundly difficult suggestion that the idea one has of God corresponds to the idea one has of one's freedom, and that in this sense religion and the formation of the state are one and the same. This book pursues what a logic of education can do in understanding this difficulty from the side of religion. The political significance of this logic requires a different book.

Note

1. I have explored this in Tubbs (2014).

Part 1
Know Thyself
Ancient Metaphysics

2   Socrates to Augustine

Ancient Sources

Eliza Wilkins rehearses eight themes in the idea of KT in the ancient world. These are: know one's measure, know one's limits, know one's place, know the limits of one's wisdom, know one's own faults, know one's mortality, know one's soul, and finally know how difficult all this is. These themes bring to light many of the references to KT, direct and indirect, in both pagan and early Christian sources.

Of knowing one's measure and limits Heraclitus says 'I make enquiry of myself' (Heraclitus, 1987, 61) while noting that 'all people have claimed to self-knowledge and sound thinking' (1987, 67).[1] Pindar advises 'Take measure of thyself' (Wilkins, 2013, 141),[2] while knowing one's limits is found in Xenophon's *Hellenica*[3] where Thrasybulus suggests the generals might learn of themselves more fully in relation to the qualities of the poor. Xenophon's *Memorabilia* includes a discussion regarding KT as knowing one's own abilities.[4] Diogenes the cynic warns Alexander that his hardest struggle in life is with himself, and that his lack of self-knowledge may be the root of his recklessness.[5]

Wilkins relates knowing the limits of one's wisdom to the virtue of *sophrosyne*. It is 'probable that γνῶθι σεαυτόν was often given as a definition of virtue in the ethical discussions of fifth-century Athens' (2013, 33). If self-knowing is a virtue, it means that a lack of self-knowing may well be the madness in which one thinks one comprehends what in fact one does not.[6] Timaeus records that it is not the man of divine frenzy but the man of sound mind who can know his own mind.[7] Wilkins notes both Origen and Olympiodorus conjoining KT with virtue.

Flattery is the great enemy of knowing one's own faults. Plutarch in 'How One May Discern A Flatterer From A Friend' says if truth is a divine thing then 'the flatterer is likely to be enemy to the gods, and especially to Apollo, for he always sets himself against that famous saying "Know thyself," implanting in everybody's mind self-deceit and ignorance of his own good or bad qualities' (Plutarch, 1898, 154). In the same piece, Plutarch says self-love and conceit make one an easy prey for the flatterer. This can be resisted if we obey the god

> and recognise the immense importance to everyone of that saying "know thyself," and at the same time carefully observe our nature and education and training, with its thousand shortcomings in respect to good, and the large proportion of vice and vanity mixed up with our words and deeds and feelings. (1898, 185–6)

Aristotle, Horace, Seneca, and Plutarch all draw attention to how hard we find it to avoid repeating in ourselves the faults we find in others, and the benefit of having these faults brought to our attention by others. Plutarch adds, 'upon no one is the God so likely to have enjoined the γνῶθι σεαυτόν as upon him who is going to find fault with another' (Plutarch, 1898, 207).[8] Wilkins also notes Aesop's Fable of the two sacks Jupiter placed upon us, the one with other people's faults hung before us, and the one with our own faults hung behind us.

One of the most fundamental themes of KT is learning of human mortality, an extension of knowing one's limits. Wilkins argues that it is not until Menander (4th–3rd century BCE) that KT and knowing the necessity of death are clearly brought together.

> When thou dost wish to know thyself—what thou art, look at the tombs as thou dost pass along the street. In them live the bones and the light dust of men . . . Look into these things, know thyself—what thou art' (Wilkins, 2013, 55).[9]

Wilkins notes that Christian and Jewish writers also cited this relationship. Clement of Alexandria, for example, says that among the things that KT shows is that you were born a human being and 'that thou art mortal' (Clement, 1885, 449). Philo Judaeus says that in the impossibility of fully comprehending the creator, so 'know yourself and be not carried away with impulses and desires beyond your power' (Philo, 1993, 538).[10]

On the seventh theme, Porphyry in his Γνωθι Σεαυτον[11] finds in Philo that 'the perfect νούς of which each of us is a likeness distinguishes the inner self, where the real man dwells' (Wilkins, 2013, 63) from the outer image of the body and one's possessions. In his letter to Marcella he says, unless one views the body only as an outer membrane, and works instead on the pure region of the mind, 'thou wilt not know thyself' (Porphyry, 1910, 50). The Emperor Julian makes a similar observation in his fourth oration, 'To the Uneducated Cynics'. KT means knowing the body as well as the soul because, although the body is composite and not a single substance, nevertheless while this distinguishes it from the divine, it still requires a knowledge of 'its harmony and the influences that affect it' (Emperor Julian, 1913b, 11).

Cicero also says that the road to self-knowledge requires us 'to know the powers of body and mind, and to follow the path of life that gives us their full realisation' (Cicero, 1913, 443). The precept KT is so powerful and significant that it was ascribed 'not to any mortal, but to the God of Delphi' (Cicero, 1853, 118). It befalls man to find this divinity through education regarding 'what part of them is mortal and perishable, and what is divine and everlasting' (Cicero, 1853, 119).[12] Similarly, Julian says that to KT 'a man must come completely out of himself and recognise that he is divine, and not only keep his mind untiringly and steadfastly fixed on divine and stainless and pure thoughts, but he must utterly despise his body' (Julian, 1913a, 129). The catharsis of such theoretical work is that in philosophy one comes 'to know oneself and to become like the gods. That is to say, the first principle is self-knowledge, and the end of conduct is the resemblance to the higher powers' (Julian, 1913a, 127).

The last of Wilkins' themes is on the difficulties attendant to KT. As we will see below, Alcibiades says that he thinks it is sometimes hard and some-times easy to KT.[13] Euthydemus in Xenophon's *Memorabilia* says it gives the impression of being easy (Xenophon, 1897, 186). Croesus in Xenophon's *Cryopedia* says that on hearing the Oracle say 'Know Thyself, O Croesus, and happiness shall be thine,' he was comforted because 'the God has laid the lightest of tasks upon me and promised me happiness in return' (Xenophon, 2009, VII, II).[14] In contrast, a fragment of Ion's suggests self-knowledge can be interpreted as being 'impossible' (Wilkins, 2013, 79). Wilkins notes that as an ethical precept KT 'was not conceived as being beyond the attain-ment of each and all' (2013, 81), but taken as an injunction to know one's soul, 'it became possible for the wise man only, and even for him perfect self-knowledge was unattainable, for it is God alone who fully knows him-self' (2013, 81).[15] Returning to Aristotle's distinction between divine NN and human KT, and of the unbridgeable gap between them, Julian the Apos-tate notes that 'what we are sometimes, God is always. It would therefore be absurd that God should not know himself . . . For he is himself everything' (Julian, 1913b, 15–17).[16]

Wilkins also explores KT in early ecclesiastical literature and reveals something of the struggle to claim its origin. Clement of Alexandria, in the tradition of Jewish writers who saw the source of Greek wisdom as Hebraic, 'maintains that γνῶθι σεαυτόν and certain other apophthegms really origi-nated in the Old Testament' (2013, 89). There is evidence that some of the Church Fathers ascribed the wisdom of KT to Moses and to Solomon. Clem-ent is prominent here. He lists some of the Greeks to whom the expression is claimed to belong, noting that of the list only Thales 'seems to have met the prophets of the Egyptians' (Clement, 1867, 392). He later argues that the third maxim on the temple of Apollo, εγγύα πάρα δ'ἄτη, give surety and trouble is at hand, comes from Solomon, *Proverbs*, VI, 1, 2, saying that a pledge to a neighbour gives one's hand to a stranger. KT he ascribes to Moses when he says 'take heed to thyself' (*Deuteronomy* 4.9, and *Exodus* 34.12).

Clements's pupil, Origen, also looked to Solomon for the origin of KT. Believing KT to be the 'noblest task of philosophy' and the 'prime maxim of wisdom' (Thamaturgus, 1920, 73), Origen relates KT to the *Song of Songs* 1.8., 'If thou know not [thyself], O fairest of women'.[17] But he also makes a much wider claim. In his *Commentary on the Song of Songs* he notes the three books of Solomon are acknowledged by the Church as the 'three general disciplines by which one attains knowledge of the universe' (Origen, 1979, 231), namely, morals, physics, and the speculative. The Greeks, he says, have tried to claim these as their own discoveries, but Solomon first distinguished them and set them out in logical order as the Books of *Proverbs*, *Ecclesiastes*, and the *Song of Songs*. In doing so, Solomon 'was not unaware that he was laying the foundations of the true philosophy and founding the order of its disciplines and principles' (1979, 232).

Ambrose claimed KT for Moses and Solomon in his *Hexameron*, and Wilkins notes that Cyril of Alexandria, in his reproach of Julian,[18] says that Pythagoras and Plato offer interesting and reasonable ideas about God and the cosmos 'because they collected their teaching or rather their knowledge during their stays in Egypt, where the very wise Moses is held in great regard, and where his doctrines are held in reverence and admiration' (Cyril, II.16). Eusebius of Caesarea says that Plato 'imitated not only the thought, but also the very expressions and words of the Hebrew Scripture' (Eusebius, 1903, 465).[19] He appropriated the Hebrew doctrine where all things can be referred to one beginning, declared to Moses as I am that I am, and in Solomon's doctrine of 'the origin and decay of all things corporeal and sensible' (1903, 465).[20]

In Philo Judaeus KT is linked to Hebrew purification rites. He says, 'The lawgivers intention is that those who approach the service of the living God should first of all know themselves and their own essence' (Philo, 1993, 559).[21] In *Exodus* 33.18 Moses asks God to show his face, and Philo interprets the reply as saying that such knowledge cannot be granted to a created being. As such, God commands 'know yourself[22] and be not carried away with impulses and desires beyond your power' (1993, 538).[23] Specifically this education is carried in the purification rite in which ashes from the sacred fire are mixed with water and sprinkled over those being purified. One is reminded here that the individual's bodily essence is merely earth and water, and therefore to know this is to KT in relation to the perfect God. 'When a man is aware of this he will at once reject all vain and treacherous conceit, and, discarding haughtiness and pride, he will seek to become pleasing to God' (1993, 559).[24] This rite commands 'the first principle of wisdom not to forget one's soul and always to keep before one's eyes the materials of which one has been compounded' (1993, 384).[25]

In his *Kuzari* (1130–40) Halevi records a rabbi saying that Solomon conversed on all sciences, and that many travelled to him for such wisdom. As such,

> the roots and principles of all sciences were handed down from us [the Jews] first to the Chaldaeans, then to the Persians and Medians, then

to Greeks, and finally to the Romans. On account of the length of this period . . . it was forgotten they originated with the Hebrews, and so they were ascribed to the Greeks and the Romans. To Hebrew, however, belongs the first place. (Halevi, 1964, 24)[26]

* * * *

This serves as a broad sweep of references to KT in Antiquity. We will now turn to a deeper engagement with the relation between NN and KT in Socrates, Plato, Aristotle, Plotinus, and Augustine. Our companion on parts of this journey is Edward Booth, whose PhD and subsequent books, notably *Aristotelian Aporetic Ontology in Islamic and Christian Thinkers,* are pathfinders for following aporia in the tradition.

Socrates (469–399 B.C.E.) and Plato (429?–347 B.C.E)

In *Alcibiades* 1[27] Socrates argues that since man's body is mastered by the soul, and the body is incapable of ruling itself, so KT means 'we should know our souls' (Plato, 1997, 589)[28] and cultivate virtue. Self-control therefore comes by way of KT, and virtue is the human equivalent of what Aristotle will see as the self-governing first principle or NN. As such, KT means avoiding 'whatever is appropriate for slaves' (1997, 595).[29] But in the *Sophist* Plato rehearses the aporia of KT emulating NN. To know something is to be changed in the knowing. Thus KT can never know the in-itself. This is to know and not-know at the same time, and the philosopher becomes 'like a child, begging for "both"' (1997, 271)[30] the unchangeable and the changeable.[31]

This aporia is taken up in *Charmides*. Critias suggests that KT means be temperate or do good things. Socrates is wary, questioning the distinction between a science of self-knowing and the understanding within it of what is known and not known. Critias replies that unlike any other science KT, or temperance, is a science of itself and of other sciences. Socrates introduces the line of questioning that one might expect from the midwife and gadfly: Can this science, the knowing of knowing, also know the absence of knowing, can it know not-knowing, and can it know what it does not know of itself? Booth says here that for Critias KT is the 'science of science' (1997, 657)[32] or the knowledge of knowledge,[33] and with the subject being identical with its object, is 'true wisdom' (Booth, 1977, 381). But Socrates, notes Booth, cannot reconcile Critias's version of the science of self-knowing with the dialectic of knowing and not-knowing. Without the latter the self learns of itself incompletely by not understanding how its learning is incomplete.

Here we arrive at a key moment for our study of God and education. Aristotle solved this problem by means of the unchangeable nature of the highest knower of self, the NN. Speaking of this exchange in *Charmides*, Booth says, 'Aristotle saw an intuition of enormous value in this discarded Platonic aperçu: for him it was in the nature of thought to be primarily self-thinking, and this in fact was the divine' (1977, 382). Aristotle 'was willing to accept an unbridgeable divide in human subjectivity between pure thinking and everything else in order to preserve intact the valuable insight of the *Charmides*' (1977, 382) of the unchangeableness of NN. For Aristotle, 'there is nothing else which it need know, for it is completely absorbed by and completely satisfied in itself' (1977, 382). It would desire nothing else. Here then, Aristotle alights upon the distinction between the pure and the compound, and upon truth in-itself as independent self-identity and self-mastery.

If Booth is correct, then from the *Charmides* Aristotle preserved scientific *elenchus* as the means of philosophical enquiry, and preserved pure thought from corruption by such enquiry. Booth notes that thereafter the Neoplatonist tradition wrestles with this problem of the relation of self-knowing in-itself (NN) to the KT of a differentiated subject and object. Νοῦς and its objects, the intelligible ideas, were related in 'a paradoxical one-in-manyness' (1977, 383), an aporia that haunted Neoplatonism for centuries to come.

At times, ψυχη (soul) is 'the intermediary between the changeless νοῦς and the changing world, in which all change is a demonstration of falling short and imperfection' (1977, 384). For Booth the problem in Plotinus is that true knowledge surpasses discursive thinking, so, when one knows oneself as νοῦς then 'one knows oneself no longer as a man but as a being quite different from a man' (1977, 385). We will return to this below.

Summing up the aporia of NN and KT, in the *Phaedrus* Socrates says 'I am still unable, as the Delphic inscription orders, to know myself; and it seems to me ridiculous to look into other things before I have understood that' (Plato, 1997, 510).[34] When I look into myself I ask, 'Am I a beast more complicated and savage than Typhon, or am I a tamer, simpler animal with a share in a divine and gentle nature?' (1997, 510).[35]

Booth on Aristotle (384–322 B.C.E.)

Booth traces the development of the divine self-moving NN of Aristotle through to the KT of Augustine's *notitia sui*.[36] The latter, grounded in the mind (*mens*)[37] and memory of individual personality, was, says Booth, a model of subjectivity which 'lasted right into modern times' (Booth, 1975, 7). He notes that while Aristotle was happy to divide pure NN and compound KT, nevertheless Aristotle also accepted the nature of this relation as aporetic rather than completely resolved.[38] It is this aporia in Aristotelian thinking that Neoplatonism suppressed thereafter, and it is this suppressed version that Augustine inherits.

The aporia can be demonstrated in what Booth identifies as the ontology of the *Metaphysics*, Book XII, chapters 7 and 9, and the subjectivity of *De anima* III. The *Metaphysics* suggests that the intellect is excited and moved to activity by already existing *noeta*. Here 'thought thinks itself because it shares the nature of the object of thought' (Aristotle, 1984b, 1695).[39] Pure will and pure knowledge coincide. It is a 'state of self-equality with thinking as activity and as object . . . its thinking is a thinking of thinking' (Booth,

1989, 8).[40] *De anima* offers a more subjective account involving thinking as 'a dynamic spontaneously creative process which creates the object of thought' (Booth, 1975, 28). Aristotle saw the problem here of an apparently creative role for the individual intellect against the divinity of the *Metaphysics*. The problem is that if the divine intellect is purely its own creation (*Metaphysics*) then individual νοῦς stands little if any chance of learning of its own truth (*De anima*). Equally, if thought is both 'divine and timeless in itself but temporally and individually embodied' (Booth, 1977, 98) then this ambiguity contradicts the nature of the divine. One response to this by Aristotle is to distinguish potential and actual knowledge of things where only the latter 'is identical with its object' (Aristotle, 1984a, 684).[41] If the soul contains both passive and active intellects then it can hold within it the capacity to be moved by something external (νοῦς παθετικος), and the actuality of being already itself in act (νοῦς ποιητικος).[42] This relation is as that of art (τεχνη, techne) to its material, or of light to what makes potential colors actual. Here Aristotle is not avoiding working with the aporia of divine and human.

Neoplatonism was less accommodating to such contradictions. Because mind is divine, 'a human subjectivity structure could not be based on it' (Booth, 1989, 8). It would be Augustine who would achieve a coherent structure of subjectivity which, in recollection, could KT. Booth concludes that the 'divergence between thought in itself and human thinking was thus made the basis of a moral orientation' (Booth, 1977, 98–9) in which, for Plotinus, 'a man must strive to unite his own thought into divine self-thinking and be absorbed into it' (1977, 98). What was established here was a strict separation between God and man such that God remained uncompromised by the sublunary world, and man's gaze was fixed on the One, disregarding any lower concerns.

Faced with this seemingly irresolvable opposition, Booth says that Neoplatonists bequeathed a tradition in which the difficulty was erased in favor of the logic of non-contradiction, or the logic of the independence and mastery of the in-itself. Aristotle, however, does not simply erase such uncertainties. There is no intention on the part of Aristotle (or Booth) to 'liberate us from overall discord' (Booth, 1983, ix). Aristotle relished working with the incompleteness of aporia. As such, aporia is an education: it not only facilitates 'entrance into the subject matter' (1983, x), it also *is* the subject matter of God and the individual. Aporia was to become Aristotle's 'pedagogical method' (1983, 268) in which subject matter is 'barely distinguishable from the method' (1983, 268) or in which aporia is self-formative.

Against Plato's transcendental forms and earthly shadows, Aristotelian actuality gave independent existence to material objects. But it did so through the aporia of form and matter. This encouraged later Neoplatonists to seek their reconciliation, despite Aristotle claiming in the *Metaphysics* that the logic of demonstration or *apodeixis*, in detaching proof from the thing itself, repeated the 'greatest' (Aristotle, 1984b, 1717)[43] of aporias, therein thwarting 'a satisfactory union between the way of universals and the way of concrete facts' (Booth, 1983, 2–3). This illustrates the 'noetic aporia' (1983, 3) where abstracted essence and individual substance become irreconcilable. More complex still is the 'corresponding ontological aporia' (1983, 3) of universal forms and the being of each material individual. How can the unique also be universal? Booth says that one might conclude that Aristotle hoped that the empirical and the intuition of essence 'could be so brought together that there would be an επιστημη (*episteme*/knowledge) which would grasp things in their universality and individuality at the same time' (1983, 5). But how could this be achieved 'if the individual substance had a primary existence as ουσια (*ousia*/essence)' (1983, 5)? Indeed, the idea that objects are primary substances is part of Aristotle's radicalism.

However, 'a gap remained' (1983, 5) between the characteristics that made the individual different, and the characteristics it shared with similar individuals. How do you keep these two aspects in the same individual apart? Aristotle attended to this in *Metaphysics* VII. 10, distinguishing συνολον as a complete compositum, 'such and such a form induced in this flesh and these bones' (1983, 5),[44] from a 'kind of compositum (συνολον τι) composed of this particular logos and in this particular matter regarded as universal' (1983, 5).[45]

Aristotle kept noetic and ontology close here. He knew that if universal knowledge was 'a creation of the mind he still needed to find an explanation of the universality in things' (1983, 6). It is this that Aristotle describes as 'the greatest difficulty (aporia)' (1984b, 1717);[46] namely, reconciling universal knowledge with the principle of existing things. It is repeated in *Metaphysics* XIII where potentiality is described as 'universal and indefinite' (Aristotle, 1984b, 1718)[47] and actuality as a 'this' (1984b, 1718),[48] a definite object. But the demonstration that each actuality is derived from universal principles would only mean that 'there will be nothing capable of separate existence—i.e. no substance' (1984b, 1718).[49] Thus, Aristotle's aporetic conclusion: 'evidently in a sense knowledge is universal and in a sense it is not' (1984b, 1718).[50]

Having surveyed more examples of aporia in the *Metaphysics*, Booth's conclusion is that Aristotle hoped 'that an aporetic initiation would enable the reader simultaneously to retain and to suppress the distinctiveness of what was universal in the individual, in which alone it is always found' (1983, 20). As we will come to see, negating truth and preserving it in the experience of aporia anticipates a modern metaphysical education.

Before leaving Booth, we can summarize the remainder of his thesis. The radical Aristotelian tradition, the one critical of Plato and the transcendental forms, and the one holding to the actual existing compositum of matter and form, became in Neoplatonism a victim of 'standardization and simplification' (1983, 26). The search for immediate clarity 'obscured the pedagogical necessity of aporia' (1983, 34). Plotinus ignores the radical tradition. Porphyry privileges the 'original common principle' (1983, 47) of

existents. Proclus resolves aporia 'in favour of the primacy of universal fac-
tors' (1983, 53). The Islamic philosophy of al-Farabi, Avicenna, and Averroes
work with 'unaporetic doctrinaire clarity' (1983, 94) and like so many commentators take up the challenge of 'tying up Aristotle's loose ends' (1983,
123). Booth's conclusion is that 'Aristotelian aporetic ontology died with
Aristotle. Henceforward the pedagogical method lost its near-identity with
the material' (1983, 268). The Greeks and then the Arabs, seeing aporia as
an error to be overcome, sought uniform commentary and interpretation.
Equally, Christianity sought to unify Platonic and Aristotelian themes, and
for Booth it is only Augustine who succeeds in formulating 'a view of human
personality that we still accept today' (1983, 121), one grounded in KT as
notitia sui. Finally, Booth turns to Hegel arguing that the principle of NN
becomes for him the entelechy of all thinking. We will explore this in more
detail below.

* * * *

Aporia, then, is our entry point into the difficult relation between God and
individual, pure and compound, universal essence and individual substance,
and unchangeable and changeable. In the remainder of Part 1 we now pursue the fate of this aporia as it appears in the relation between NN and KT.

Plotinus (204/5–270CE)

If in Plato the relation of NN and KT begins in the cave, leads to the Forms,
and returns again to the cave, this same work is found in reverse in Plotinus.
Where in Plato the self rises to the Forms, in Plotinus the self loses its wings
and descends to earth. Where in Plato the enlightened self descends again
to the city to work for justice, in Plotinus the self, having fallen away from
its unity, will strive to achieve that unity once again. Both of these struggles
characterize the relation between NN and KT.

  Booth holds that Plotinus reached for the NN of *Metaphysics* XII rather
than the more troublesome embodied version in *De anima*. Of its three
hypostases the first is the One, the Unity, the True, defined strictly according
to the Aristotelian logic, which states that the truth of an object is that which
can be reduced to no more simpler form, and is its own principle. From this
One comes the second hypostasis, an emanation, an overflowing exuberance
in which the One creates itself as its own principle. This is νοῦς, the being of
the divine mind, or the NN. It is contemplation of the One, but nevertheless
differentiated from it.

  Already the question of self-knowing arises here, and Plotinus is deeply
concerned to establish this difference. In a relatively late treatise of *The
Enneads*,[51] he notes the Aristotelian aporia: if self-knowing of an uncompounded being—the One—is not possible, then we lose any idea of true
self-cognition; but if the uncompounded can know itself, will this not introduce the duality of knower and known, and corrupt the simplicity of the

One? His answer is that the One is above the need for knowing, for, being perfect, it can have no lack and no need for anything. This includes not needing to know itself. Thus the transcendent 'neither knows itself nor is known in itself' (Plotinus, 1991, 381).[52] The One is repose, tranquillity; it has neither form nor being; it is not place or time; it is a first principle 'void of self-knowledge' (1991, 506)[53] and self-awareness; it is neither quality nor quantity; it is neither intellect nor soul, neither in motion nor in rest; it is present and not present. It is 'unity accomplished' (1991, 542).[54] If the One needed to know itself 'that would imply a previous ignorance' (1991, 543)[55] which as a simple unity logically it cannot have. 'Yet this absence of self-knowing, of self-intellection, does not comport ignorance . . . in the Solitary there is neither knowing nor anything unknown' (1991, 543).[56] It does not even know itself as good, for no such alien content is present to it: 'it can have only an immediate intuition self-directed' (1991, 507).[57]

For Plotinus then, KT

> is a precept for those who, being manifold, have the task of appraising themselves so as to become aware of the number and nature of their constituents . . . The First, on the contrary, if it have content must exist in a way too great to have any knowledge, intellection, perception of it. To itself it is nothing. (1991, 510)[58]

The One is 'in full possession of its being before Intellect exists . . . the utterly undifferentiated remains self-centred and makes no enquiry about that self' (1991, 377).[59] Restating the logic of identity on which his whole system is based, Plotinus concludes that 'anything capable of analysing its content must be a manifold' (1991, 377)[60] and cannot, by the very structure of this logic, be its own independent first principle capable of terminating infinite regression to absurdity. Alexander Altmann says here that KT addresses itself 'only to those beings that are multiple and have to learn which of their parts is the dominant one and causes them to be "themselves"' (Altmann, 1969, 29). For Booth, Plotinus makes the soul so divine and the One so transcendental that it was difficult to conceive of the One in contact with man without losing its transcendence. But we note too that Plotinus keeps both NN and KT apart from the unity of the One. Even νοῦς, the divine mind, is a falling away from or an emancipation from the One which reigns uncompounded by any desire or knowledge.

Plotinus asks why the One issues itself into a knowing principle at all. His answer is that it is of the Supreme that its production of mind is like that of the sun in relation to its light. Light is ceaselessly produced from the unchanging sun, as mind is ceaselessly produced by the unchanging Unity. What is added to this analogy, however, is that a mind is drawn to return to the One in a way that light is not perhaps drawn to return to its origin.

In the second hypostasis, then, the all-perfect produces 'nothing less than the very greatest that is later than itself' (1991, 354).[61] This is the divine mind; it sees 'The One on which it leans while the First has no need whatever of it' (1991, 354).[62] Everything else, the manifold of the universe, follows upon this second element as an act of the intellectual principle. As light is that by which the sun is seen, so the intellectual principle is the vision of the One. This implies that in an immediate sense, seeing itself is how the One 'returns' to itself without having left itself or, also in an immediate sense, that it is part of its immediate nature to see itself but not to see itself as a cognized object. Because the intellectual principle is the whole of existence *and* part of the One, its aporetic character is named as the 'One-Many' (1991, 357).[63] This intellectual principle, νους, holds within itself the aporia of NN and KT, acting as a protector of the One against the error of division or being compound. This aporia knows itself in the experience of objects which are, in relation to the intellectual principle, both distinct and identical. Each differentiated idea is a 'Reason-Principle' (1991, 376)[64] and the self-knowing of νους needs the experience of these objects. If there is nothing external, no knowing of an object, then the divine mind (conception) 'exists in vain' (1991, 376).[65]

Plotinus is working hard here to show how the intellect has to have multiplicity, and argues consistently that even when the intellect or divine mind knows the One, it does so via multiplicity and therefore never 'knows' the One in the immediate way that the One 'exists'.

The third hypostasis is that of the soul (ψυχη) from the intellect (νους). Booth says here that ψυχη is 'the intermediary between νους which is unchangeable and the changing world' (1975, 122). Its Janus-face is turned partly to νους and partly to the material world. This duality persists so long as the soul is attached to an earthly body. When the soul is united with νους it will have no memories of itself as having been a personality. In this ecstasy, as Plotinus puts it, one becomes *alone with the alone*.[66]

He describes this in the following way:

> Many times it has happened: lifted out of the body into myself; becoming external to all other things and self-encentred; beholding a marvellous beauty: then, more-than ever, assured of community with the loftiest order; enacting the noblest life, acquiring identity with the divine. (1991, 334)[67]

For Booth this is the primary problem with Plotinus's metaphysics. For Plotinus, ruled as we are by the divine mind, we only truly know ourselves when we become 'actually identical with the principle' (1991, 368).[68] The nature of the ecstasy in which the individual is lost to its noetic truth is where the nature of knower and known, subject and object, is transformed into a different idea of identity. This new identity is that in which the intellectual object 'is itself an activity' (1991, 369).[69]

> As an act—and one whose very being is an act—it must be undistinguishably identical with its act . . . It possesses self-knowing, thus, on

every count; the act is itself; and the object, seen in that act-self, is itself. (1991, 370)[70]

But for Booth the problem is clear. When the soul conforms to νοῦς 'then one knows oneself no longer as a man but as a being quite different from man, raised on high, taking there only the superior part of the soul, which alone can go out to thought' (Booth, 1977, 385).[71] The problem for Booth is that if this is self-knowing, if this is the zenith of KT, it is not the human individual self that is known, but rather something very different. This is further emphasized in that the One has no knowledge of itself at all. Even though, in 'reminiscence' (Plotinus, 1991, 365)[72] the soul discovers that intellect is available to it—a discovery it experiences as an 'agony for a true expression' (1991, 398)[73] of the One—nevertheless any learning about the One in the soul goes only so far as the first principle of νοῦς and no further. In order to reach the supreme One, one must 'put aside all . . . learning' (1991, 505).[74] Learning, as a first principle, would be an infinite regression, for it would always have to be learning of itself. Instead, the One will 'know neither itself nor anything else but will hold an august repose' (1991, 507–8).[75] The Supreme is the goal of education but also the termination of education. 'To itself it is nothing' (Plotinus, 1991, 510).[76] Teaching and learning are only 'of the road and the travelling' (1991, 540).[77] They are not the active arrival. 'To find ourselves is to know our source' (1991, 544).[78] But 'knowing' here is really the unity of the vision which sees itself. There will be

> a time of vision unbroken, the self hindered no longer by any hindrance of body . . . It is a knowing of the self restored to its purity . . . In this seeing . . . there is no two. The man is changed, no longer himself nor self-belonging; he is merged with the Supreme . . . [This] vision baffles telling. (1991, 547)[79]

It is the light that is alone with the alone. Again, for Booth, this is no longer a KT of the individual.

Augustine (354–430CE)

Booth's concern with Plotinus is that illumination requires the gradual obliteration of the subject in the object and is a 'progressive extinction' (Brehier, 1958, 189) of the individual mind.[80] It is also an extinction, or flattening, of the undulations of Aristotelian aporetic thinking. Booth turns to Augustine as being able to do justice to such aporias, negating and yet preserving the individual mind with its knowledge of God.

For Booth, Augustine's unification of νοῦς and ψυχη is the foundation of Western Christian subjectivity. Contrary to Plotinus, self-memory, *memoria sui*, is an image of a self-conscious deity. Addressing Socrates' point in the *Charmides*, memory here knows that it understands, that it is the condition for understanding anything else, and that it can know that it knows some-thing unsuccessfully. This is to risk uncertainty in knowing God, but the prize was a self-consciousness that was 'personal' (Booth, 1975, 182).[81] The primacy of self-knowledge for Augustine was a 'metaphysical neces-sity' (1975, 183) in the memory which acted as 'the total commander of cognition' (1975, 202). Where Aristotle bequeathed a division between pure thought and material subject, and in turn divided νοῦς into the passive and active intellects, Augustine found unity in the embodiment of thought in memory, which housed self-thinking, self-knowing and self-loving as a 'simple and complete conception of subjectivity' (1975, 307). Where Neo-platonist thought resorted to a hierarchy of hypostases, with each element 'drawn into unity by desire for [its] source (1975, 307), Augustine ensured 'the independence of self-knowing mind' (1975, 308).

Alongside Booth, here, a case can be made that in Augustine's best-known writing on KT in *De trinitate* 8–15, there are elements of a logic of education which, as we will see in Part 2, share characteristics with the logic of KT in modern metaphysics. In his own logic, Augustine works with aporias of presupposition, repetition, infinite regression, and faith in ways that do not sacrifice difficulty to the systematic, doctrinaire clarity or imposed resolu-tions that suppress the radical Aristotelian tradition.

For Augustine the question (or presupposition) of beginning arises in the conundrum that 'no one can in any way love something of which he is absolutely ignorant' (Augustine, 2002, 42),[82] and so, for example, what a seeker pursues in study cannot be entirely unknown and must be loved already. This is not just the recollection of the knowledge which is held unknown until recollected. It is also a logic of education, of preserving what is not present, which expresses itself as love of itself. What, says Augustine, does the seeker love in his studying except 'what the beauty of learning is' (2002, 43).[83]

This logic of presupposition as education is also a logic of faith, for to search for truth in advance of its being known is a search predicated not only on a faith in the existence of God, but crucially on a faith that learning to KT expresses the divinity of NN. In the contradiction of beginning and faith, it is learning which learns of itself, and which expresses the divinity in the creature. Learning, for Augustine, is the inner word of the trinity in the individual mind. Already in the *Confessions* Augustine had expressed the wish for critics to 'reflect upon the triad within their own selves' (Augustine, 1998, 279).[84]

Where curiosity wishes only that nothing be unknown, love and faith as learning also love knowing the unknown, and express this love as study-ing. This mind knows learning as the whole, and knows too that it has not learned everything there is to know about the whole. This negation and preservation of the whole in individual learning is a key feature of the mod-ern metaphysical logic of education. This is the logic in which the learning mind 'knows itself as seeking and not knowing, while it seeks to know itself'

(2002, 48).[85] In knowing that it does not know itself 'it is more known than unknown to itself' (2002, 48).[86]

In the later books of *De trinitate* the outer man, the inner man, and God Himself all have truth in an educational logic of KT. The trinity of the outer man sees the will direct the mind's attention to images/thoughts of external objects which are stored in the memory. The trinity of the inner man recalls not images of objects but words which proclaim faith in the invisible. When the inner man recalls what these words signify, and 'when he believes them to be true and loves those things there which are to be loved, then he already lives according to the trinity of the inner man' (Augustine, 2002, 134–5).[87] Nevertheless, even the trinity of the inner man, 'the retention, contemplation, and love of this same temporal faith is not such a trinity as to be now called the image of God' (2002, 139)[88] for, unlike God, the inner man 'does not see anything everlasting' (2002, 139).[89] The trinity of the recollection, contemplation, and love of faith will not survive after this earthly pilgrimage. In the city of God, 'Faith will no longer be that by which those things that are not seen are believed, but rather the sight by which those things are seen which were believed' (2002, 139).[90] Since this faith will be seen to be something of the past, and not enduring, its finite nature shows that it was not able to count as the image of God. Instead the image of God must now be sought in that which is eternal and immortal, and that is the rational or intellectual soul.

It is in Book 14 that Augustine explains the trinity that is the image of God found in the soul or mind. It is the memory in which the mystery first unfolds itself, for the memory is that in which the mind can know itself even when not thinking about itself. In the love that is the inquiry, or in the work of KT, learning binds together the begetter and the begotten, or binds together thinking and thought. Here, in love, as in learning, the mind 'sees itself through thought, it understands itself and recognises itself' (2002, 145).[91] This is an immanent trinity, for mind 'begets this, its own understanding and its own knowledge' (2002, 145).[92] It is 'finally an image of God' (2002, 148).[93]

But there is a particular problem here. Memory can only recall an object after the object has been placed in it. If this were also the case for recollecting mind or thought, it would mean the mind did not exist before it was recalled, as if the mind were not there 'before it knew itself' (2002, 152).[94] Augustine deals with this by means of a non-sequential educational logic, in which memory can pertain to present things:

> in a present thing, which the mind is to itself, that is not unreasonably to be called memory, by which the mind is present to itself, so that it can be understood by its own thought, and both can be joined together by the love of itself. (2002, 153)[95]

For this claim to make sense to us, we have to accept that there are two logics here. The sequential logic of cause and effect is the temporal logic in which memory can only pertain to things past, for remembering something is only possible after it has been placed in the memory. The non-sequential logic, the logic of education, is different. Whereas in sequential logic mind is *already* recollection of past things, in educational logic mind is *always already* a recollection (or as we will see in Part 2, also a repetition[96]) of past things. The present is no longer a moment, it is a relation, and a relation often called actuality, for it negates and preserves itself in and as the recollections from which it derives. The present, in fact, is the mediation—always and again—of itself. This is a modern metaphysical logic of education in contrast to the ancient logic of mastery, in which the eternal is unknowable and any mediation of identity is error.

The wisdom that arises from this recollective logic does so because the mind can recollect in the present the eternal conditions of its own possibility. Augustine says here 'this Trinity of the mind is not on that account an image of God because the mind remembers itself, understands itself, and loves itself, but because it can also remember, understand, and love Him by whom it was made' (2002, 153–4).[97] In this knowing of knowing, the mind 'becomes wise' (2002, 154).[98] Here the mind knows itself as the image of God. In sum, 'the rational and intellectual nature which is the mind of man . . . has been made according to the image of Him who made it' (2002, 154).[99] This is an 'inward teaching' (2002, 159)[100] by which 'even the godless [can] think of eternity' (2002, 159).[101]

When Augustine turns to the trinity of God himself, he warns in advance that no man will be able to comprehend all things in the way God does, in his 'eternal, unchangeable and ineffable vision' (2002, 180).[102] This retains the Neoplatonic logic of identity in which NN is unknowable to the changeable activity of seeking God in KT. It is found too in Augustine's distinction between the chronological time of the human mind, in which knowledge cannot be eternal, cannot be without privation (we do, after all, forget things) and the eternity of God whose eternal word is 'co-eternal with Himself' (2002, 197).[103] The differentiation of changeable and unchangeable saves the Word as substance from the error of subjectivity, while nevertheless defending the presence of the divine in subjectivity, or as KT. One should seek the highest as it lives in him, but should remember too 'the great unlikeness that there also is' (2002, 210)[104] between creator and created. Where the inner word is begotten, the word which does not belong to the language of any nation, there is the 'knowledge of knowledge, the vision of vision, and understanding of understanding' (2002, 211).[105]

Nevertheless, it remains the case for Augustine that KT is the image of God in each human subjectivity. Such is the power of KT that for him it stands against the academicians, offering irrefutable proof that I know that I live. Skeptics argue that the infinite regression to absurdity of such proof—I know that I live, and I know that I know that I live *ad infinitum*—shows that nothing is true. But Augustine turns this on its head, arguing that it shows skeptics unable to disprove that I know that I live. Here Augustine displays another feature of modern educational logic, in which infinite regression is not interminable error, but an education about the truth found in learning.

Booth, then, champions Augustine not for resolving but for finding truth in the aporias bequeathed by Aristotle and 'within the philosophical tradition of thought being in itself self-thinking: νοησις νοησεως [NN]' (1975, 307). We have tried to complement this with features of a logic of education in Augustine regarding presupposition, recollection, faith, and infinite regression, which hold the truth of learning able to negate and preserve itself. This enables Augustine to hold together in the aporia of learning and of KT, the word of God both eternally and eternally in time. Truth here is faith in education. What does an individual who is seeking truth love 'except that he knows and beholds in the reasons of things, what the beauty of learning is' (2002, 43).[106]

Augustine never loses sight of this truth in enquiry, in faith, and in love. It is present at the end of *De trinitate* when he says he has 'desired to see with my understanding that which I believed' (2002, 223).[107] Asking why the mind was commanded to KT Augustine answers, so that 'it might consider itself and live according to its nature, that is, that it might desire to be ruled according to its own nature, namely, under Him to whom it ought to be subject, and above those things to which it is to be preferred' (2002, 49),[108] or perhaps so that the creature might have the desire to know God and be improved by the search.

Notes

1. Fragments 101 and 116 respectively.
2. *Pythian* II.34.
3. II.IV. 40–1.
4. IV. 2.
5. αφροσυνη, *aphrosune*: perhaps 'the opposite of σωφροσύνη: *sophrosyne* (Wilkins, 2013, 20n).
6. See Xenophon (1897) *Memorabilia*, III.9. 405.
7. *Timaeus*, 72a.
8. From 'How a Man May Be Benefitted By His Enemies,' *De capienda ex inimicis utilitate*, chapter 5, Plutarch (1898, 207), using Wilkins translation here, (2013, 49).
9. Menander, fragment 538. See Menander (1921). Here Wilkins' translation is used, (2013, 55).
10. From 'Special Laws I' VIII.44.
11. Found in fragments in the Floregium of Johannes Stobaeus.
12. This emphasizes the distinction between mind and body to the extent that Porphyry recalls of his teacher Plotinus that he seemed embarrassed to be living in a body at all (Plotinus, 1991, cii; MacKenna's Introduction). We will explore Plotinus separately.
13. *Alcibiades 1* 129a.
14. Lines 20–2.
15. Below we will follow the aporetic experience of this impossibility.
16. IV Oration, 185b-c.
17. The Greek here in the *Song of Songs* is γνῶθι σεαυτόν.

18. Book II. chapter 16.
19. Book 11, chapter ix.
20. Book 11, chapter ix.
21. *The Special Laws* I, 263.
22. γνῶθι δη σαυτόν, (Wilkins, 2013, 58)
23. *The Special Laws* I, 44.
24. *The Special Laws* I, 265.
25. *On Dreams* I, D11.
26. Wilkins prioritises Delphi here over all similar claims for the origin of KT.
27. It is not agreed that this dialogue can be attributed to Plato.
28. *Alcibiades* 1, 130e.
29. *Alcibiades* 1, 135c.
30. *Sophist* 249d.
31. In this passage in the *Sophist* Plato says that what *is* contains soul, life, and intelligence. Booth suggests that this may be the origin of the Neoplatonic triad of *esse-vivere-intelligere* found especially in Proclus's system of emanation; see Booth (1983, 270). Booth also suggests (1975, 83) that Plato's Second Letter might contain an early idea of triadic emanation: 'Related to the King of All are all things, and for his sake they are, and of all things fair He is the cause. And related to the Second are the second things and related to the Third the third' (Plato, 1966, 312e).
32. *Charmides* 170a.
33. επιστημης επισημη; *Charmides* 169b.
34. *Phaedrus* 230a.
35. *Phaedrus* 230a.
36. I will follow themes in Booth from his PhD in 1975, from the reproduction of the thesis in *Augustiniana* 1977–9, from the book on the Aristotelian aporetic published in 1983, and finally from the Villanova lecture of 1986 (published 1989).
37. Gareth Mathews (2005, 49) notes that in translating *mens* as 'the mind' we should remember that in Augustine's Latin there are no definite or indefinite articles. As with Booth, Mathews sees *mens* in Augustine referring to individual minds.
38. Aporia is mentioned only once by Booth in his PhD. but his 1983 book develops the idea of aporia out of the PhD.
39. *Metaphysics* 1072b 19–21.
40. *Metaphysics* 1074b 33–4.
41. *De anima* 430a 20.
42. Passive and active intellect respectively.
43. *Metaphysics* 1078a 13.
44. *Metaphysics* 1034a 5–7.
45. *Metaphysics* 1035b 28–30.
46. *Metaphysics* 1087a 10–13.
47. *Metaphysics* 1087a 17.
48. *Metaphysics* 1087a 16–19.
49. *Metaphysics* 1087a 24–5.
50. *Metaphysics* 1087a 25.
51. V.3.
52. *Enneads* V.3.13.
53. *Enneads* VI.7.38.
54. *Enneads* VI.9.6.
55. *Enneads* VI.9.6.
56. *Enneads* VI.9.6.
57. *Enneads* VI.7.38.

58. *Enneads* VI.7.41.
59. *Enneads* V.3.10.
60. *Enneads* V.3.10.
61. *Enneads* V.1.6.
62. *Enneads* V.1.6.
63. *Enneads* V.1.8.
64. *Enneads* V.3.10.
65. *Enneads* V.3.10.
66. *Enneads* I.6.7.; V.1.6.; and VI.7.34.
67. *Enneads* IV.8.1. Note that Plotinus, in his ecstatic moment, is lifted out of the body into himself. This means that it is not true to see the soul as residing in the body, but rather it is the body that resides in the soul. If soul were in the body, this would disturb the logical order of the emanation, for soul would be a hypostasis of body. Instead, it is the body that enters the soul when the soul descends to the material universe. Soul, self-contained in the intellectual principle, 'is the container of the body' (1991, 401; *Enneads* V.5.9.).
68. *Enneads* V.3.4.
69. *Enneads* V.3.5.
70. *Enneads* V.3.5.
71. *Enneads* V.3.4.
72. *Enneads* V.3.2.
73. *Enneads* V.5.6.
74. *Enneads* VI.7.36.
75. *Enneads* VI.7.39.
76. *Enneads* VI.7.41.
77. *Enneads* VI.9.4.
78. *Enneads* VI.9.7.
79. *Enneads* VI.9.10.
80. For Emile Brehier it is only ecstasy that can 'reveal us to ourselves' (Brehier, 1958, 163), something that is no longer accountable to rational explanation; see Brehier (1958).
81. Having shown how the three persons of the trinity belong to the one individual, Augustine could not explain how those three things were also three persons. Augustine speaks of his failure to comprehend 'why the Holy Spirit is not the Son when it proceeds from the Father' (Booth, 1975, 215; *De trinitate*. XV. 25. 45), something that will be revealed only in heaven. The cause of the uncertainty, and perhaps of the imperfection compared to Plotinus, is that Augustine in particular, and Christianity more generally, has a 'discontinuity between Creator and creature, the timeless and the time-bound' (1975, 251), which means that the completeness attained by Plotinus cannot here be achieved in the same way.
82. *De trinitate* 10.1.1.
83. *De trinitate* 10.1.2.
84. *Confessions* XIII.xi.12.
85. *De trinitate* 10.3.5.
86. *De trinitate* 10.3.5.
87. *De trinitate* 13.20.25.
88. *De trinitate* 14.2.4.
89. *De trinitate* 14.2.4.
90. *De trinitate* 14.2.4.
91. *De trinitate* 14.6.8.
92. *De trinitate* 14.6.8.
93. *De trinitate* 14.8.11.

94. *De trinitate* 14.10.13.
95. *De trinitate* 14.11.14.
96. Taking recollection and repetition from Kierkegaard; see below Chapter 7.
97. *De trinitate* 14.12.15.
98. *De trinitate* 14.12.15.
99. *De trinitate* 14.12.16.
100. *De trinitate* 14.15.21.
101. *De trinitate* 14.15.21.
102. *De trinitate* 15.7.13.
103. *De trinitate* 15.15.25.
104. *De trinitate* 15.20. 39.
105. *De trinitate* 15.21.40.
106. *De trinitate* 10.1.2.
107. *De trinitate* 15.28.51.
108. *De trinitate* 10.5.7.

3   Aquinas and Maimonides

Christianity

Etienne Gilson has argued that between Socrates and Pascal there is a form of 'Christian Socratism'.[1] It appears after Plotinus and particularly concerns the individual learning of its place in the universe, somewhere between brute and angel. Being between earthly toil and heavenly bliss, a form of Christian mysticism sought the possibility of 'a higher order of its own spontaneity' (Gilson, 2012, 218), while Aquinas emphasized the idea of the individual as a microcosm, 'a whole universe in little' (2012, 219).

Gilson illustrates here the kind of aporia that characterizes the radical Aristotelian tradition. In the individual seeking to know God, he says, 'The trouble is that he [the individual creature] is himself involved in the mystery' (2012, 219). As such, and emphasizing the absolute divide between unchangeable substance and changeable individual matter, the quest for self-knowledge is something that 'calls for investigation but at the same time resists it' (2012, 224). For Gilson this means especially that the soul cannot apprehend itself immediately because it is always compromised by intermediaries.

On the path to Aquinas we note the motif of KT in Boethius for whom the lack of self-knowledge in the beasts is a 'moral blemish' (Boethius, 1999, 31); Hugh of Saint Victor, who argues that the maxim at Delphi is necessary because the individual has clearly 'forgotten his origin' (Hugh of Saint Victor, 1991, 46) and needs to learn 'not to seek outside [himself] what [he] can find within' (1991, 47); but especially Richard of Saint Victor who, in his *Benjamin Minor*, expresses the education of KT in symbolic form as a family tree. Jacob, the rational soul, has two wives, reason (Leah) and affection (Rachel), or wisdom and virtue, which are the soul's principal powers. Leah's children are the seven virtues (fear of God, grief, hope, love, joy, anger, and shame) while Rachel's children are Joseph and then Benjamin. Joseph is the education that pertains to the soul's education; he embodies the work of KT, that is, 'to knowledge of God, through knowledge of himself' (Richard of Saint Victor, 1979, 141). Benjamin comes to symbolize divine contemplation, rising above all reason (his mother) and even 'beyond himself' (1979, 145). Of particular interest for our own study, the *difficulty* of the ascent, likened to climbing a mountain, is a struggle in which one learns the 'admiration of difficulty . . . and joy' (1979, 134–5). Richard states, 'Ascend this mountain; learn to know yourself. For he descended from heaven when he said γνῶθι σεαυτόν; that is, "Know yourself"' (1979, 136).

Struggle is also a feature of Peter Abelard's essay *Ethics—Know Thyself*. It is, he says, only because the vices exist in us that the struggle for good can be fought. Within us this means withdrawing consent from doing wrong things, and from avoiding doing good things. Sin is the consent to vice; it is not the willingness to sin, but the consent to this will. Intention and not performance is key here, and the struggle to KT aims at having a deeper understanding of one's intentions.

Aquinas (1225–1274)

Aquinas is concerned with the same aporias of KT as we saw in Augustine and before him Aristotle. His thinking on this has been rehearsed recently by two commentators, Richard Lambert[2] and Therese Scorelli Cory.[3] Both show Aquinas trying to negotiate his way through the first principle of NN and its appearance in the human intellect as KT.

Aquinas states the aporia in *Summa Theologica* I.87.1. With Augustine, the intellect can know itself differently from any other object because the intellect can know intelligible substance as its own self-knowing. With Aristotle comes the suggestion that intellect understands itself, as it does other objects, through representation and not therefore according to its own essence.[4]

Aquinas responds with a hierarchy of levels of actuality. God is the pure and perfect actuality of NN, an act with no division between knower and known. Angels share this substance as their own actuality, but not in the pure sense that God does. The angel's act of self-knowing is 'not completed by his essence' (Aquinas, 1922, 217).[5] The human intellect is only potentially self-knowing, but requiring actuality to be so, and is dependent here upon the active intellect. It knows itself not by its essence but by its act.[6]

There is not just a hierarchy of intellects here, i.e., of God, angels, and the human individual; there is also a hierarchy within the human intellect. It can be self-knowing in the sense of being aware of itself, of knowing that it has understanding. This, says Aquinas, is the KT of Socrates and Plato. It teaches the soul *that* it exists. But as to *what* the soul is, this requires specialist enquiry. This is found more explicitly in *Summa Contra Gentiles*. We know that the soul is through its acts and we seek 'to discover what it is, from a knowledge of its acts and objects, by means of the principles of the speculative sciences' (Aquinas, 1975b, 158).[7] This is to say that the human intellect can be present to itself habitually as the immediate principle of the possible intellect. But in the acts of the intellect there has to be some distance between passive and active intellects, 'with the result that the mind can never understand itself through its essence' (Aquinas, 1953);[8] and again, the soul 'goes out from itself in the understanding, and through things outside returns to knowledge of itself. Thus it does not understand itself through its essence' (Aquinas, 1953).[9] In short, the problem is that 'there is more composition in the understanding of the soul than in its existence' (Aquinas, 1953).[10]

For Lambert these are the definitive statements from Aquinas on self-knowing; 'our mind cannot so understand itself that it immediately apprehends itself. Rather it comes to a knowledge of itself through apprehension of other things' (Aquinas, 1953).[11] Lambert's conclusion here is that self-awareness in Aquinas is only a 'secondary form of knowledge' (Lambert, 2007, 276) because knowledge of self is derivative of knowledge of objects and therefore 'neither original nor foundational' (2007, 276). This is a very clear restatement of the ancient logic of the in-itself and the errors that accrue to any mediation.

Cory takes a different view. For her, the most mature statement on KT in Aquinas comes in the *Book of Causes*, proposition 15, written near the end of his life and restating the hierarchy of intellects. She too draws on *De Veritate 10.8* to distinguish between self-awareness that the soul exists and the philosophical knowledge of what the soul is. However, where Lambert remains unconvinced regarding the soul having direct access to itself in Aquinas's thinking, Cory is perhaps more ambitious in trying to work through the aporia of NN and KT in terms of a theory of the actuality of dependency. She finds in Aquinas an attempt to see KT as intellectual but 'in a human way' (Cory, 2014, 41).

If *De anima* is correct and the intellect knows itself in the same way as it knows other things, then it will always be dependent upon the form—the actuality of the thinking of—the object. However, what is here a limitation in the extent of self-knowing will be developed by Aquinas into a theory of the true science of self-knowing. Actual knowing will be seen as the intellect taking the actual form of the object. Might we say here that the thinking of the object forms matter and provides the intellect with its self-knowing as its own *self-in-formation*.[12] This expresses how Aquinas makes the case that the active self-knowing is always embodied and that this does not prevent the immaterial intellect from understanding its own self-in-formation.[13]

What Cory is alluding to here is a theory of dependency that can also be a theory of actual self-determination. In his *Commentary on the Soul*,[14] Aquinas takes up Aristotle's claim that the intellect is intelligible in the way other things are. Since the potential intellect, like a blank tablet, is ready for the impression upon it of form or actuality, so it becomes intelligible in the same way as other intelligible objects. Not only does the potential intellect ensure that the intellect cannot know its own essence, because it always requires the separation of potential from actual, it also guards against the threat of infinite regression of an intellect cognizing itself as a representation of a representation of a representation *ad infinitum*, never arriving at a knowledge of itself. This is the insight in Cory's work: actual dependency as a form of KT that fits within the hierarchy of intellects.

When the intellect is in-formed by an intelligible species of an external object, not only is the object actually known, but the intellect also becomes aware of itself, knowing the intelligible species. If the knowledge of the first intelligible is dependent upon external sensory experience, the second knowledge is dependent upon this dependence. What is crucial here for Aquinas and Cory is that both the cognized object and the cognizing intellect are cognized in the same way. One species does 'double duty' (2014, 56), says Cory, but in the same vein, one species does double dependence. Thus, KT is of the same kind of truth as NN because here the cognized intellect 'is both its existence and its essence solely "by its act"' (Cory, 2014, 56, emphasis removed).[15] Cory calls this a 'phenomenological experience of self-knowledge' (2014, 56) as part of the case for understanding KT as intellect but in a human way. It addresses the question she asks, namely, 'How can one affirm the dependence of actual self-awareness on cognition of extramental objects without undermining the intimate, first person character of our ordinary self-awareness?' (2014, 69) It is also close to Booth's concern to hold Augustine's KT to human subjectivity. Cory is asking here, how can the immediacy of essence and the mediation of actuality be reconciled to allow for the truth of self-knowing? How can the double dependency in which 'I understand myself to understand' (2014, 71) claim to be anything other than a composite truth and therefore in error when compared to pure truth in-itself?

The key to understanding this understanding of understanding lies in the nature of *actual* self-knowing. For Corey, the mind is not seen by Aquinas to be a vessel into which is dragged information about the world.[16] On the contrary, all understanding is the single formation of two elements, cognizer and cognized, in which cognizer and cognized are actually the one act of understanding. This means there is no 'bare self' (2014, 105) which has thought as its own instrument or property or tool. There is only, always and already, the self-in-act, the thinking self that is always already actual. Cory states that Aquinas 'does not think of an act as something independently perceptible' (2014, 108). Instead, the I and the act of thinking are the one actuality, the one existing and cognizing subject. This 'immediacy of actuality' (2014, 109) is a self-awareness even more intimate than the immediacy of sensation. It is such a powerful awareness of self that it provides for an implicit self-awareness capable of carrying an obvious and perhaps quotidian notion of a first-person agent, a selfhood, or an I that is present to us as the awareness of existing. Importantly for Cory, this is the same immediacy of actuality that the divine and angelic intellects enjoy. But whereas they are always already in act and require no species from outside, the immediacy of the human intellect is species-dependent.

Dependent actuality and double duty express the dualism in Aquinas between implicit and explicit self-awareness. Implicit self-awareness is the 'formal principle' (2014, 150) of actual intelligibility, while explicit self-awareness is the process of actuality which actualizes both the cognized and the self-actuality of the cognizer. This is the human KT of the divine NN in a hierarchy of intellects.[17]

What is radical in Cory's interpretation is perhaps also modern. The idea that there is no bare self, only an actual self, opens up the problem of the infinite regression of the actual self being just an eternally changing essence and therefore not an essence at all. Slavoj Zizek has recently argued against any such idea of a bare self, preferring instead the priority of recollection, or actuality, over essence. What is perhaps conservative, and ancient, in Cory's interpretation is that actuality is not made its own rational principle of the instability it presents for essence. If 'dependent actuality' is a fixed idea then it is immune from itself, immune from its dependency upon itself, and immune also from the (perceived) threat of infinite regression. If dependent actuality is not immune from itself then it is never fixed and is never in-itself because it is always another actuality in being known again. If there is no bare self, there is no potential intellect, for both are ideas made by dependent actuality only retrospectively to compensate for the vulnerability of dependent actuality. When Cory says 'I can presumably isolate a bare notion of "myself" by means of the conceptual separation" used in discovering metaphysical notions like "substance" and "being"' (2014, 171) this allows the bare self immunity from its dependency upon the actuality that thinks it. Why does it have such immunity, unless it is to defend dependent actuality against its own infinite regression in the repeated negation of even the possibility of essence? If there is no science of the logic of dependent actuality, then it is not rational in the sense of modern metaphysics.[18]

Judaism

Alexander Altmann has explored KT in Islamic and Judaic thinking up to the earliest period of the European Renaissance according to three motifs. The first is the likeness of a soul to God, with Delphi seen as a 'warning against hubris' (Altmann, 1969, 4–5) and a reminder of the virtue of *sophrosyne*. According to Werner Jaeger this is 'converted into its opposite' (Jaeger, 1962, 165) when the individual emerged from Aristotle's cave and saw the likeness of God to the individual soul. Altmann sees here the Empedoclean motif of life being known only by life.

The second motif is of man as microcosm, mirroring God, creation, and the universe in both body and soul. It is found in Democritus, Aristotle, Philo, and Egyptian astrology and rabbinic literature.[19] Altmann suggests that Porphyry is the first to attest to the microcosm motif and the Delphic Oracle in his *On "Know Thyself"*. Haberman[20] suggests that the origin of the parallel between man and universe goes back to the oldest Babylonian literature. The Talmud and Midrashim also mention similar analogies, having no direct dependence on Greek philosophy.[21] In *Timaeus*, Plato says that the world is a living thing of which all other living things are parts and that the gods imitated the shape of the universe in the shape of a man's head.[22] Aristotle was first to use the term 'microcosm' (*Physics*, VIII. 2. 252b 26–7) but did not employ the idea in his writing. The Hebrew for microcosm is *olum qatan*, meaning small world. It is first found in the Midrash Tanhuma.[23] In *The Fathers According to Rabi Nathan*, Rabbi Yose, the Galilean, says that whatever God created in the world 'He created in man' (Goldin, 1955, 127). Abraham Bar Hayya quotes Job 19:26 at the start of his *Meditation of the Sad Soul* (c. 11th–12th) to emphasize that in knowing one's creation one can 'comprehend the wisdom of your Creator' (Altmann, 1969, 38).

The third motif is that of the Neoplatonic (aporetic) relation between soul and intellect, or between the individual and the universal. For Philo, Socratic self-knowing, equivalent to Terah, the father of Abraham, does not go far enough. It subjects the self to philosophical speculation, but Abraham knew also to renounce self-knowing in order to attain to an exact knowledge of God.[24] Abraham, in truly knowing himself, renounces this self. Similarly Philo notes Moses' intention is that 'those who approach the service of the living God should first of all know themselves and their own essence' (Philo, 1993, 559).[25]

This motif is also taken up by Porphyry in *On "Know Thyself"*, by Augustine and by Proclus, and in the *Theology of Aristotle*. Porphyry is the first to use the term 'inner man', found also in Augustine's *Confessions*.[26] For Porphyry the immortal inner man requires to be known so that the outer man, which is an image of this immortality, might also be known. This is philosophical work, and 'since a human is a microcosm of the cosmos, knowing oneself leads to knowing the universe' (Johnson, 2013, 311). Ignorance, he says, is 'utterly evil when it disparages the divinity in oneself' (2013, 311). Therefore if we 'are eager unerringly to philosophize, we shall desire earnestly to know ourselves, and we shall attain a true philosophy, proceeding from our own perception towards the contemplation of the Whole' (Altmann and Stern, 2009, 204).

We will not pursue Altmann's three themes separately. Instead we will explore them as a whole from the Jewish perspective of Isaac Israeli, Maimonides, and Joseph ibn Saddiq.

Isaac Israeli (ca. 855–ca. 955)

The importance of Isaac Israeli's Neoplatonic thinking on KT is stated in the following terms by Altmann and Stern.

> At the dawn of the second millennium of the common era, Isaac Israeli (c855-c955) bears witness to the adoption and adaptation of Greek philosophy in Islamic culture, and gives evidence of an interest in philosophy not seen among Jews since the time of Philo Judaeus in the first century CE. (Altmann and Stern, 2009, vii)

Israeli's *Book of Definitions* defines the four types of enquiry necessary to arrive at knowledge of things. Borrowed from Aristotle's *Posterior*

Analytics[27] these are: whether a thing exists, ει εστι; what the thing is, its quiddity, τι εστιν; whether it has a certain attribute, το οτι; and why it has a certain attribute, το διοτι. These match the four causes: movement, logos, material, and final cause.[28]

Then Israeli defines philosophy as 'the love of wisdom' (2009, 24) but ties it immediately to KT. Philosophy may well be 'the assimilation to the works of the Creator . . . according to human capacity' (2009, 24), *but* it is also the case that philosophy is 'man's knowledge of himself' (2009, 27). Indeed, man, 'if he acquires a true knowledge of himself, viz. of his spirituality and corporeality, comprises the knowledge of everything, viz. of the spiritual and corporeal substance, as in man are joined substance and accident' (2009, 27). He reiterates,

> It is clear that man, if he knows himself in both his spirituality and cor-
> poreality, comprises the knowledge of all, and knows both the spiritual
> and the corporeal substance, and also knows the first substance which
> is created from the power of the Creator without mediator. (2009, 27)

In sum, if a man knows all things, 'he comprises the knowledge of every-thing and is worthy to be called a philosopher' (2009, 27).

Altmann and Stern interpret this, and Israeli's work overall, in terms of emanations out and back from the divine source. Israeli insisted on creation from nothing, which was a 'fundamental concept in orthodox-rabbinic Juda-ism' (2009, 152). They see here the Platonic influence of turning the soul away from sense perception and toward spiritual substance. They tie Israeli closely to the idea expressed in the *Phaedo* that one must pursue truth in life by pursuing the death of the corporeal life. Here, to know death in life is to KT.

They also tie Israeli to the microcosm motif in KT found clearly in Al-Kindi and the Ikhwan, and in al-Mas'udi. Their common point of reference might have been Porphyry's *On "Know Thyself"*, which they state can be 'regarded as one of the sources for the definition of philosophy as self-knowledge' (2009, 204). They argue that Al-Kindi and Israeli would have followed Por-phyry, Proclus, and the Ikhwan, in agreement that 'the ultimate purpose of self-knowledge is to understand the true nature of the soul and its ascent to the upper world' (2009, 207). Israeli might be taken to mean that this even-tually leads to 'union with the supernal wisdom' (2009, 207) but not that this is equated with a knowledge of God. Israeli 'does not quote the famous saying "he who knows himself, knows his Lord", which is well-attested in 10th-century Islamic and Jewish sources' (2009, 208).[29]

Maimonides (1138–1204)

The Eight Chapters of Maimonides' Introduction to his *Commentary on the Mishnah* and his *Laws Concerning Character Traits* from *The Book of Knowledge* both advise the soul to live in the way of the middle, for it is the way of the wise man, and it is the 'way of the Lord' (Maimonides, 1983, 30). Recovery from disease of the soul is achieved by moving from one extreme character trait to its extreme opposite, and to accustom itself there until able to return to the middle way. Moderation, nothing in excess, 'is one of the good actions, and the state of the soul that produces moderation is a moral virtue' (1983, 67). Such virtue is KT to the extent that

> the perfect man needs to inspect his moral habits continually, weigh his actions, and reflect upon the state of his soul every single day. Whenever he sees his soul inclining toward one of the extremes, he should rush to cure it and not let the evil state become established by the repetition of a bad action . . . he should attend to the defective moral habit in himself and continually seek to cure it, for a man inevitably has defects. (1983, 73)

These inevitable imperfections persist in keeping man's soul slightly off center. Maimonides insists that man subordinate all the soul's powers to attaining knowledge of God through his thinking. Like Augustine, he believes that study in general, and to study oneself diligently, are 'among the greatest acts of worship' (1983, 75).

In the eighth chapter of the *Laws* Maimonides rehearses a theme found in *The Guide of the Perplexed* that God is not to be known according to human attributes. He does not know by means of knowledge, nor live by means of life as we understand it. To know by knowledge would be to find multiplicity in the One. Instead, God is 'identical with His attributes and His attributes are identical with Him, so that one says that He is the Knowledge, the Knower, and the Known' (1983, 94), or NN. There is no genitive here. God therefore knows and understands himself in a way that finite beings are incapable of. As such, 'the actions of man are entrusted to him . . . it is up to him to be virtuous or wicked, without God compelling him to either of these conditions' (1983, 95).

A recent study of Maimonides' *Mishneh torah* by David Gillis enables us to pursue the aporia of KT and NN in Maimonides, in particular through the macrocosm/microcosm motif. Gillis's interpretation, suggestive of an aporetic reading, we rehearse now.

There are various ways in which Gillis establishes the case for the *Mishneh torah* as a microcosm of the macrocosm. Structurally its four books on Commandments/civil law and its 10 books on the Commandments between man and God imitate the four sublunar elements and the 10 immaterial angelic substances of the spheres above the Earth. The inference is that the Commandments of the Torah are designed to bring the human being 'into line with the ideal order of the cosmos' (Gillis, 2015, 6). As the ascent through the spheres, for example in Dante and Avicenna, is an educational journey, so in the *Mishneh torah* the knowledge of God at the end has developed from what it was at the beginning. In short, macrocosm/microcosm works here as a model of *imitatio*; 'to be so perfectly like the cosmos as to inspire in others the love and fear of God, and the desire for knowledge, that contemplation of the cosmos itself inspires' (2015, 35).

In line with the Aristotelian notion of virtue as the middle way, the Commandments of the Torah translate the perfect order of nature 'into norms of human behaviour that avoid excess or deficiency' (2015, 39). Gillis observes that Maimonides is nearer to Plato in seeing God as external to nature but nearer to Aristotle in holding that God can only be known by his works. Similarly, in line with the Aristotelian notion of actual substance, if the intellect in knowing an object also merges with that object, as actuality, then knowledge of God could 'entail some kind of likeness to God' (2015, 81).

Maimonides's problem is in accepting Genesis 1:26, 'Let us make man in our image, after our likeness'. To avoid anthropomorphic images of God made in man's image Maimonides retains the notion that for us God is ineffable. But the ideas of macrocosm/microcosm and imitation seem to require that man really be like God. Gillis describes this problem in the aporetic way that Aristotle described his own similar difficulties. The problem for Maimonides, says Gillis, is that both intellectual and moral virtue require likeness to God, whilst He remained unknowable. Gillis concludes 'a way must be found in which human beings are like God, yet not like God' (2015, 81), imitating precisely Aristotle's own expression of this aporia in the *Metaphysics* that 'There cannot then be a definition of anything; or rather in a sense there can be, and in a sense there cannot' (Aristotle, 1984b, 1640).[30] It is this aporetic thinking that perhaps drives Gillis's own interpretation of Maimonides's notion of intellectual and moral virtue. We will see below to what extent he thinks he can find a way out of this difficulty.

Gillis explores the relationship between the first two parts of Maimonides's *Book of Knowledge,* which is Book 1 of the *Code.* These two parts are 'The Laws Of The Foundation Of The Torah' and the 'Laws Of Ethical Qualities' (hereafter FT and EQ).[31] Gillis reads the structure of these parts as grounded in the model of macrocosm/microcosm. FT moves through the sequence of God, angels/stars/spheres to sublunary material and action. EQ moves from mind to emotions/appetites to the body and behavior. If FT imitates the cosmic hierarchy, then EQ and especially the human being, is the microcosmic likeness of that macrocosm.

Pursuant of the aporia concerning the likeness of man to God, Gillis discerns a correspondence between intellectual and moral virtue, based on a further correspondence between the pedagogical structure of the *Mishneh torah* and the theme of ascent and descent expressed in the final chapter of the *Guide.* Central to Gillis's account is the idea that thought can change behavior, and desire (behavior) can change knowledge (thought). Both human and heavenly bodies see the universe (physics), desire to understand it (metaphysics), and experience love for the Creator whose goodness should now be imitated (ethics). This is a path from theoretical virtue to moral virtue where the former replicates the desire and activities of the cosmic order. In reverse, those pursuing moral virtue in the sublunary realm, in obeying the commandments, will open the soul to the order and knowing of creation, to the desire to live according to one's intellectual understanding of creation. Here ethics leads to physics and to metaphysics, where moral behaviour now becomes 'a dictate of reason at the end of the *Guide*' (2015, 108). Moral virtue is a kind of knowledge of God, and the knowledge of God is a kind of moral virtue.

This employment of the macrocosm/microcosm model expresses the aporia of knowing and not knowing God; it represents 'both moral virtue as preparation for intellectual virtue and moral virtue as consequent on intellectual virtue' (2015, 109). In terms of the *Book of Knowledge*, FT is theoretical perfection, EQ is moral perfection, but only in an aporetic interplay, each with the other. If moral self perfection is 'equivalent to a kind of knowledge of God' (2015, 111) then Gillis thinks Maimonides has established 'considerable mobility between the two' (2015, 111).

But employing the NN from Aristotle, Gillis also argues that, since in actuality the form and its thought are a unity, so each of us is actually what we think. We are not God, and yet, in thinking him, we are also like him. God is beyond human comprehension,[32] nonetheless,

> Despite this unbridgeable, incomprehensible gap, when your intellect is active, your subjective self, your intellect, and the thought you are thinking are in a state of unity and analogous to the unity that is God, and in that sense you are one in God's likeness. (2015, 115)

If we do not rule out aporia as error here, then this KT as thought thinking itself is an aporetic way of knowing God. But Gillis refines aporia into analogy. He notes Maimonides's view that this kind of actuality of KT as NN happens only very rarely in the acquired intellect, and means that much time is spent only in the potential intellect. When it does happen, the best that can be said of it is that it is a likeness to God not as 'identity' but as 'analogy' (2015, 117).

Gillis concludes his attempt, within the aporia of knowing and not knowing God, to create a model that relates intellectual and moral virtue in a likeness to God, in the following formula: 'the *operation* of human intellect is God-like by analogy; the *product* of that operation, at its highest level, is angel-like by identity' (2015, 118). In FT intellectual virtue is God-like by its identity with the separate intellects, while moral virtue and moral action in the microcosm/macrocosm model is God-like by analogy. This model of macrocosm/microcosm employed in knowing God means that the more one establishes

> the role of intellect over all his faculties, making unity out of multiplicity [and] thus reflecting the unity in the multiplicity of the cosmos . . . [so] the more closely he approximates the condition of the one who possesses a unity that passes understanding and for whom all knowledge is

self-knowledge. That approximation is perhaps as much knowledge of God as is to be had. (2015, 122–3)

KT here both is and also is not the knowing of God.

But perhaps Gillis is not true to this aporetic reading when he says that, at this point, 'We thus have a solution to the problem with which we started, of how to fulfil the command to know a God who is unknowable, and without violating the doctrine of negative attributes' (2015, 130). Calling this 'a circle completed' (2015, 130), and a 'solution' is perhaps underestimating the persistence of, and the truth of, the aporia, which is not resolved but practiced as the incompletion of analogy and identity. Can this aporetic *incompletion* instead be understood as the truth of metaphysical, physical, and ethical education in, of, and for itself? If so, perhaps this questions the logic and structure of the 'philosophical principles' (2015, 134) that Gillis believes Maimonides has not violated in producing a God who can be known neither in himself nor anthropomorphically.

Another correspondence of macrocosm/microcosm is that between the Commandments which mediate man and God and the spheres. Both are 'intermediary between the non-corporeal and the world of matter' (2015, 165). As the stars influence matter, so Commandments influence earthly life. The man-God Commandments, like the spheres, are a ladder to God. Gillis argues that the desire to be close to God comes through the knowledge of the creator of the laws, accompanied by the fear of their prescriptions. Awe experienced at the cosmos is not so much for its size, for awe at the cosmos without a love of God is idolatry, but rather at the difference between God's knowledge and human knowledge. This is where 'cosmology becomes epistemology' (2015, 193), a 'dawn of consciousness' (2015, 186) and a way of knowing that is awe, fear, and love. The prophet enjoys a much more direct form of relationship. The Torah's Commandments 'represent Moses' unsurpassed, and unsurpassable prophetic understanding of the cosmos translated into norms of behaviour' (2015, 189). The Commandments enact 'a human being's microcosmic form' (2015, 191). As cosmology becomes epistemology, so epistemology becomes love of God, and both intellectual and moral virtue are *imitatio Dei*. The Commandments 'dissolve the Aristotelian partition between moral and intellectual virtue, directing, even converting, experience to knowledge' (2015, 207). Their mediation of man and God preserves what the aporia, at first glance, appears to destroy.

The direction of travel here is from God to man by means of emanation. The universe directs forms onto the human mind by means of the agent intellect. Here the universe '*is* intelligibility' (2015, 193). It is 'the complete manifestation of God's wisdom, and it actively communicates that wisdom, each mind comprehending it according to its capacity' (2015, 193). Logic is the means by which the mind, through emanation, can receive God's wisdom in the cosmos. By the end of the book, Gillis makes it absolutely clear that the *Mishneh torah*, as a work of art, has an educational goal, and that its design is its pedagogy. The *Mishneh torah* is not a book about education; it is a book that does education.

The first 10 books of *Mishneh torah* move in a hierarchy from higher to lower and can be read as Neoplatonic emanation or 'the successive levels of hypostasis in the Plotinian system, as adopted by Al-Farabi' (2015, 208). Gillis argues that each book in the *Mishneh torah* emanates from the preceding one. The self-perfect *Book of Knowledge* overflows into the remaining books. 'Just as the universe emanates from God, so *Mishneh torah* emanates from its opening assertion of God's existence, which is like a stone thrown into a pond, the ripples expanding to cover all of reality' (2015, 260). *Mishneh torah* also has a hierarchy of holiness, where rank depends upon distance from the absolutely holy. The *Book of Knowledge* is the contemplative mode, which does not imitate God in his relation to the world, but is instead 'intellect intellecting itself' (2015, 234).

In the structure of the *Mishneh torah*, Jacob's dream becomes the working of the cosmos and the education of the prophet and his community. Jacob's dream is a ladder of ascent and descent. The first 10 books of *Mishneh torah* ascend this ladder of knowledge and perfection, the last four books descend to the human realm. This notion of Neoplatonic return is a Judaic concept of repentance. 'It is a dual moment of introspection and retrospection, in which the hypostasis forms a thought of itself and the thought of the First Cause . . . it is a dual process of self-examination and of reconciliation with God' (2015, 264).

For Gillis, then, instead of an empirical model of the universe, which would be anachronous because grounded in emanation, *Mishneh torah* is to be seen as a work of art. It becomes a site where its own inner workings can educate the reader to divine truths. The experience of *Mishneh torah* is 'the kind of guided subjectivity that is the experience of art. In this way, the book is re-born in every reader' (2015, 380). But more than this, Gillis is able to retrieve the emanationist cosmos in Maimonides as specifically and deliberately an educational universe. God works enlightenment through nature. Objects are not created specifically for man, but for their own sakes. The educational significance here is that things glorify God most when they become what they truly are by discovery and then following their own laws. It is this overall educational aim of the created universe and its pedagogy in Maimonides that for Gillis is the artistic. It is in the aesthetic, in the sympathetic movement of the mind of the image of divine unity, that there is generated a '"form in the soul"—a subjective, integrative process that goes beyond ideas, resembling more and more, though never reaching, the ineffable unity of God' (2015, 381). What more can we ask of *Mishneh torah* as a work of art 'than that it should thus teach us to value existence' (2015, 385) by means of an 'educated wonder' (2015, 383) that can reunite NN and KT without necessarily losing the divinity of the one and the humanity of the other.

Joseph Ibn Saddiq (d. 1149)

Finally here we mention briefly the work of Joseph Ibn Saddiq who lived in the Jewish community of 12th-century Cordoba and died in 1149. In his *Microcosm* he states that his work is founded on his love of philosophy. The only path to wisdom is to understand the philosophers and the scholars, and this can only be achieved through knowledge of the four branches of wisdom: arithmetic, geometry, music, and astronomy. Retaining this emphasis on education, after study in the quadrivium are required dialectic and the art of inference from analogy.

Specifically on KT Saddiq is as bold as anyone on the relationship between microcosm and macrocosm. He says, 'from knowledge of himself he may come to know all' (Ibn Saddiq, 2003, 54).[33] Man can be called microcosm because 'there is in him a likeness to everything there is in the world, his body in respect of the physical world and his rational soul in respect of the spiritual world' (2003, 54). Philosophy is precisely this: 'man's knowledge of himself' (2003, 54).

KT is discussed specifically in part two of the *Microcosm*, beginning with Job 19:26, 'from my very flesh shall I perceive God' (2003, 77). Nothing remains in the physical world 'that does not have its counterpart in man' (2003, 82); indeed, the Brethren of Purity aligned the face and its features to the separate elements of the cosmos. With regard to the spiritual universe, whatever reason finds 'to be valid to a single soul will be valid in regard to the Universal Soul in its totality' (2003, 101). In sum, 'man was created, so to speak, in "God's image", that is, complete, in that he has in him the likeness of everything that the Creator, may He be blessed, created; and hence he is called a microcosm' (2003, 103).

On theological issues Haberman, his translator here, explains that Saddiq refutes doctrines that lead 'to a regressus in infinitum' (2003, 29), which is clearly 'absurd' (2003, 29). He also refutes proofs for the eternity of the world which are grounded in 'the Aristotelian definition of time as the number of motion, according to the prior and the posterior' (2003, 29). Saddiq instead says that there is no before or after. Time is created with the world and as such time and the movements of the celestial bodies are not eternal, for 'before the production of the spheres time did not exist' (2003, 29). God created the world *ex nihilo* as 'an act of love; the diffusion of God which produced a perfect world' (2003, 29). But Saddiq avoids emanation here perhaps because 'it is inconsistent with the belief in creation ex nihilo'. Like Maimonides, who knew Saddiq (2003, 18), the latter maintained that 'all positive attributes, whether essential or inessential, are to be understood in a figurative way. Only negative attributes may be applied to God, who is indefinable' (2003, 29).

Notes

1. This had been the title of a book by Jean-Louis Guez de Balzac (1597–1654) *Socrate chrétien, par le S. de Balzac*, published 1661.

2. Lambert groups Aquinas's writings on self-knowing into seven works. These are *Summa Theologica* I. q. 87 a. 1–4; *Summa Contra Gentiles*, III.46; *The Book of Causes*, Prop. 15; *Writings on the Sentences of Peter Lombard*, I.d.17.q.1a4, and III.d.23.q. 1a2; *Quodlibetal Questions*, VIII, q.2 a2; *Disputed Question on the Soul's Knowledge of itself*; and *Disputed Questions on Truth*, q.10, a, 8–10.
3. Between 1252–72 Cory sees Aquinas refining his version of KT so as to legitimate the opacity of the self to itself through a sophisticated theory of dependent actuality. She identifies three distinct but related phases in this refining. First his work in the *Sentences* (I.3.4.5 & III.23.I. 2 & 3); second in *De veritate* (10.8) and *Summa Contra Gentiles* (3.45); and third, a mature phase in *Summa Theologica* (1a. 87. 1), in *De anima* (III.1.3) and *The Book of Causes* (prop. 15).
4. Where essence here is interpreted as that which is immediately itself and without the distinction of knower and known.
5. *Summa Theologica* I.87.1.
6. See Aquinas (1922, 218).
7. *Summa Contra Gentiles* 3.1; ch. 46. 11.
8. *De veritate* I.q10.Art VIII.8 at http://dhspriory.org/thomas/english/QDdeVer.htm
9. *De veritate* I.q10.Art VIII.10.
10. *De veritate* I.q10.Art VIII.12.
11. *De veritate* I.q10.Art VIII. Reply.
12. My phrase, not Cory's.
13. This requires the distinction, unique to Aquinas, says Cory, between a self-awareness brought about by knowing the species of the objects, and essential self-knowledge that is possible in philosophical and scientific reasoning. It is perhaps the kind of distinction found much later in Hegel between natural and philosophical consciousness.
14. Specifically on *De anima* 429a 22–430a 9.
15. See *Summa Theologica* I. 87.1. (Aquinas, 1922, 217).
16. See Cory (2014, 70).
17. Cory argues that the distinction between understanding the intelligible and understanding that I intelligibly understand the understanding is found in *Sentences* I.2.1.ad1, and 1.10.1.5. ad2; in *De veritate* 1.5. ad5; in *Summa Theologica* 1. 87. 3. ad2 and 1. 93.7. ad4 among others; (see Cory, 2014, 143)
18. Our own view of modern metaphysics in Part 2 takes up this challenge of a modern rational human science of the logic of KT and its relation to the truth of NN. What this offers is not ever-more intricate and scholastic *distinctiones* or citing of an *exceptiones*, but a redefinition of essence and truth according to the educational logic that Cory's dependent actuality expresses but which is not pursued as its own aporetic subjective substance, or as the modern logic of KT.
19. See Altmann (1969, 21).
20. In his Introduction to his translation of *The Microcosm of Joseph Ibn Saddiq*; Ibn Saddiq (2003).
21. It is also present in the pre-Socratics. See, for example, Collingwood (1960), *The Idea of Nature*.
22. *Timaeus* 30d and 44d.
23. Section Pequde, §3; see Saddiq (2003, 24).
24. See Philo, *On Dreams* I.X. 57–9, in Philo (1993, 370).
25. *The Special Laws*, I.XLIX. 263–4.
26. *Confessions* X.6.9; Augustine (1998, 184).
27. II.1. 89b 22–5
28. See Altmann and Stern (2009, 13).
29. They note that Ibn Saddiq, in his *Microcosm*, 'adopts the doctrine, if not the actual formula, of the Islamic hadith, "he who knows himself, knows his Lord"'

(Altmann and Stern, 2009, 208). The microcosm motif could perhaps be claimed for Judah Halevi, in *The Kuzari*, when he says that God arranges order and harmony for humankind 'in the same systematic way as God has done for the universe' (Halevi, 1964, 209–210).

30. *Metaphysics* 1039a 20–2.
31. This differs from the translation by Russell and Weinberg, who have 'The Foundation of the Torah' and 'Discernment'; see Maimonides (1981).
32. *Guide*, i. 57; Maimonides (1963, 132–3).
33. Altmann and Stern argue that Saddiq derives his version of KT from Israeli's *Book of Definitions* (2009, 30n).

4 Avicenna to Ibn Arabi

Al-Kindi (c. 800–870), in his *On the Definitions and Descriptions of Things*, includes within his summary of the ancient definition of philosophy not only the familiar Alexandrian definitions—love of wisdom, awareness of the soul's need for the death of the body and of its desires, and the idea of philosophy as the first science—but also an idea not apparently adopted by the Alexandrians, *know thyself*. Al-Kindi states here that the ancients said, 'Philosophy is man's knowing himself' (Altmann and Stern, 2009, 28) and that this is a 'saying of noble scope and great profundity' (2009, 28). When a man discovers that he has a soul which is substance, distinct from the body, which is corporeal, then 'he knows everything. For this reason the philosophers called man a microcosm' (2009, 28).[1]

Altmann suggests that Islam draws on three related versions of the motif of KT. As we will see, Ibn Arabi notes the Hadith, which attributes to the prophet the saying 'He who knows himself knows his Lord', as well as 'He who knows himself best knows his Lord best'.[2] The Brethren of Purity quote both of these, while Altmann suggests that the first record of the saying as a *hadith* is by Yahya ben Mu'adh (d. 871). Avicenna and Al-Ghazali suggest that the interdependence of knowledge of the soul and of God is found in the Qur'an, 59:19, 'Do not act like those who have forgotten God, so that he has caused them to forget themselves'.[3]

The third version of KT is not a *hadith*, and is quoted by Avicenna and Averroes as KT and thou will know the Lord. Ascribed to a Greek temple, this version is of Greek origin.[4] It is Avicenna, however, building on the emanationist cosmos of Al-Farabi, that we will explore first, and here our guide will be Henry Corbin.

Avicenna (980–1037)

In Avicenna the emanationist cosmos is educational in itself, primarily through emanation and an 'angelic pedagogy' (Corbin, 1990, 46) in which the individual is able to reorient itself from its earthly form to a spiritual and esoteric journey of KT. In Avicenna's angelology the universe of emanation contains the path of self-knowledge. As Corbin argues, Avicennan symbols and recitals are 'the place of a personally lived adventure' (1990, 4) in this universe. The imagination is required to create the symbolisms that carry the *imago mundi*, which is the image of an individual's own inner world and expresses 'the deepest being of the person' (1990, 7).

In contemplating itself, and telling the story of itself, it embarks on a journey of self-knowing. Central to this is the idea of the Orient, where the self is reoriented to a spiritual world and away from the material world, which appears, now, as a way of living only in exile, and as a stranger in a strange land. The journey from stranger consciousness to the Orient is told in a trilogy of Avicennan Recitals. In the first, *Recital of Hayy ibn Yaqzan*, 'the meaning of the Orient is announced to the adept by a messenger from the Orient itself' (1990, 123). By the end of this illumination into KT the pilgrim is invited to follow his guide. The *Recital of the Birds* remembers the 'psychic event of the inwardly experienced celestial ascent' (1990, 123), and at its completion what is revealed to each of the birds is 'the mystery of its own Self: a self that overflows its terrestrial and exiled ego' (1990, 203). The final recital is that of *Salaman and Absal*. This concerns the exile from Paradise 'and the Progressive return to the original state of bliss and perfection' (1990, 207). It is 'the autobiography, the adventure, of the mystical soul' (1990, 235). In self-consciousness the soul can know the angel, the active intelligence, who appears as a definite individual, acting as a guide into the spiritual world on a journey oriented to returning home from exile. Here Occident and Orient are not found 'in our atlases' (1990, 16), but in meaning.

When the soul learns of itself in exile this is the beginning of Avicenna's version of KT, according to a dual nature of earthly self and celestial transcendental self. It involves a guardian angel appearing to the individual, which individualizes 'the relation of the soul to the Active Intelligence' (1990, 21). It is where the soul, aware of itself in exile, meets itself in νους.

This return from exile has its structure and its movement in the emanation model of the universe. While holding the primordial unity as unchangeable, eternal, and indivisible, Avicenna explains how from this divine unity 'there precedes a First Intelligence, or a First Archangel-Cherub whose being already contains a duality, since its own being is distinct from its necessity for being' (1990, 25). For Avicenna here, emanation allows the many to proceed from the One without compromising or corrupting the unity of the One,[5] and in turn this allows the soul of the One to know itself able to return to the One. There is a trinity here, for the archangel is able to know itself by seeing its principle, but it is a trinity of emanation, not of the modern rational self-consciousness of subject and object. Emanation—the one, the duality, and the principle (νους)—is the creativity of the One, achieved without reducing itself in any way. Emanation is the apprehension of its own necessity. As such, the universe in its structure and its movement is its *knowing itself*.

The first triadic emanation leads to a second, culminating in the ten spheres, 'until it terminates with the active intellect which governs our selves'

(Avicenna, 2005, 331). In this triadic emanation of self-re-creation, the first being is the first knowing or intellection of the first principle by itself. Darkness is part of this process because there is a desire in the soul to return to the archangel 'from whom it emanates and of whom it is the thought' (1990, 61). From within this first archangel there proceeds the second archangel, the celestial soul, and the orb that it moves. Archangel, soul, and heavenly sphere are the hypostatization of the One. This continues to the heaven of the fixed stars and then through the seven planetary spheres until the ninth archangel emanates a tenth intelligence and the soul which moves the heaven of the moon. It is the active intellect, which, being exhausted, splinters into human souls and elementary matter. In each case, it is the desire of the soul for the intelligence from which it emanates that creates motion. The hierarchy of emanation is created because, as each heavenly intellect looks up to its source, the effect of this perception is to create another lower sphere. Corbin refers to this process of emanation, consisting of desire and the resulting body and soul, as one which seems to cast a shadow of itself, a shadow that is 'propagated from heaven to heaven until, after the Tenth Archangel, the shadow itself becomes the Active Intelligence and demiurge of our sublunary world, the nocturnal zone of matter or terrestrial "Occident"' (1990, 25).

Corbin draws from this a form of phenomenology that resonates with a *bildungsroman*, a study of self-realization and education. It is a phenomenology in which the mediation of immediate light is the shadow cast as soul and body in the universe. As the intellectual universe is driven by the necessity that re-creates itself by knowing itself, a necessity and knowing that drives it ever further from its source, so it enacts this educational drama in which origin is related to its being as light is to shadow. As terrestrial matter, the shadow has emanated as far away from its origin as it is possible to go. This is the exile on earth of the intellect from its own principle.

For Corbin here, the idea of intellect 'falling' is not an appropriate way of describing emanation. In contrast to a universe marked by a fall from good to evil, the Avicennan angelic cosmology is one of pathos. 'Each heaven is the thought of an Archangel, not of an Archangel fallen from his station, but rather an Archangel "saddened" by the limitation of his being' (1990, 26). The celestial motions here are 'an immense symphony of desire and nostalgia for a boundless perfection' (1990, 26). The souls of the exiles are not the result of an original sin, and the cosmos does not have a demonic character. Rather, these souls share this drama of the sadness because the exile is one of 'the same celestial race as the original dramatis personae' (1990, 26). It is for the human soul on Earth 'to decide whether its angelic or its demonic' (1990, 60) side is to flourish.

Thinking of the Avicennan universe as this triadic emanationist phenomenology, we see a universe enacting the imperative: *cosmos: know thyself*, according to the conditions of the possibility of its own self-developing, self-educating first principle. Emanation is the triadic and creative process

of intellect knowing itself, moved by pathos and nostalgia (rather than negation and separation). This education is the whole of the first principle being
what it is, namely, a self-longing to return from exile in the necessity to KT.
This education becomes lost to itself in the material conditions of the occidental world of exile. But the cosmos has left a trail of celestial breadcrumbs
by which the exile who learns of truth in sadness can return to this truth
through another educational journey, reoriented away from the Occident to
the spiritual.

Corbin says this KT of the exile begins in a 'phenomenology of the stranger-consciousness' (1990, 27) or in 'the soul's awakening to its consciousness
of being a Stranger' (1990, 27). Here the stranger can turn to *ta'wil,* which
consists in '"bringing back," recalling, returning to its origin, not only the
text of the book but also the cosmic context in which the soul is imprisoned'
(1990, 28). *Ta'wil* is an inner spiritual exegesis, an exodus from the Occident
of exoteric appearance 'to the *Orient* of the original and hidden Idea' (1990,
29). The truth that is to be returned to is symbolized in visions and recitals.
The symbol is not an allegory; it is 'the *unique* expression' (1990, 30) of
arriving at 'the experience of the soul to which a soul has attained' (1990,
31), reminding us here of Corbin's emphasis on *talem eum vidi qualem
capere potui,* the implication of which is that one sees that which one is
able to understand. It is this uniqueness of the symbol for each individual
that means it cannot be allegorical, and opposes any rational, general, and
abstract equivalence.[6] It is not a story that happens to others; it is 'the soul's
own story . . . personally lived' (1990, 33). Because it is told in the first person, it must be recited. Thus, in essence, the KT of this Oriental philosophy
is the reorientation of the one who has his home in this world becoming the
stranger in this world who has his home in the spiritual world. The stranger
will be open to the guide who will help to reorient the intellect to its true
source, the angel-spirit. This is the path to the symbols that will allow each
individual uniquely to see the ineffable in the conceptions open to this individual. On this path of cosmic and spiritual self-knowing the Occidental
philosopher becomes an 'Oriental philosopher' (1990, 36).

But Corbin does not merely find KT in the individual journey. As mentioned above, emanation in Corbin's Avicennism is the KT of the whole
universe, something similar to that which Dante would offer in the *Divine
Comedy* over 200 years later.[7] The triadic nature of emanation issues in an
angelic pedagogy. It is a 'sort of phenomenology of the angelic consciousness' (1990, 51). For Corbin this angelic pedagogy offers hermeneutics
against a relation of servitude between angel and God. This hermeneutics
is an 'annunciation and epiphany of the impenetrable and incommunicable
divine transcendence' (1990, 55). It is this hermeneutic function of the angel
that explains how, 'by knowing itself, the Soul knows the Angel and the
world of the Angel—that is, the world of the Souls and the world of the
Active Intelligences' (1990, 55). For Avicenna and Corbin here, knowing is
not a dialectic or a negation that separates into subject and object. Angelic

pedagogy instead is characterized by continuity, marked by the expression of emotion and of going and returning. In this sense emanation and reorientation of stranger consciousness toward the One is essentially a creative self-realization, or KT.

Corbin also argues that the philosophy of the angel as the 'hermeneut of the divine silence' (1990, 55) is able to 'destroy the dilemma' (1990, 55) of the plurality of prime movers expressed by Aristotle in *Metaphysics* XII. The division into monotheism and polytheism is only a 'splintering of abstract monotheism' (1990, 55), a multiplicity of monotheistic divine centers, whereas the angelic pedagogy is revelation in, of, and by emanation, which does not divide into the abstract opposition of the One and the many that plagues the Western *cogito*. For this soul, 'knowledge of itself is consciousness of the Angel' (1990, 56), and the Angel is of the One, not a human intellectual construction, or object. Crucial here is the fact that emanation is a continuity, while the mind in exile appears to be disconnected and seeks only exiled/rational ways of restoring its relationship to truth. Sadness and shadow are at their peak when the active intellect, the tenth cherub, no longer has the strength, in its turn, to reproduce itself as the trinity of one intellect, one soul, and one heavenly sphere. Instead, the triadic emanation splinters into 'the multitude of our individual souls' (1990, 56). From here it is the combination of sadness and angelic pedagogy—sadness looking up at the distance between the soul and its truth, and pedagogy as the structure of education that lies within the sadness of this distance—wherein 'the human soul can grasp the trajectory and the terminal mystery of the cosmic process' (1990, 56). Pedagogical sadness is the one continuity of the irradiation and emanation of the one truth. 'It is by acquiring consciousness of the structure of the angelic universe that the *anima humana* learns to behave as a soul *ad imitationem Animae coelestis*' (1990, 56).

Corbin's reading of the Avicennan pedagogy of the emanationist cosmos addresses directly the relation we are exploring between KT and NN. It offers a very different interpretation than that of Aristotle, Plotinus, or Augustine. Where Aristotle struggled with the aporia of the one and the many, where Plotinus resolved this in yielding individual KT to NN, and where Augustine preserved individual KT perhaps at the expense of a precise knowledge of NN, Corbin's Avicennan cosmos struggles with this aporia or dilemma in a different way. For Avicenna it is only in the land of exile that separation from the One appears total to a *cogito* that mistakes darkness for the logic of rational thinking. This *cogito* tries to avoid the infinite regression that its own reasoning creates in relation to absolute truth and subjectivity by positing something external that it then argues requires to be healed of this 'fall'. Against emanation, exiles in the zone of darkness take themselves and their rationality as the first principle and reduce the celestial pedagogy to superstition, or dismiss it empirically as speculative and theological nonsense. Here the NN is grounded in the identity of each exile. But for Corbin and Avicenna this NN has its true non-exiled being in emanation. The first caused is the intellection that the first principle has of itself. As such, 'the First Caused is precisely the Thought eternally thought by the Thought that thinks itself' (1990, 57), and emanates this self-knowing into a universe moved by the necessity of KT that such thinking carries.

The claim, then, is that Avicennan philosophy finds a way of expressing the One knowing itself without dividing into subject and object. This pure thought 'that thinks itself . . . is at once also sovereign Beauty and Goodness and primordial Love' (1990, 57). The unity of the One here, knowing itself, is an eternal procession or emanation out of itself, but in a way which, although creating the duality of knowing itself, does so as 'an Epiphany of the First Principle eternally revealing itself to itself' (1990, 58). When finally the active intellect appears, there begins a relation, 'personal and conscious, confiding and loving' (1990, 67) with the soul whose contemplative intellect is herein activated. In a theology that discards angels or celestial souls there would be no pedagogical reorientation toward pilgrimage from Occident to Orient, and KT would be left isolated and alone in the darkness of its own human rationality.

Al-Ghazali (c. 1056–1111)

The *Munqidh* of al-Ghazali (c. 499/1105) describes his personal struggle with self-knowing, and in other works, notably *The Alchemy of Happiness*, he describes this self-knowing in terms of a guide for knowing God and the self. *The Alchemy* begins with the hadith 'He who knows himself knows God', and adds from the Qur'an that 'We will show them Our signs in all the regions of the earth and in their own souls, until they clearly see that this is the truth' (Koran, 2003, 338). Al-Ghazali sees this in educational or pedagogical terms. 'Know thyself and you know God' refers not to physical appearance but to one's purpose on earth. Learn first that you have a body and soul, and that the soul is the key to the knowledge of God. Reason, the highest faculty, can purify the heart of greed and anger, contributing to an alchemy of happiness that will enable man to rise from the beasts to the angels.

Man is seen here as a microcosm of all the wondrous intricacies of God's creation. He is a 'little world in himself' (al-Ghazali, 2008, 18). Man needs to learn that the earth is our schooling in regard to the existence of God. Man did not make the earth; man is a microcosmic conversion of God's power and wisdom. His creation cannot be improved upon. To know beauty or perfection in ourselves is to know God. To see the world provide for man's needs is to know God. To know the attributes of the soul as indivisible, not of space and time, not of quality or quantity, having no shape, size, or color, is to know the attributes of God. The universe leads man to ask the questions how and why. These questions take man to God. Those who see no God here fail to understand the educative trail of breadcrumbs left by God on earth that lead to Him.

Man's time on earth should therefore be spent pursuing the knowledge of self and God. The soul must care for the body but not indulge it in false needs. The world is deceitful and will try to entice the soul away from God. Man must learn not to be distracted by the things of the world. Goodness and knowledge can be found on Earth, and learning and doing good in this world will ensure one possesses learning and good character in the next world. Those who do not believe in their future life attach themselves to earthly things and store up misery and punishment for themselves after death. In the spirit of Dantean *contrapasso* every sinner carries with him to the next world the instruments of his own punishment. Al-Ghazali acknowledges that some will never learn to know God but asks that, even for skeptics, is it not reasonable to give the benefit of the doubt to the existence of God and the future life 'considering the tremendous issues at stake' (2008, 44).

In short then, the judgment that awaits in the future life demands rigorous and disciplined self-examination in this life. Recollection of God is man's remembering that God observes all actions and thoughts. The saints, who know only God, are permanently absorbed in the recollection of God. Those who are not saints can have a second level of recollection in which they are always requiring themselves to remember that they are permanently under God's observation. For this, as with Avicenna, a spiritual guide may be needed. All life is educative if, as part of that education, the individual learns what to look for. The legacy of this learning lies in asking the big questions: how and why.

Al-Ghazali's *Letter to a Disciple* opens up complementary themes in the work of KT. The dominant theme in the letter is perhaps the need to ensure that what one learns externally is fully absorbed internally, so there is no gap between what one says one believes and what one does believe. He warns his disciple against book learning, both in Islamic tradition and especially in relation to its Neoplatonic influences, because the philosophers believe that redemption can be achieved by understanding and without the need for action. 'The essence of knowledge is to know what obedience and worship are' (al-Ghazali, 2005, 22). He draws attention to the antinomy that strikes those who would presume to know how to walk the correct spiritual path. 'Whoso believes he will reach his goal by the expending of effort is presumptuous' (2005, 12). His advice here is not to give up action, but to give up calculating its possible rewards, leading to a Kantian-type observation: 'knowledge without action is madness and action without knowledge is void' (2005, 16). If one lives right, then there is little need for academic learning. He offers eight lessons that should guide the disciple: do good deeds, restrain the ego, give possessions to the poor, find nobility in God-consciousness, have no envy, have no enmity, trust God to provide, and rely on him. These eight lessons, he says, are common to the Torah, the Psalms, and the Qur'an.

The education of a disciple by a master requires the disciple never to disagree with the teacher, and to ensure that external lessons are internally absorbed.

This is the only way to avoid hypocrisy. At a more general level al-Ghazali's *Revival of the Religious Sciences* has as its aim 'to counter insincerity through systematically internalising the religion' (al-Ghazali, 2005, xx).[8] If the disciple should become a teacher or preacher, he must learn how to inspire questioning in others and how to answer those questions, but to do so without pretentiousness, and without the need to incite excitement for appearances' sake. Rather, the intervention of the teacher must be 'to lead man from the world to the hereafter, from recalcitrance to obedience, from acquisitiveness to renunciation, from stinginess to generosity, from doubt to certainty, from indifference to vigilance, and from illusion to God-consciousness' (2005, 50). The student needs always to monitor the state of the relation between the internal and the external (theory and practice) and always to struggle against hypocrisy and for sincerity. Al-Ghazali ends by describing the way in which death can be the universal teacher of KT;

> if you read or study knowledge, your knowledge must improve your heart and purge your ego—just as if you learned that your life would only last another week, inevitably you would not spend it in learning about law, ethics, jurisprudence, scholastic theology and suchlike, because you would know that the sciences would be inadequate for you. Instead you would occupy yourself with inspecting your heart, discerning the features of your personality, giving worldly attachments a wide berth, purging yourself of ugly traits, and you would occupy yourself in adoring God. (2005, 56)

In *The Correct Balance* Al-Ghazali enquires into self-knowing but without mentioning the motif of *homo imago Dei*. Here knowledge is weighed against the concepts in the Qur'an of equivalence, concomitance, and opposition. The implication of this balance is again to ensure the relation between the external and the internal. An example of such balancing is where self-knowing rejects mere conformism to the authority of the Imam, and requires that each soul see things clearly for itself. No one can receive knowledge from the Prophet 'without knowing the balance' (al-Ghazali, 1980, 269). As well as religion, cognition can also be weighed against the sciences—arithmetical, geometrical, medical, legal—in order to distinguish true from false.

Al-Ghazali left a unique record of how his own life lived out this struggle to KT by knowing God, or of how he put this theory into the practice of his whole life. The *Munqidh* describes his own deliverance from error to truth, and is often compared to Augustine's *Confessions*. In his early life al-Ghazali says he had a thirst for understanding the many things that troubled Islam, but a thirst compromised by a 'servile conformism' (al-Ghazali, 1980, 55) to inherited beliefs. This conformism dissolved when he experienced the relativism implied by people adhering to religious truths on the basis of their birthplace rather than on the truth of religion itself. Behind such contingency he sought that to which 'no doubt clings' (1980, 55), where there is no pos-sibility of error and deception. 'During this time I was a skeptic in fact, but not in utterance or doctrine' (1980, 57), and plagued by an incorrect balance between outer and inner.

A prerequisite of servile conformism is that one does not know thyself to be so. But when a man recognizes this, 'the glass of his servile conform-ism is shattered—an irreparable fragmentation and a mess which cannot be mended by patching and piecing together: it can only be melted by fire and newly reshaped' (1980, 59), that is, melted in the educational fire of KT. As such, he rejects the Mutukallimun as merely conserving the orthodox, and the philosophers as 'incapable of grasping all problems or of getting to the heart of all difficulties' (1980, 71). The Sufis, however, offered al-Ghazali a unity of theory and practice that appeared to counter the hypocrisy where inner truth and outer appearance contradicted each other. In pursuit of KT he left his home and his family, spending years in solitude and spiritual exer-cise according to Sufi practice. A final lesson in KT reveals to him that even seclusion might be motivated by laziness and self-aggrandizement, and he returns to teaching some eleven years later, desiring only 'to reform myself and others' (1980, 92).

The Story of Hayy Ibn Yaqzan

Written by Ibn Tufayl (1105–1185), *Hayy Ibn Yaqzan* is a tale resembling somewhat the ambition of Rousseau in *Emile*. It sets an individual's educa-tion within an environment left free of corrupting influences, so that what-ever necessity is present can emerge uncompromised.

The story begins with Hayy Ibn Yaqzan's birth. One account is of his spontaneous generation from clay, another that he was born to parents on a different island who could not keep him. In either case, Hayy is found and nurtured by a doe, and he then lives among deer learning their ways. At age seven he learns of death when the doe dies, and he learns of the organs by vivisecting it, learning to make the necessary instruments in doing so. He reasons that death must be due to some kind of missing being in the body. It is the search for this missing being that is the motivation behind the meta-physical education that lies ahead for him. Even at this stage life and death prove to be the most formative experience. He learns that heat and fire must be the missing animator of the body, and some kind of animal spirit.

At age 21 he is learning of natural science, seeing the whole animal king-dom as one being, leading him to seek for objects with the fewest predicates. The forms of objects, apprehended not by the senses but by reason, are part of his metaphysical education. This principle of life over and above corpore-ality he sees as the soul. Since everything has a cause, the soul must have one too. Here he awakens to the idea of the necessary existent, or God. At age 28 he turns his attention to the starry spheres since he reasons that earthly bod-ies cannot be the cause of all change. Musing on the differences between a creation of the universe *ex nihilo*, and an eternal universe, he says that both required a non-corporeal author who was somehow not matter, and yet the cause of all matter. He reasons that such an other can only be consummate perfection whose essence 'is necessary existence' (Ibn Tufayl, 2003, 134).

At age 35, having 'gained an awareness of this eternally existing Being, Whose existence is uncaused, but Who is the cause of all existence, Hayy wished to know how this knowledge had come to him' (2003, 135). It was not through the senses, so it must be by some non-physical means. Hayy reasons that since life knows life, there must be something about his own self that can recognize itself in the divine. This is a self-realisation that the self that comes to know the necessary existent is his true self and true identity. To know God is to know one's true self.

Above the decay and generation of the earthly realm, stars and spheres seemed unchangeable and undisturbed by distractions of material bodies. He also sees that he alone among the animals is aware of this necessary existent. This distinction resides in the conscious part of Hayy.

> This conscious part was something sovereign, divine, unchanging and untouched by decay, indescribable in physical terms, indivisible to both sense and imagination, unknowable through any instrument but itself, yet self-discovered, at once the knower, the known and knowing, the subject and object of consciousness and consciousness itself. (2003, 141–2)

We recognize this awareness in Hayy as the *hadith*, to know God is to know the self. Indeed, it was 'his obligation to become the Necessary Existent because he was (and to the extent that he was) himself, that is to the extent of his identity with that self which brought him his awareness of the Necessarily Existent Being' (2003, 142–3).

Putting these statements together, we see that in Hayy the intellect has produced the thought of itself as something separate from the changeable and corporeal and has recognized that it has a relation to itself that constitutes its own self-discovery. The intellect is able to learn about itself from itself in a way not available to anything known through the senses. To the idea of the spirit that is responsible for life, and which is missing from the dead body, and to the necessity of a non-corporeal first cause or necessary existent, is now added the metaphysical nature of each of these—spirit, intellect and God—which are seen to be of the same substance. None of them have predicates, and none of them can be conceived or imagined in their oneness and unity.

This education in knowing God and knowing the true self is seen as a moral education in its own right. Hayy's dietary regimen respects the work of his creator by trying not to oppose his work. He eats only that which is abundant, and he is careful to make no species extinct. In emulating the planets, he cares for suffering, both plant and animal; he makes sure to be clean; and he moves in circles. He contemplates the One, shutting out the senses, and sometimes spinning so that 'the action of his true self, which transcended the body, would grow more powerful' (2003, 147).

In the union of macrocosm and microcosm, Hayy learns that God's self-awareness is not distinct from himself, and that his self-identity is his self-knowledge (NN). Thus, Hayy reasons that 'if he himself could learn to know Him, then his knowledge of Him too would not be distinct from His essence, but would be identical with Him' (2003, 148). To know him positively meant not attributing predicates to him, while to know him negatively required removing all physical hindrances to the ecstasy in which he could appear in his pure form. He achieves this ecstasy in a state in which memory and mind have disappeared, and in which he dies to himself, 'drowned in ecstasy' (2003, 149). For Hayy, here, 'whoever gains consciousness of His essence wins that essence itself' (2003, 150). Hayy, drowned in ecstasy, 'must be identical with Him' (2003, 150).

But Ibn Tufayl now has to rehearse the contradiction of man claiming to know God in this way. It is 'specious thinking' (2003, 150) to believe that God and man are united, for Hayy has not become non-material and remains the one called Hayy. Faced with the logical truth that the divine could not be described without misrepresentation, Hayy abandons the rule of reason. Now, says Ibn Tufayl, if the reader can avoid giving words their ordinary meaning, what Hayy sees in his ecstasy can be spoken of.

> Passing through a deep trance to the complete death-of-self and real contact with the divine, he saw a being corresponding to the highest sphere, beyond which there is no body, a subject free of matter, and neither identical with the Truth and the One nor with the sphere itself, nor distinct from either . . . He saw it to be at the pinnacle of joy, delight and rapture, in blissful vision of the being of the Truth. (2003, 152)

The story ends with Hayy arriving on another island, one that has symbolic religion but only sought to know God in a human way. He returns to his own island, having understood all-too-well the human condition, and stays there until his own death.

Ibn Arabi (1165–1240)

We again take Corbin as our guide to the phenomenology of KT found in the work of Ibn Arabi. This will enable us to rehearse Corbin's view that the West lacks a notion of spirit that can still hold God and man together in a way that does not assign the difficulty of the relation to a third party, namely, the church. At stake here for Corbin is nothing less than the need to retrieve a community of spiritual problems and vocabulary through which East and West might be able to talk to each other.

Ibn Arabi's treatise on self-knowing was the first of his works to appear in a Western language.[9] It is a concise statement on the *hadith* 'whoso knoweth himself knoweth his Lord.' For Ibn Arabi this is to be taken to mean that the self is not the self, and that this non-self is God. 'If thou knowest thyself without existence . . . then thou knowest God' (Ibn Arabi, 1976, 5).

He explains that for the Sufi there is death before death. The first death is of the self who does not know himself as God. Here the ego is removed, and the Sufi learns that he is nothing but God—that 'thou art not, wast not, and never wilt be' (1976, 13).

One does not take refuge here in the dualism that either one is or one is not. Both existence and nonexistence are His existence. To 'know thyself after this fashion, is to know God, without wavering and without doubt, and without compounding anything of what is of recent origin with what is original' (1976, 15). One knows God by God, not by one's self. The self that does not KT is the ignorant self who believes that it exists in and of itself. When this ignorance is dispelled, so a union is formed, but this is a union without union because 'the knower and that which he knows are both one' (1976, 17). To believe in God being divided is polytheism. Instead, to know union without union is precisely to understand the saying 'Whoso knoweth himself knoweth his Lord.'

Corbin reports three aspects of Ibn Arabi's life that have symbolic significance. The first is his attending the funeral of Averroes, having met him in Cordova in his youth.[10] The second is his pilgrimage, beginning at the age of 30, after a vision telling him that a guide—Gabriel—was waiting for him, a pilgrimage that takes him around the near East, including Mecca, before settling in Damascus for the last 17 years of his life.

The third symbolism is his being a disciple of Khidr. Khidr is an 'invisible spiritual master, reserved for those who are called to a direct unmediated relationship with the divine world'.[11] In the Qur'an Khidr is the companion of Moses who revealed to him a divine science above the law (*shari'a*). For Corbin Khidr can be 'experienced simultaneously as a person and as an archetype, as a person-archetype' (Corbin, 1998, 60). This 'resolves the dilemma presented in terms of formal logic' (1998, 65) between universal and particular. His role can be related to KT for Khidr undertakes 'to reveal each disciple to himself' (1998, 61). He does not dogmatically lead all disciples to one common good. In turning each man to himself he guides him away from legal or authoritarian servitude.

This 'individual ministry' (1998, 62) of Khidr threatened the orthodox dogmas of the West with a radical individual angelology. The Avicennan angel does not simply transmit orders. Rather, expressing KT, it holds that 'the idea that the Form under which each of the Spirituals knows God reveals Himself to Himself in that man' (1998, 60), a self-knowing of NN that needs no church or material mediator in the individual's experience of God. The master can only guide *each* man individually to what he alone is capable of seeing, and not bring him to any collective pre-established dogma: *Talem eum qualem capere potui* (1998, 75–6), or, 'I saw him in such a form as I was able to see him.' The angel is the relation between man and revelation, without which God would remain unknowable.

The key to his phenomenological KT is the active imagination. It transmutes sensory data into symbols, and it is symbols that carry meaning that would otherwise remain unknowable. Shi'ism holds that for everything external there corresponds something internal. Even though the work of the angel of prophetic revelation has ended, the task of the interpretation of meaning, or hermeneutics, remains the same. This openness of prophetic hermeneutics within a completed revelation is played out in the individual way that each self learns of God. Christianity, says Corbin, closed down this esoteric gnosis when the church substituted itself as a 'dogmatic ministry' (1998, 82) over individual inspiration and experience. In Islam there is no such 'pontifical authority' (1998, 82). In addition, where in Christianity God's incarnation on Earth is a historical fact, the divine manifestation of esotericism takes place 'on the plane of the angelic universe' (1998, 84), whose time does not coincide with historical time.

Summing up the idea of Khidr in Ibn Arabi as KT Corbin says:

> He who knows himself knows *his* Lord. Knowing one's self, to know *one's* God; knowing one's Lord, to know one's self. This Lord is not the impersonal self, nor is it the God of dogmatic definitions, *self*-subsisting without relation to *me*, without being experienced by *me*. He is the he who knows himself through myself, that is, in the knowledge that I have of him, because it is the knowledge that he has of me; it is alone with him alone . . . that it is possible to say *thou*. (1998, 95)[12]

Corbin's account of Ibn Arabi suggests that his KT, advancing from the angelology of Avicenna, rejects the Aristotelianism of Averroes. Moving East, and away from Latin Averroism, Ibn Arabi's self-knowing of the one God carries with it an 'integral humanism' (Corbin, 1998, 36), which for Corbin can still be a hope for a renewed dialogue between East and West. This argument rests to some extent on Corbin reading a version of Heideggerian phenomenology into Islamic hermeneutics.[13] In his Nemo interview Corbin says that hermeneutics

> practised in the Religions of the Book put into play the same themes and vocabulary familiar to phenomenology . . . [therefore] if I lay claim to phenomenology it is because philosophical hermeneutics is essentially the key that opens the hidden meaning (etymologically the *esoteric*) underlying the exoteric statement. (Corbin, 1976)[14]

Here then, Western (Heideggerian) phenomenology opens itself to Oriental spirituality. Phenomenology, says Corbin, allows the Western mind to examine experience and self-experience without reducing it to sense data. In this vein, Corbin advises us away from the view that Arabic philosophy terminated with Averroes. In fact, Avicennan spirituality continued to thrive at the other end of the world, in Iran, to be developed by Suhrawardi and Ibn Arabi. He writes that 'The return of Shi'ism to the spiritual horizon . . . might actually change the conditions of dialogue between Islam and Christianity, provided the interlocutors were Spirituals' (1998, 9).

Summarizing Corbin here, Avicenna's Neoplatonic angelology alarmed mediaeval scholasticism. It heralds an intermediate world of pure imagination, leading to the spirit of symbolic exegesis or *ta'wil*: the carrying back to a principle. While Avicennan angelology 'provides a secure foundation for a radical autonomy of the individual . . . in a theosophy of the Holy Spirit' (1998, 12), Averroes restored Aristotelianism, rejecting emanation as 'crypto-creationism' (1998, 12). Averroes did not see the eternal belonging to the individual because the individual perishes. Elsewhere Corbin states that for Averroes and for the Latin Scholastic tradition, 'all one can say is that there is eternity within the individual, but what is "eternalizable" in him belongs wholly to the active Intelligence alone, not to the individual' (2006, 248). Corbin finds a lack of individualism in this Latin Averroism, because Averroes, in accepting matter as the principle of individuation, can only identify the individual with the perishable and corruptible, and is left with a notion of immortality which cannot be individual, only 'generic' (2006, 248). By removing angel-souls Averroes excludes the world of active imagination and symbolic visions, which are essential to the view of macrocosm and microcosm in Ibn Arabi.

> The magnitude of the loss becomes apparent when we consider that this intermediate world is the realm where the conflict which split the Occident, the conflict between theology and philosophy, between faith and knowledge, between symbol and history, is resolved. (1998, 13)

Corbin also claims that Aquinas does away with the 'transcendent dimension of the individual as such, that is, his immediate and personal relationship with the Angel of Knowledge and of Revelation' (1998, 17). As Averroes denies the possibility of the individual being eternal, so Aquinas 'grants the individual an "active intellect," but not a separate intellect; the intellect of the individual is no longer a transcendent or celestial Intelligence' (1998, 17).[15] It is in the nature of this imaginative immediacy that we see Ibn Arabi's notion of KT. Corbin says that the role of this immediacy, rejected in the West, is then taken over by the church or Magistery, with all its attendant implications of sovereignty over the path to God. Corbin notes that even though there is no church or Magistery in Islam, there is still 'a clash between official Islam and the initiatory movements' (1998, 16).

The significance of *ta'wil* as the movement of returning to a principle is also excluded by the West. *Ta'wil* is the 'essential symbolic understanding, the transmutation of everything visible into symbols, the intuition of an essence or person in an Image which partakes neither of universal logic nor of self-perception' (1998, 13). Without the imagination, symbols cannot be returned to that which they symbolized or indeed, understood as symbolic at all.

Corbin's view of the implications of the Oriental for the Occidental here, and for its notion of KT, are, he would say, profound and far reaching. If Western scholasticism removes the immediate relationship between God and man, then the vital link has been broken in the truth wherein he who knows himself knows God. Where Plotinus had in a sense overcome the individual in a transcendence to the One, and Augustine had returned KT and knowing the Holy Trinity to the individual mind, Avicennan angelology cuts through the distinction between them as being a false one, and restores to the imagination the immediacy of knowing self and God in a 'union without union' (Ibn Arabi, 1976, 15). For Corbin, the divide between the individual and God, whether it is overcome or not overcome, is a false debate, one having serious consequences for Western religion. This 'alienation of the individual's transcendent dimension' (Corbin, 1998, 18) becomes a laicization and transfers spiritual authority to a church which in itself provokes the soul to rebel against it. Suhrawardi and Ibn Arabi on the other side of the world see philosophy and mystical experience as 'inseparable' (1998, 20). Iran, he says, knows no disappearance of celestial souls or of the intermediate world of symbols or of the imagination. Indeed, the Iranian tradition goes back well beyond 'the schematic notion of "Arabic philosophy" with which Western thinkers have too long contented themselves' (1998, 19). Zoroastrian angelology, and the Suhrawardian dualism of light and dark, seeing life as light, and material as death, 'precludes the possibility of a physics in the Aristotelian sense of the word' (1998, 22). Corbin's overall project holds at its centre the idea that 'the conditions for a spiritual dialogue between Islam and Christianity change radically accordingly as Christianity addresses itself to Shi'ite Islam or to another branch of Islam' (1998, 25). Corbin states that within 'Arab' philosophy and 'Arab' science,

> there *is* a sum of human experience, ignorance of which is not without its bearing on the desperate difficulties besetting our times. No dialogue is possible without common problems and a common vocabulary; and such a community of problems and vocabulary does not arise suddenly under pressure of material events, but ripens slowly through a common participation in the questions that mankind has asked itself. (1998, 37)

Notes

1. Altmann and Stern surmise here that 'obviously Al-Kindi had access to some lost Alexandrian commentary which . . . included "knowing oneself" in the list of definitions' (2009, 29–30).
2. William C. Chittick believes that this *hadith* is 'not found in the standard collections and is rejected by most *Hadith* experts, some of whom ascribe it instead to the Prophet's cousin Ali ibn Abi Talib' (Chittick, 2015, 1743).

3. Note that '"knowing one's self" is understood here as "knowing one's soul", the Arabic *nafsahu* having both meanings' (Altmann, 1969, 2).
4. See Altmann (1969, 3).
5. See Netton (1994, chapter 4).
6. The emphasis on the individual also recalls Augustine's attempts to retrieve the individual *mens* from its vanishing into Plotinian ecstasy.
7. On the Arab-Islamic sources for Dante's *Divine Comedy* and the controversy surrounding them, see Asin (2008) and Menocal (1987).
8. From Mayer's *Introduction*.
9. The work has been attributed to Ibn Arabi, but Cecilia Twinch notes that it may be written by one of his contemporaries, Awhad al-din Balyani. The work is also known under a variety of titles. See Ibn Arabi (2011, 3).
10. Asked by Averroes if he could reconcile mystical illumination and spiritual thought, Ibn Arabi is reported to have replied 'yes and no'—adding that between yes and no 'the spirits take their flight beyond matter, and the necks detach themselves from their bodies' (Ibn Arabi, 1980, 2).
11. Avicenna's Khidr was Hayy Ibn Yaqzan: see Corbin (1990).
12. This process is unfolded by Corbin in parts one and two of the book *Alone with the Alone*. I follow this up below in a later chapter: The Logic of Tears.
13. See Bligh (2012) for a discussion of this, and below, Chapter 8.
14. There are no page numbers in this version of the interview.
15. See Aquinas (1975a, chapter 76), Copleston (1962, 105–7), and Aquinas (1922), Q79, 5th article.

5   Cusanus to Pascal

Wilkins finds many of the themes from Antiquity regarding KT present in the European Renaissance. KT as knowing one's measure, and knowing what one is and is not capable of, is employed by secular writers, often exhorting the reader to 'form a true estimate of his capacities and virtues' (Wilkins, 2014, 88). Knowing one's limitations will induce humility and moderation and protect against pride. For other writers, the secular and the religious could be brought together around these themes. Thomas Elyot, for example, arguing that *nosce te ipsum*, although found in Greece, must surely have 'proceeded of God' (Elyot, 1962, 164), finds in the maxim the necessity to love God, and to love one's neighbour, and therein to accomplish justice.

Taking one's measure is also represented by Hobbes in his introduction to the *Leviathan,* where he observes how men will judge others before themselves. To do so without first knowing ourselves is 'to decypher without a key' (Hobbes, 1968, 83). John Donne's 'Ode'[1] notes how ignorance of one's faults only comes to light in the punishment of them. Richard Baxter warns against excessive zeal in KT, arguing that God does not wish man to KT any more than is necessary for his humility and self-control. When KT is seen as belonging to the paganism of the pre-Christian Greeks, then, for Thomas Browne it becomes 'the counsel of the Devil himself' (1965, 14). In such Christianity, KT emphasizes repenting one's sins and at times is synonymous with 'conversion.' Seeing KT as a matter of self-reflection, Luther speaks of Christ as a mirror,[2] and Francis Bacon in *De augmentis scientiarum* argues for both a divine mirror and a political mirror for self-education.[3] An example of learning from adversity is the poem *Nosce Teipsum* (published in 1599), written by John Davies having been expelled from Middle Temple after a brawl.[4] Another example is found in a poem by Christian Wernicke (1661–1725) which deserves repeating here.

> How many a man, when all is fair, thinks he is made of hero stuff,
> Who fainteth in the hour when trouble draweth nigh!
> 'Tis trouble alone that pierceth to the false heart's most innermost reaches,
> And bringeth the soul of the misguided wretch to self-knowledge.
> A piece of transparent glass revealeth only the light;
> But darken its surface beneath, and it showeth to thee thy face.[5]

A broader theme of KT in the Renaissance is pursued by Jakob Burck-hardt. He claims that in the Italian Renaissance, for the first time, 'man became a spiritual individual (Burckhardt, 1944, 81), no longer defining himself as merely a general category defined within a larger classification.'[6]

Robert Procter has recently compared ancient KT with Renaissance KT. In broad terms, when facing life's tribulations Cicero looked upward for solace, while Petrarch and Bruni looked within. The ancients 'experienced their individual lives as *parts* of a greater whole, the whole of the cosmos, the whole of the *polis*, the whole of the *civitas*' (Proctor, 1998, 109), whereas, for Bruni, 'the individual becomes the whole' (1998, 19).[7] The disciplines of the *studia humanitatis* serve to 'personalise' (1998, 21) the individual, and as such the nature of KT undergoes a radical transformation. Petrarch particularly demonstrates this inward turn when facing contingency and death, and becomes 'a physician to his own soul' (1998, 43). For Roy Por-ter new cultural genres, the soliloquy in drama, 'the portrait (above all the *self*-portrait), the diary and the biography (especially the *auto*-biography) reveal heightened perceptions of individuality, the ego glorying in its own being' (Porter, 1997, 3). As Polonius says in *Hamlet*, 'this above all, to thine own self be true.'[8]

Cassirer on Cusanus (1401–1464)

The aporia of knowing God through self-knowledge reemerges powerfully in Nicolas Cusanus's idea of learned, or self-educating, ignorance. It expresses the difficulty of KT that is both a separation (χωρισμος) from and a par-ticipation (μεθεξις) in NN, or of the individual that is both in the cosmos and apart from it. As such, learned ignorance expresses the clash of the independent mind with the model of emanation. The emerging shape of KT here will forego yielding destiny to fortune, to the planets, and to astrology, and take responsibility for itself in a natural world whose regularity and harmony will be expressed by science and observation rather than religious dogma.

While not rejecting the religion of the age, Cusanus practices a profound skepticism wherein the finite work of KT is unavoidably relativistic when measured against the unchangeable and unknowable NN. If the gap between finite and infinite is absolutely inviolable, then all finite logic, categorization, movement, and judgment are merely relative to each other, unable ever to close the gap to the infinitely true.

Here the continuity of the emanationist cosmos is destroyed. The logic of absolute transcendence overcomes the logical need for emanation, and rea-son and theology threaten to separate from each other. For Cusanus every-thing finite is ultimately the same, i.e., not true. While on the one hand this leaves human knowledge humble and resigned, nevertheless, says Cassirer, it is 'a completely new *movement* of thought' (Cassirer, 2000, 20). What is new is that the aporia between the finite (the same) and the infinite (the absolutely different) is now seen as the way in which God is thought. In *De sapienta* Cusanus says that the difficulty of such separation and participation is the necessary presupposition of God and the knowing of God. Doubt is how God is known because 'all doubt is certainty' (Cusanus, 1962, 118).

His thinking here has an aporetic logic of positing which Hegel and Kierkegaard will take up four hundred years later. 'If that which is presupposed in every question is in matters divine the answer to the question, then there cannot be, properly speaking, any question concerning God, since the answer coincides with the question' (1962, 118). But true to the religion of his age, Cusanus has to distinguish between truth for-us and truth in-itself. Hence, God is negation and doubt to us (participation) but He is above contraries (separation) and is neither affirmation nor negation, for either of these would reduce Him to the same, to multiplicity and difference.[9] Here KT is the knowing of the self for whom God is negative while NN is above any such relativity or contingency. God remains 'beyond all comparison' (1962, 136)[10] with things in the world of multiple equivalence.

In *De visione dei*, it is the contradiction of the for-us and the in-itself, or ignorance regarding God, and God in-himself, which is our *learning* about God. The more one learns this ignorance, 'the greater his learning will be' (Cusanus, 2007, 9). Learned ignorance here is the aporia of separation and participation, and is the door leading to God. But the aporia is not overcome in being known. Jesus, alone, is the 'absolute mediator' (Cusanus, 1962, 169) uniting divine and human intelligence. It falls to the rest of humanity to know learned ignorance as its own movement, a movement that is the condition of the possibility of knowledge, and of a mind which 'can come to *know itself* and to measure its own powers' (Cassirer, 2000, 44).[11] KT here means learning that it is participating in separation that 'guarantees the validity of experience' (2000, 22). In learned ignorance 'there is no otherness for us that does not in some way point to the unity and participate in it' (2000, 23).

This new movement of thought implies tolerance to the differences in other religions since all are finite and therefore the same. Now no one person is closer or farther from the divine, original source of being than any other' (2000, 28). It also reforms the relation between the individual and the cosmos. If the universe is the creativity and productivity of divine intellect forming matter into individuality, objective science becomes the expression of the order of its work. Here the newly forming self-consciousness of participation and separation sees itself as the microcosm of the divine order of the macrocosm. To learn of one is to learn of the other. What nature achieves without intellect man comes to understand through scientific principles.[12] Cassirer says of this, 'What we call "wisdom", therefore, is not really a knowledge of external objects but a knowledge of our own selves' (2000, 90). Here the newly formed KT can 'taste the truth' (Cusanus, 1962, 105) in the contradictions between the finite and the infinite; it is participation and separation in and as the taste of learned ignorance.

At stake here is the reforming of Renaissance individuality, where its knowledge of itself overpowers astrology and emanation (precisely what Corbin regretted), and discovers the creative and autonomous powers of man's own intellect, which comes now to define his *humanitas*. The destiny of man no longer flows to him from the stars but 'arises from the ultimate depths of his innermost self' (Cassirer, 2000, 120).

Cassirer also employs Bovillus[13] to make an Hegelian-type observation here regarding subject and substance. In the Middle Ages subject is related to substance only through intermediaries who are 'external' (2000, 127) to the isolated individual. Renaissance humanism still rides this ambiguity between subject and substance but, taking Petrarch as exemplary here, at the same time it extols 'the inexhaustible wealth and value of "individuality"' (2000, 129). In turn, Christianity tries to defend individuality against Averroism, which it perceives as making individuality accidental rather than essential. If subject and substance participate with each other, even in their separation, then the external natural world is no longer purely base or evil. So Ficino, for example, 'reconciles and resolves the *substantial* diversity of the elements of being by letting them be recognized as subjects' (2000, 133).

Subjective substance here is a different and negative version of KT in relation to NN, for 'to know an object means to negate the distance between it and consciousness . . . it means, in a certain sense, to become *one* with the object' (2000, 134). Nevertheless Cassirer adds here that it does not overcome the distance, despite Neoplatonic claims that it can, because as learned ignorance has shown, participation is always accompanied by separation, and as much as knowledge negates the distance between object and consciousness, at the same time it also preserves it. We will see below how negation and preservation reappear in the educational logic of modern metaphysics.

Erasmus (1467?–1536)

It is instructive in reading Erasmus to see how the theme of KT bestrides the Renaissance and the Reformation. KT is central to his *Enchiridion*, which he describes as outlining 'the pattern of a Christian life' (Erasmus, 1971, 215)[14] and a 'guide for spiritual living' (Erasmus, 1964, 28). It declares that KT requires the self to lay siege on itself in a state of warfare against the seductive vices. The crown of wisdom requires that 'you know yourself' (1964, 40). In the *Adages* he says that the three maxims at Delphi are 'the most famous of all the utterances of wise men' (Erasmus, 2001, 97), and that the first of these, KT, recommends 'moderation and the middle state' (2001, 97).[15] That it requires a struggle no one should be in doubt about, for even Paul did not know himself well enough.[16]

In this struggle of KT lust, lechery, and envy are to be brought under control by reason, and its accompanying affections of piety, charity, benevolence, compassion, and honesty. There is nothing harder than this, but it is 'the only road to happiness' (1964, 46). When Erasmus describes this as a war between the inner and the outer man, he observes the strange nature of the truth that emerges in KT. Those who live by the flesh in fact die to spirit; and those who live by the spirit mortify the flesh. In this sense KT teaches 'a new order of [dialectical] things: to seek peace in war, war in peace, life in death, death in life, freedom in slavery, slavery in freedom' (1964, 48).

Erasmus believes liberal learning (*bonae litterae*) is a way of learning the spiritual Christianity advocated in the *Handbook*. This is not just because learning the classical style is itself a humanist and therefore virtuous pursuit. In the *Handbook* he also draws attention to how the macrocosm and microcosm, conjoined with the invisible and visible worlds, would be an important contribution to KT. The invisible world of the angels and the intellect is where true piety can be maintained, while the visible world refers to the stars, planets, and heavens. Man will KT if he sees himself as 'a third world participating in both of the others, the visible world referring to his corporeal part, the invisible to his soul' (1964, 62). An examination of the self here will 'advance from the body to the spirit, from the visible to the invisible, from things sensible to things intelligible, from things compound to things simple' (1964, 71).

The spirit of the Reformation is carried within this KT for Erasmus. To KT is to learn that good works 'do not make the Christian' (1964, 69). Such works 'are of little value unless they are accompanied by internal piety' (1964, 69) which, as we have seen, requires the individual to be aware of himself as always in a state of self-war. 'Examine yourself' (1964, 65) to see what your inner motivations are in prayer and in church attendance. 'What does it mean if you perform good deeds in public but allow evil deeds to dominate your mind?' (1964, 70). 'You could rush off to Rome or Compostella and buy up a million indulgences' (1964, 91) but that falls short of the need to 'examine yourself in all honesty' (1964, 49).

Luther (1483–1546)

In Luther's Reformation KT exemplifies the aim both to recognize and to reform within the soul of each person what had become only an outward show of glittering penances and indulgences. In a sermon from 1522 for the Sunday after Easter he summarizes the way self-knowing can act as a remedy and cure for the disease afflicting the clergy. There are, he says, two classes of men who seek to fulfil the law. The first performs outward works, making a show 'with their glittering fabricated service of God' (Luther, 2010, 365). In believing that men can be made righteous through outward adherence to laws, they fundamentally misunderstand the law. The other class knows a different way to become righteous, 'which commences by teaching us the laws of God, from which we learn to know ourselves' (2010, 365).

The relation between law and self-knowledge is itself pedagogical. One learns to KT in rage at the law because, against it, one learns increasingly of one's own sin. Hypocrites can be seen obeying the law, but the righteous despair of themselves and learn to surrender themselves entirely to God. Law, when preached properly, teaches one to KT. The law places us in a position of failure in regard to it in order 'to show us our inability, and that we may learn to know ourselves and to see ourselves as we are, even as one sees himself in a mirror' (2010, 365). This is a dramatic education. In an earlier sermon of 1519 he says of it that man is 'terrified and crushed' (Luther, 1989, 168) by learning of himself in this way. Without this terror, one will neither 'derive much benefit from Christ's Passion' (1989, 168), nor give oneself to God entirely. But with this educative terror one begins 'to burn with the divine love and become quite another man, completely born anew' (Luther, 2010, 368). Such a man is no longer the hypocrite who, in fear of the terror of self-knowing, strives to be rid of his sins by 'running from one good work or penance to another, or by working their way out of this by means of indulgences' (Luther, 1989, 170). Rather the reborn come to a deep knowledge of themselves through which God 'gives us a joyful and secure conscience' (Luther, 2010, 371).

Much of this is to be found in the *Theologia Germanica*, which Luther twice edited prior to 1520. In the Preface he wrote that 'he had learned from it more than from any writing save the Bible and the works of St Augustine' (Bainton, 1978, 133). Chapter IX contains the kernel of the ideas expressed by Luther above in the two sermons. It states that all types of virtue and goodness will never make a man virtuous or good or happy 'so long as it is outside the soul' (Luther, 1893, 31). Instead, it continues, one is required to 'withdraw into himself and learn to understand his own life, who and what he is' (1893, 31), and of the ways in which God is working within him. Self-knowledge, even more than all the wonders of a liberal arts education, is above all 'the highest art' (1893, 31). 'For it is said, there came a voice from heaven, saying "Man, know thyself"' (1893, 31).

Calvin (1509–1564)

Calvin, like Luther, advises that the proverb KT should be seen not in the ancient sense of revealing to man his excellence and his dignity. Rather, self-knowledge allows us to see 'how great the excellence of our nature would have been had its integrity remained' (Calvin, 1989, 210). Echoing the terror that self-knowledge unleashes for Luther, and in the light of self-knowledge of the Fall, 'all confidence and boasting are overthrown, we blush for shame, and feel truly humble' (1989, 210). In the presence of God, self-knowing sees those 'who previously stood firm and secure so quaking with terror, that the fear of death takes hold of them [and] they are, in a manner, swallowed up and annihilated' (1989, 39). Such self-knowledge reminds us of 'the spectacle of our ignominy and corruption' (1989, 210) and inspires us to seek after God and 'so incline us to submission' (1989, 211). Calvin notes how man is apt to remain blind to his faults, and to credit himself with the foolish notion that he is 'perfectly sufficient of himself for all the purposes of a good and happy life' (1989, 211). The loudest applause is always reserved for those who flatter, leading man to 'rush headlong to destruction' (1989, 211). This is not self-knowledge, but rather 'the most pernicious ignorance' (1989, 211). The individual, practicing self-knowledge by the standard of the divine rather than the human, will meditate on the end to which he was created, will become humble and weary at a dignity lost, and will therein learn of his duty to God and his limitations in performing it.

This relationship between self-knowledge and knowledge of God opens the *Institutes* as a whole. In self-knowledge 'there exists in man something like a world of misery' (1989, 38) but, in being stung by this, he 'necessarily obtains at least some knowledge of God' (1989, 38). As with Luther so with Calvin, 'we cannot aspire to Him in earnest until we have begun to be displeased with ourselves' (1989, 38). The man who is not known to himself is apt to rest in the illusion of his own worth, content with his human endowments. The man who is known to himself 'is not only urged to seek God, but is also led as by the hand to find him' (1989, 38). Having God as the standard, true self-knowledge reveals man's 'injustice, vileness, folly, and impurity' (1989, 38). Even human wisdom itself, within the purging power of self-knowledge, would only appear as 'extreme folly' (1989, 39).

Book I of the *Institutes* also relates self-knowledge to the question of the education about God that is to be found in the natural world through divine ordinance. No one can open his eyes to the perfections 'in the whole structure of the universe' (1989, 51)[17] without beholding the work of the great architect. Liberal studies is assisted by religion here in obtaining deeper wisdom regarding 'the secret workings of divine wisdom' (1989, 51) in its studies of the motions of the heavenly spheres, and in its understanding of the symmetry and beauty of the human body. Both display 'proofs of ingenious contrivance as are sufficient to proclaim the admirable wisdom of its Maker' (1989, 52). Man indeed is rightly referred to as a microcosm, a 'rare specimen of divine power, wisdom, and goodness' (1989, 52). As such what need is there, in order to apprehend God, 'to go farther than ourselves?' (1989, 52) The human race as a whole is 'a bright mirror of the Creator's works' (1989, 52). But this does not prevent individuals from refusing self-knowledge of this kind, and 'appropriating as their own that which has been given them from heaven' (1989, 53); such is the 'immense flood of error with which the whole world is overflowed' (1989, 59). It is in the teeth of this flood of error, which suppresses the work of God, that self-knowledge can turn man from this madness, a madness in which 'monstrous fictions' (1989, 59) are substituted for the true God, turned that is, by way of terror at his own lack of worth to the architect of the universe.

Richard Baxter (1615–91)

The Nonconformist Richard Baxter appeared in Max Weber's thinking as representing the Puritan work ethic. Baxter is no less zealous in bringing the work ethic to the demand to KT, as illustrated now from his essay 'Mischiefs of Self-Ignorance and the Benefits of Self-Acquaintance' (2010 [1662]). Many of Wilkins's themes are apparent here. On KT in relation to one's mortality Baxter advises one to study oneself in good time so that death does not come before one has had time to discover and then reform one's sinful ways. The approach of death can often teach one just how little one knows of oneself. Regrets are common for not living a different life. Many are easily fooled by prosperity and only danger or calamity can move such souls to examine themselves. As death approaches, so does God's judgment, and so does the urgency to KT.

In terms of knowing one's measure, one's limits, and one's faults, Baxter says it is better to think less of oneself than to judge oneself too highly. Self-ignorance has its strongest hold on men who do not know of their own condition, particularly those chained to appetite and passion, who love prosperity and fame, who are young and in health, and who are atheist. Indeed, Baxter opens the book by stating 'He that is a stranger to himself, his sin, his misery, his necessity etc., is a stranger to God, and to all that might denominate him wise or happy' (Baxter, 2010, 755). Against such atheism, which is 'cherished by self-ignorance' (2010, 762) KT teaches the creature about the creator. The education that lies within the creature who knows itself is that the truth of intellect, free will, society, and the universe, lie in the absolute creator. The atheist may use as a weapon that God is only ever described anthropomorphically. But even these faculties that deny God are the effects of the almighty cause. 'As if a fool should ever write a volume, to prove that there is no ink or paper in the world, when it is ink and paper by which he writes' (2010, 763).

KT for Baxter is also practical. Self-inquiry teaches one to know one's physical nature and one's relation to God's law via duty and punishment. It teaches one compassion, and to doubt one's own understanding. This would make for better rulers and subjects. It would make them merciful, just, faithful, and comforted by joy within. Nevertheless, many remain ignorant of self-knowledge and believe themselves blessed when in truth they are not. In terms of education, given that one is nearest to one's self, this is what one should be best acquainted with. Studying the cosmos, the earth, other societies, history, medicine, etc., is just a distraction from KT. Not only will KT tell one what to study, and why, but it will also help one to manage political and economic affairs wisely; 'the country that you should survey and travel is within you' (2010, 789).

Baxter also preaches KT in moderation. Quoting Anselm on the difficulty of KT—that if a man does not inquire into himself he cannot know himself, and if he does he cannot endure what he finds—Baxter advocates avoiding the extremes of knowing oneself too little or too much. There is also a stoical strain with Baxter noting that since comfort lays in one's own hands, one is one's own tormentor. The wise will talk to their troubled souls, aiming to bring them peace. The one who does not KT will push the blame for despair, injury, and misfortune anywhere but within. The internal hindrances to self-knowing are deep-rooted pride, unreasonable self-love, and a self-deception engineered by judging oneself in good times rather than in life's trials. Property and the flattery that comes with it are to be avoided. Reminding one of the part Baxter plays for Weber, he says that if one finds oneself in property not by desire but by the will of God, then use this wealth not to 'the pleasing of the flesh' (2010, 855) but rather in ascetic denial.

Baxter also brings KT specifically to the life of the Christian. Second Corinthians is where Paul says 'Examine yourselves'[18] in case you do not see how Jesus is within you. As such, 'If you know not yourselves, you cannot be Christians' (2010, 779). To be open to Christ one must already have received 'the sentence of death in thyself' (2010, 780). In a theme seen above in Erasmus, the death of the non-Christian self is required to give birth to the Christian self, with this death being the stimulus to and the teacher of self-knowledge. This death brings the self out of the world of error, the world of Satan, who designs to keep one ignorant of one's self. KT is needed not just to teach men how to pray, what to ask for, and how to listen to the answers to their prayers. It is also a way to more earnest prayer, and to greater knowledge of one's own weaknesses and for seeking help against sin which goes unobserved. He speaks too of the hindrance to KT caused by the poor practice of ministers. In short, Baxter suggests that one who does not know God does not know himself, and the one who knows only himself knows nothing. They must be known together 'or nothing can be known' (2010, 790).

Baxter knows both well enough to end the essay with the necessary judgment of his own limits. He writes on KT convinced that all should agree with him but knows too that so few heed the words, leaving him and those who agree with him standing by and watching the division of the church and the work of Satan carried in error, violence, and pride, and an abundance of hypocrisy. The remedy is easy and available: 'to know themselves, till they are driven to study, and seek and know the Father and his son Jesus Christ. And yet is the salvation of most as hopeless almost as if there were no remedy' (2010, 864).

Montaigne (1533–1592)

Montaigne brings Socrates and the pedagogy of knowing that one does not know to self-enquiry in ways that are stoical, skeptical, natural, religious, and philosophical.[19] Most of Wilkins's themes are represented in Montaigne: know one's limitations, one's faults, one's soul, and all of these particularly in relation to death.

Montaigne is clear that one learns best from difficulty, and responds best to difficulty with a stoical frame of mind. Life is composed of discords, but it is difficulty 'which makes us prize things' (Montaigne, 2003a, 696).[20] Oppositions are formative, and learning is keener when it is from discord rather than harmony. One learns more from bad examples than from good ones. Contradictions are a stimulus to learning. Indeed, philosophy he says has become a refuge for avoiding the natural pains that accompany life, pains that need to be felt.

Socrates and the Socratic life is exemplary in showing how to make difficulties a way of life. Too often man wears learning as a mask for status rather than for its worth in life. 'There is a plague on Man: the opinion that he knows something' (2003a, 543).[21] More outstanding men are to be found among the ignorant than the wise. Men of learning often lack integrity, humility, fear, and goodness, which can spring from KT, requiring a soul that, in not thinking too much of itself, remains empty and teachable. Socrates is exemplary of this ignorance and simplicity. Only God can know himself, and one's best route to knowing God is through ignorance, which is to say that to KT as ignorant is to know the divine. Ignorance that is aware of itself is not complete ignorance, for complete ignorance does not know itself. Hence, in Socrates we find the philosophy of ignorance: know thyself as the true condition.[22] From this, Montaigne criticizes school learning, which crams knowledge into students with little or no regard for the virtue and wisdom, the self-improvement, that should be the good of education. Those who take pride in how much they know suffer from the plague of deceit and illusion. They know neither themselves nor anyone else. Those teachers are best whose minds are not well-filled but well-formed, and such was Socrates's commitment to Apollo, 'he alone was worthy of being called The Sage' (2003a, 427).[23]

Philosophy may hide its own difficulties behind the mask of knowledge, but like everything else, it will not be able to avoid KT in the final scene played out between death and the self. All actions in life will be judged against the touchstone of death, for the death-day is where one will come to see the strength and character of one's soul. 'The assay of the fruits of my studies is postponed unto death. Then we shall see if my arguments come from my lips or my heart' (2003a, 87).[24] Drawing on Socrates belief that philosophy's task is to practice dying[25] Montaigne sees death as a great teacher of self-knowing. To carry this education every day is to carry an education regarding freedom, for a 'man who has learned how to die has unlearned how to be a slave' (2003a, 96).[26]

In the face of death as one's teacher, something of a stoical mind is helpful. Pain and difficulty rule one only to the extent that one lets them. 'No one suffers save by his own fault' (2003a, 72).[27] The soul cannot escape itself, and so one does well to know this constant companion as well as one can. Tranquillity of mind, temperance, and restraint accompany the vocation of self-knowing. But this requires isolation as the soul knows itself best when it is not distracted by everyday activities. In seclusion, ambition and glory play no part, but tranquillity is at home. In becoming a crowd of one, one is drawn into the self-conversation of KT.

It is in Montaigne's natural theology that we find the relation of KT to God, or to NN. His fullest statement is in his *Apology for Raymond Sebond*.

Sebond's *Prologus to The Book of Creatures*, or *Book of Natural Theology*[28] was translated by Montaigne and published in 1569. The preface announces this natural theology to be a scientific doctrine of man in which, after only a month's study, and requiring no prior knowledge of liberal education, a man can know himself, his creator, and what he needs for his eternal salvation. Without this self-knowledge, the knowledge gained from the liberal arts is mere vanity and can only be used badly for one's own harm. Since man has, by the creator, been given the capacity for learning, it would be wasted were one not also able to instruct himself about himself and his place in the created universe 'naturally' (2003a, lviii) and by himself.

Regarding the relation of all created things, Montaigne argues that in natural theology the creatures and the creations share life in the creator. As such, God can be known from the things he has made. The man who holds himself master of the universe, with no external assistance, is laughable and ridiculous, for he is not even master of himself. Reason cannot be assumed to be equal with the principle of the heavens. To believe so is mere vanity. This vanity is apparent also in the way man assumes his own nature to be superior to that of other animals. Montaigne makes a long defense for the reasoning of the animal kingdom and demands that the genus man links us not only to animals but to trees and plants as well (2003a, 488).[29] In relation to living things, we should reflect on whether we are 'neither above them nor below them' (2003a, 513).[30]

> Beasts are born, reproduce, feed, move, live and die in ways so closely related to our own that, if we seek to lower their motivations or to raise our own status above theirs, that cannot arise from any reasoned argument on our part. (2003a, 524)[31]

Montaigne's natural theology demonstrates here how self-knowledge leads to knowledge of the universe as a whole, and to the equality of all created life. He concludes, 'we do not place ourselves above other animals and reject their condition and companionship by right reason but out of stubbornness and insane arrogance' (2003a, 541),[32] but this is known only to the man who knows himself.

If human reason lives impermanently in the soul (and permanently in God), what can human reason know about itself and the soul? Montaigne notes that anyone who 'makes repeated examinations of himself, internally and externally' (2003a, 623)[33] will find that without the presence of the divine, man is only redolent 'of death and dust' (2003a, 623).[34] Montaigne reaffirms, 'what can anyone understand who cannot understand himself?' (2003a, 628).[35] Protagoras made man the measure of all things, ignoring the fact that man cannot even know his own measurements. 'Man is so full of contradictions and his ideas are so constantly undermining each other' (2003a, 628)[36] that such arrogance is laughable. So, beware the mind that thinks itself clever. It is likely to break out into licentiousness. The mind is a tool that does not take kindly to moderation and order. As such, it needs to be held in check by laws and religious customs and to be kept under tutelage. In knowing the self in such ways we learn that 'our intellect is adequate enough to bring us to the knowledge of some things but that there are definite limits to its power, beyond which it is rash to use it' (2003a, 631).[37]

The relativism of human knowledge leads him to ask 'What kind of truth can be limited by a range of mountains, becoming a lie for the world on the other side?' (2003a, 653).[38] It seems that we cannot receive from nature just one truth that commands universal assent. There is nothing received by the mind of man which he does not change, for nothing reaches man 'except as altered and falsified by our sense' (2003a, 678).[39] No objective judgment regarding these objects of sense is possible because the judges transform them in their own image. In looking back to Sextus Empiricus and forward to Kant and Hegel, Montaigne says here 'We register the appearance of objects; to judge them we need practical proof; to test that proof we need an instrument. We are going round in circles' (2003a, 679).[40] Reason fares no better, for one reason requires to be verified by another *ad inifnitum*. The lack of any universal agreement on even one single proposition is a sure sign that

> our natural judgement does not grasp very clearly even what it does grasp, since my judgement cannot bring a fellow-man's judgement to accept it, which is a sure sign that I did not myself reach it by means of a natural power common to myself and to all men. (2003a, 634)[41]

Such a power exists, and to know ourselves clearly enough to know that we have adulterated it is part of the self-education that advances the idea of natural theology.

The *Apology* ends by repeating Plutarch from *The E at Delphi*. Reason fails to find essence in the changeable. Even time and nature are transitions. Only God is 'according to an unchanging and immortal eternity' (2003a, 682).[42] KT can educate only so far as the limitation of the individual. This is true self-knowledge. Man will rise above KT only if God proffers His hand. 'It is for our Christian faith, not that Stoic virtue of his, to aspire to that holy and miraculous metamorphosis' (2003a, 683).[43] At the end of the *Apology* we have the view that KT is stoical when it learns of its limitations, and learns of NN when KT can 'rise above humanity' (2003a, 683),[44] reach out to the immutable God and say, 'Thou art'.[45]

Montaigne works hard to put KT as a theory into practice in his own life. He says he has spent many years preparing for death. His life is ever an apprenticeship in KT and its relation to God. He sees that no one, himself included, is as empty and needy as man; he is 'the seeker with no knowledge, the judge with no jurisdiction, and, when all is done, the jester of the farce' (2003a, 1133).[46] He sees that the vocation of self-knowing and attachment to the middle way as he understands them are not opposed to Christianity. He takes many opportunities to defend the time he spends in self-knowing.

Each man, he says, 'is an excellent instruction unto himself provided he has the capacity to spy on himself from close quarters' (2003a, 424).[47] His spying does no harm to others, and his foolishness dies with him. Perhaps, he says, it will help others. Despite the difficulties involved in penetrating the mind's inner life, nevertheless, 'For many years now the target of my thoughts has been myself alone; I examine nothing, I study nothing, but me . . . No description is more difficult than the describing of oneself' (2003a, 424).[48]

In explaining the origin of his essay writing to a bout of melancholy, he says that 'Finding myself quite empty, with nothing to write about, I offered myself to myself as theme and subject matter' (2003a, 433);[49] and finding there one's ignorance 'is one of the surest and most beautiful witnesses to our judgement that I can find' (2003a, 459).[50] But 'If you are to tell of a vice of yours you must first see it and study it. Those who conceal it from others usually do so from themselves as well' (2003a, 953).[51] In 'On Experience' he says he studies himself more than any other subject.

His natural theology, then, means 'It must be important to put into effect the counsel that each man should know himself' (2003a, 1219).[52] Wisdom for Plato 'is but the executing of that [Delphic] command' (2003a, 1212).[53] Montaigne does not hate the natural passions of the body and chastises the philosophies that do. 'I accepted wholeheartedly and thankfully what Nature has done for me' (2003a, 1265).[54] He ends his essays in praise of nature. She is a gentle guide, wise and just. In her the marriage of pleasure and necessity is a good match. And he ends, as he began, with the idea that self-knowing is the key to life as it should be lived.

> It is an accomplishment, absolute and as it were God-like, to know how to enjoy our being as we ought. We seek other attributes because we do not understand the use of our own, and, having no knowledge of what is within, we sally forth outside ourselves. (2003a, 1269)[55]

His final thought is to be spared a descent into dementia.

Pascal (1623–1662)

Conflict and opposition also characterize much of what Pascal says on KT. Man may wish that there were not a 'civil war' (Pascal, 1966, 235) within him, but if the individual is to understand itself then it will see that the oppositions exist within, and that peace for the individual is when one 'is at war with the other' (1966, 235). This peace is the lesson learned in KT. Nature, says Pascal, offers the self doubt and anxiety. The one who finds here signs of a creator, will 'peacefully settle down in the faith' (1966, 162). But for the troubled mind, finding too much of the creator to deny him but too little to affirm him, there is only the 'pitiful state' (1966, 162), in which 'not knowing what I am nor what I ought to do, I know neither my condition nor my duty' (1966, 163). Within this anxiety and doubt one learns that man 'infinitely transcends' (1966, 65) himself and is 'a paradox' (1966, 64) to himself. Man abandons God, and then seeks to find Him everywhere in nature, but nothing seems able to take his place.

It is in feelings, and not through reason, that one learns of first principles, not least in the wonder and bewilderment of a created universe. Reason depends on the heart for its premises, for the heart feels spatial dimensions and feels infinities. Faith, in the face of this uncertainty, also comes from the heart. Reason, by contrast, is only ever relative in its finite propositions. Indeed, reason 'can be bent in any direction' (1966, 216). Even though 'reason makes feelings natural and natural feelings are eradicated by reason' (1966, 239), the desire for the true and the good is natural to all men and makes itself known in its failure to be secured. The lesson here for man is from God. To KT is to know that 'you are not in the state of your creation' (1966, 78). That this education should be found in the difficulty of oppositions is testament to Pascal's insight that contradiction 'is no more an indication of falsehood than lack of it is an indication of truth' (1966, 84).

One can read something of Cusanus's idea of learned ignorance in this character of the education that Pascal finds in self-understanding and its relation to God. To be in relation to truth (NN) and ignorance (KT), but for it to be impossible to know either absolutely, is to know a perfection from which we have fallen and to which we seem unable to return. Without original sin, we remain ignorant about the duality of human nature and remain 'invincibly ignorant of the truth about ourselves' (1966, 65). This is a Socratic wisdom, in admitting our ignorance, and a Cusanian wisdom, in understanding what not-knowing means and what its significance is regarding self-understanding, i.e., that it is a learned ignorance. In both cases, and for Pascal too, 'it is not through the proud activity of our reason but through its simple submission that we can really know ourselves' (1966, 66). Such submission is the wisdom that 'leads us back to childhood' (1996, 51). Therefore, the journey of KT lies between two great ignorances,

> one is the pure natural ignorance of every man at birth, the other is the extreme reached by great minds who run through the whole range of human knowledge, only to find that they know nothing and come back to the same ignorance from which they set out, but it is a wise ignorance that knows itself. (1966, 51)

On the transition from self-knowledge to knowledge of God Pascal seeks traces that God may have left on Earth that would lead one to Him, including an innate relativity in the 'landscape' (1966, 48) of man and nature. On the one hand, the earth in relation to the infinite sphere of the universe is 'a mere speck' (1966, 89). In this relativity, the proper value of one's own landscape is duly reproportioned. But this also works the other way. A human being can be reduced to head, heart, veins, blood, humors, just as a town can be reduced to houses, trees, tiles, leaves, grass, ants, ants' legs, 'and so on ad infinitum' (1966, 48). At both the macrocosmic and microcosmic levels man exhausts the powers of imagination regarding both the very large and the very small, and has an education in the relativity of proportions while being between these extremes. Both the macrocosm and microcosm have an infinity of amplitude and minuteness. The human being is both a speck and a Colossus.

While this sheer instability may produce fear and trembling for the ever-movable identity of the living human being, Pascal believes that it can be transformed into a wonder that will open one up to an education regarding the true significance of KT. Like Cusanus, Pascal concludes that in relation to the infinities of nothingness and eternity, all finitudes are equal. But even if man cannot know the whole, he should at least know the parts to which he is related and which he carries as proportion. In finding the interdependency of the parts, he is brought into relation with the whole, even if as wonder and bewilderment. 'The eternity of things in themselves or in God must still amaze our brief span of life' (1966, 93).

Diversion from self-knowing forms a major theme in *Pensées*. Youth are unhappy unless they are diverted from introspection, and all men are happier not to think about death, wretchedness, and ignorance. Individuals avoid rest, preferring disturbance that distracts, and then valuing these disturbances as if they were necessary in themselves. It is no good 'philosophers telling us: Withdraw into yourselves and there you will find your good. We do not believe them' (1966, 73). To KT is only to open one's self up to the horrors of the dual nature of man, and especially to the realization of one's own mortality. Diversion is the only thing that consoles us in our wretchedness. But those who avoid self-knowing, and especially the fact of their own mortality, 'drift wherever their inclinations and pleasures may take them, without reflection or anxiety, as if they could annihilate eternity by keeping their minds off it, concerned solely with attaining instant happiness' (1966, 161). Pascal, somewhat like Nietzsche, laments 'I thought I should at least find many companions in my study of man, since it is his true and proper study. I was wrong' (1966, 245). Perhaps this is not surprising.

> The only thing that consoles us for our miseries is diversion. And yet it is the greatest of our miseries. For it is that above all which prevents us thinking about ourselves and leads us imperceptibly to destruction . . . diversion passes our time and brings us imperceptibly to our death. (1966, 148)

We note here that Pascal also makes a political observation regarding the relation between reason and natural law. With no natural law common to all, there is no justice in-itself, only local versions of justice. The legitimacy of authority is therefore also local. But there are dangers if revolutionaries should attempt to return law, authority, and justice to a natural first principle. Man will realise that the usurpation of natural reason came about 'originally without reason' (1966, 47). Its origin, being arbitrary and ignoble, and being might over right, is best kept hidden since we now base civilization upon this usurpation. The lack of reason that overthrew natural reason was that of private property. 'Mine, thine'—there is 'the origin and image of universal usurpation' (1966, 47). This suggests a sophisticated insight into the dual significance of such usurpation. Might and right coexist—'Right without might is helpless, might without right is tyrannical' (1966, 56)—but do so in a totality constructed upon the priority of might which overthrew natural reason and became private property. The reality of might was granted the status of right. This is an insight Rousseau builds on in his *Second Discourse*. Pascal's conclusion is stark:

> Equality of possessions is no doubt right, but, as men could not make might obey right, they have made right obey might. As they could not fortify justice they have justified force, so that right and might live together and peace reigns, the sovereign good. (1966, 51)

Notes

1. 'Vengeance will sit above our faults', Donne (1572–1631).
2. *Sermon On Christ's Suffering* 1519; 1989, 167.
3. Mirrors have often been seen in this educative role. Aristotle saw friends as mirrors in which the self might be reflected back to itself, and know itself in this way. Seneca, in *Natural Questions*, talks of mirrors as offering not only an idea of one's self but also as a counsel for actions in the world. 'Mirrors were invented so that human beings might know themselves, and this leads to many benefits— first of all self-knowledge, then guidance for particular circumstances' (Seneca, 2010, 161) including age and ugliness. Olympiodorus in his *Commentary on Alcibiades I*, 'compared the γνῶθι σεαυτόν on the Temple of Apollo to the mirrors placed on Egyptian temples, which he says are able to do the same thing as the Pythian inscription' (Wilkins, 2013, 85). In Lucian's essay on *Pantomime*, he says 'when every one of the spectators identifies himself with the scene enacted, when each sees in the pantomime (ορχησις—orchesis) as in a mirror the reflection of his own conduct and feelings . . . [then] the enthusiasm of the spectators becomes uncontrollable, every man pouring out his whole soul in admiration of the portraiture that reveals himself to himself. Such a spectacle is no less than a fulfilment of the oracular injunction KNOW THYSELF' (Lucian, 1905, 262). There is also a very significant kind of mirroring in Plotinus. When the universal Soul produces a reflection of itself in a material body, then one's soul, in a sense, gives itself a 'second glance' (Brehier, 1958, 72, *Enneads* III.9.2.), and when it likes what it sees it descends into this body, losing its wings (see *Phaedrus*, 246c). Now this soul is stuck, isolated in the body of a single object, and only a study of itself will kindle the desire to return to its source (*Enneads* V.1.; see also I.IV.10 for the idea of the mirror in relation to the imagination.)
4. For a fuller account see the Memorial Introduction, by Alexander B Grosart, in Davies (1876, xxii–xxiii). The event took place around 1597–8.
5. Wilkins (2014, 113).
6. This view has suffered much recent criticism, being seen as geographically, sociologically, and chronologically wrong. See for example, Nauert (2006), Martin (2004), and Burke (1999).

7. Italics removed.
8. Hamlet, I.3.
9. Dolan argues here that Cusanus chooses Plato over Aristotle, in terms of immediacy of contact with God, combined with the Hebraic, where 'to know' was an
active experience of the object. Cusanus's Greek metaphysics came through the
neo-Platonists, taking from Proclus the out-and-return of things to God, from
pseudo-Dionysius negative theology, from Plotinus dialectical tensions of opposites, and from Eckhart the 'reconciliation of opposites in God' (1962, 131) Carl
Jung also explored this; see Henderson (2010).
10. From *De visione dei*, chapter 1.
11. Italics added.
12. Cassirer calls on Carolus Bovillus here against the emanationist cosmos. Carolus
Bovillus (Charles de Bouelles), is author of *De sapiente* (1509); see Cassirer
(2000, 88).
13. See n12
14. In his letter to Martin Dorp, 1515.
15. In his letter to William Blount (1500) discussing his *Adages* Erasmus accuses
himself of over-proverbosity, and of forgetting the second maxim, 'nothing too
much'. See Erasmus (1974, letter 126, 266).
16. Socrates, however, is St. Socrates to Erasmus, and many likened Erasmus to
Socrates; see Herwaarden (2003, 591).
17. Book I, ch. 5.
18. XIII. 5. Similar ideas are expressed in the following: 1 Cor. xiii 11–12 'When I
was a child I spoke as a child, I understood as a child, I thought as a child: but
when I became a man, I put away childish things. For now we see through a glass
darkly; but then face-to-face: now I know in part, but then shall I know even as
I also am known.' 2 Cor. xiii 6 'Examine yourselves, to see whether you are in
the faith . . . Or do you not realise this about yourselves, that Jesus Christ is in
you?' Gal. vi 5 'Every man shall bear his own burden.' Gal. vi 1 'keep watch on
yourself.'
19. In 1576 he had a medal struck with his coat of arms and insignia of St. Michael
on one side, 'and on the other, the image of a balance, that is, a pair of scales,
with the inscription "what do I know?"' (Montaigne, 2003b, vii).
20. *Essays* II.15.
21. II.12.
22. Montaigne says here that Peripatetics, Stoics, Epicureans, and Skeptics believe in
doubt and human ignorance. Dogmatists claim knowledge out of vanity. Even
from Aristotle we learn that knowledge leads to doubt. 'You often find him
hiding behind a deliberate obscurity, so deep and impenetrable that you cannot
make out what he meant' (2003a, 566, II.12). The ancients were in error in
making gods resemble humans, with all their attendant vices. Part of the error of
humans not knowing themselves sufficiently is the degree to which they practice
anthropomorphism with regard to God, because of their 'fierce desire to scan
the Divine through human eyes' (2003a, 592, II.12).
23. II.6.
24. I.19. See Seneca (1925, 186–93); *Moral Epistles*, XXVI.
25. See *Phaedo*, 67d.
26. I.20; see also I.26 & 2003a, 170.
27. I.14.
28. Written 1487 according to Ariew and Grene (Montaigne, 2003b, 1) or between
1420s-30s according to Screech, (Montaigne, 2003a, xxi).
29. II.11.
30. II.12.
31. II.12.

32. II.12.
33. II.12.
34. II.12.
35. II.12.
36. II.12.
37. II.12.
38. II.12.
39. II.12.
40. II.12.
41. II.12.
42. II.12.
43. II.12.
44. II.12.
45. See 2003a, Introduction, xl.
46. III.9.
47. II.6.
48. II.6.
49. II.8.
50. II.10.
51. III.5.
52. III 13.
53. III 13.
54. III 13.
55. III 13.

6 Descartes to Hegel

The Writers

'I do not know myself and God forbid I should'

(Goethe, 1971, 324)

In the period between Descartes and Hegel, KT continued to be a popular theme for writers.

Jonathan Swift (1667–1745)

Among the papers of Jonathan Swift was found a sermon called 'The Difficulty of Knowing One's Self'.[1] Commenting on Elisha knowing Hazael better than Hazael knows himself,[2] Swift says it is the case that most men 'know very little of what passes within them' (Swift, 1898, 97–8), something attested to by the false repentance of past sins and the breaking of vows not to repeat them. Despite being the only creatures able to practice self-reflection, we seldom converse with ourselves and rarely undertake the 'pain and difficulty' (1898, 101) needed for KT, and which requires a temporary retreat from the senses and the distractions of the business world. One prefers a good opinion of oneself to the testing of its veracity. But even if time is made for KT, one's prejudices and appetites sabotage one's best intentions. Nevertheless, the advantages of KT include making oneself ashamed rather than proud, opening oneself up to one's true abilities and character rather than those announced in flattery, and giving one patience in the face of criticism, for one knows the evils within one far better even than one's critics. The last of these has the added advantage of making one less severe in one's judgments of the faults of others. This individual may be able to live according to the 'great comprehensive rule of Christian duty' (1898, 105), do unto others as you would have them do to you. 'Let every man therefore look into his own heart, before he beginneth to abuse the reputation of another, and then he will hardly be so absurd as to throw a dart that will so certainly rebound and wound himself' (1898, 105).

Alexander Pope (1668–1744)

Pope's *Essay on Man* (1733–4) famously says that 'laugh when we must, be candid where we can;/But vindicate the ways of God to man' (Pope, 1994, 46).[3] In terms of KT the *Essay* extols one to know one's allotted place in the great chain of being; 'Nothing is foreign: parts relate to the whole;/ One all-extending, all preserving soul/Connects each being, greatest with the least/Made beast in aid of man and man of beast' (1994, 61).[4]

One's knowledge of the whole remains imperfect, and KT reveals this imperfection. 'Snatch from His hand the balance and the rod,/Re-judge His justice, be the god of God./In pride, in reas'ning pride, our error lies;/All quit their sphere, and rush into the skies' (1994, 48).[5] To KT is to know that one cannot know the overall plan or design. He famously opens the second Epistle: 'know then thyself, presume not God to scan,/The proper study of mankind is man' (1994, 54).[6]

Pope is able to combine in his view of KT a stoicism at the present state of things (a view Voltaire would later parody) with the self-love expressed in KT, which is a condition for just social relations. There is a stoicism in the view that 'One truth is clear, Whatever is, is right' (1994, 53).[7] Thus, 'Condition, circumstance, is not the thing;/Bliss is the same in subject or in king' (1994, 71).[8] God's scheme is ultimately equal to all. But there is less tranquillity when 'The surest virtues thus from passions shoot,/Wild Nature's vigour working at the root' (1994, 58).[9] 'Virtuous and vicious every man must be,/ Few in the extreme, but all in the degree' (1994, 58).[10]

Anticipating Rousseau, Pope brings self-love and the social together at the end of the *Essay*. Self-love finds the private to be served only in the public good. As such reason and passion 'answer one great aim;/That true self-love and social are the same;/That virtue only makes our bliss below;/And all our knowledge is,—Ourselves to know' (1994, 79).[11]

John Mason (1706–63)

Mason published *A Treatise on Self-Knowledge* in 1745. Part One of the *Treatise* explores KT in the individual. By means of two soliloquies Mason asks what is man, and what shall man be? He cites three relations in which the self stands and lists the duties that accompany them. The relation to God teaches of one's subjection to God's dominion while a child to His family. The relation to Christ demonstrates one's earthly corruption. The relation to others teaches one to KT in one's appointed station in life. There follows a series of observations on the adventures of the soul that lie ahead for the individual committed to knowing itself. To KT means to know Providence; to know one's strengths and weaknesses, one's vices, one's temptations, one's prejudices and governing passions, one's motives for action, and one's knowledge and its value. One needs to drive out angry, anxious, revengeful, extravagant, chimerical, lascivious, and melancholic thoughts, and indulge in rational, religious, and moral thoughts. Above all, KT means examining one's soul to see in what condition one will die.

Part Two lists the advantages of KT. It brings a stoic-like calm and constancy against adversity by granting one self-possession against a disorder of the passions. It forms individual humility, charity, moderation, and self-denial. It makes one wise and cautious in one's judgment and conduct, and breeds decorum, dignity, and discretion. Perhaps above all it prepares for death and maintains 'a constant guard against the surprise of it' (Mason, 2012, 189).

In Part Three Mason says KT is to be achieved by self-introspection, self-scrutiny, and self-examination. He offers the soul a soliloquy that will help it into this examination, through questions about the meaning of one's life, and advises that such an exercise be undertaken regularly, calling on Pythagoras and Seneca for support. The mind's eye can turn inward to see itself as in a mirror. In seeing into the 'bottom of our hearts' (2012, 217) we can then discover 'those secret prejudices and carnal prepossessions, which self-love would hide from us' (2012, 217).

The first step to achieving self-knowledge then, is to 'examine, scrutinise, and to judge ourselves, diligently, leisurely, frequently, and impartially; and that not by the false maxims of the world, but by the rules which God hath given us, reason and scripture' (2012, 217–18). This requires constant watchfulness. In addition, to be open to self-knowledge one must not be plagued by pride or obstinacy, but rather display humility. Indeed, the 'very means of attaining humility are the properest means for attaining self-knowledge' (2012, 229). Similarly, a 'proud man cannot know himself' (2012, 230). One must be ready to 'unlearn' (2012, 233) many things which are held to be the case regarding the self, a lesson often effectively learned not from friends but from enemies. Finally, the best means to self-knowledge is frequent and fervent prayer, so that one can converse not only with oneself in meditation, but also with God.

Laurence Stern (1713–1768)

Stern attends to KT in a sermon of 1760 entitled 'Self-Knowledge'.[12] Beginning with David's unwitting condemnation of himself (2 Samuel XII. 1–8), illustrating his own lack of self-knowledge, Sterne, in the guise of Mr Yorick, asks how is it possible for a man to be able to deceive himself about himself, and not know himself. Man 'is the only creature endowed with reflection, and consequently to know the most of himself—yet so it happens, that he generally knows the least . . . [regarding] his own disposition and true character' (Stern, 1973, 67). His answer is that self-knowledge and the reason necessary to it are compromised by passions and inclinations. Indeed, when it comes to judging oneself, one is judging that which is so much and so long beloved and of whom one has 'so early conceived the highest opinion and esteem' (1973, 68). As such self-examination is 'one of the hardest and most painful lessons' (1973, 68). So difficult did the ancients find it that they supposed KT to be a divine instruction regarding both the knowledge and duties required of individuals. Those who found it difficult to look directly within were not necessarily discouraged from recommending it to others and had to find ways around the barrier of self-love, using parables, fables, and other methods of indirect communication to do so. Self-deceit in so great a man as David happens daily to the rest of us, as does the propensity to examine others before ourselves. We have the ability, always, to find some 'secret and flattering circumstances' (1973, 71) in our favor that act as barriers to real self-interrogation. Who speaks more against pride than the proud man? We cheat ourselves and torture our reason to 'bring us in such a report of the sin as suits the present appetite and inclination' (1973, 73).

The remedy is to converse 'more and oftener with ourselves, than the business and diversions of the world generally give us leave' (1973, 73). We need to set aside a small part of each day to retire into ourselves and search into 'the dark corners and recesses of the heart, and [take] notice of what is passing there' (1973, 73). We will discover our errors and faults and, with David, ask God to cleanse us.

Dr. Samuel Johnson (1709–84)

Dr. Johnson wrote two pieces on KT in 'The Rambler'.[13] In the first piece he acknowledges that KT is the most famous of ancient maxims and wisdoms, and the most important, containing all that is needed to guide a moral agent. To KT is to know one's beginning, one's end, one's duties, and one's relations to others. The ancients would have needed a lesser understanding of KT than this, for it asks for more than a heathen world can offer. Nevertheless, Socrates is due praise for trying to turn man from 'the vain pursuit of natural philosophy to moral enquiries' (Johnson, 1825, 119). Despite this, men still reject this precept, and Johnson bemoans Gelidus (a pseudonym for a Mr. Coulson of University College, Oxford[14]) who, having lost in his interest in natural philosophy, is closed to all human emotions and sensations, and thus avoids man's first responsibility to practical virtue. Many people are to be found struggling against nature with their academic studies, a struggle grounded in the 'absurdity of pride [that can] proceed only from ignorance of themselves' (1825, 121).

In the second piece Johnson opens with two thoughts on death. From Seneca, 'on him does death lie heavily who, but too well known to all, dies to himself unknown',[15] and from the 17th-century English poet Abraham Cowley, the same thought that to one known to the world yet unknown to itself 'the face of death will terrible appear' (1825, 129). Self-love and overestimation of one's self are easy; they are arts of hypocrisy. But they spring from self-ignorance and are not always to be judged as wilfully fraudulent, although they do require exposure, for example, to the person who, in acting virtuously once, deems himself a virtuous soul. Such error only magnifies such vices. Similarly, many can talk of virtue without actually practicing it. Some excuse their own errors because more errors have been committed by others. Friends are not necessarily a boon to self-knowing, for they are often unwilling to share hard truths. Johnson says that some advise that enemies are more useful for KT, and with Mason, Johnson agrees that 'adversity has ever been considered as the state in which man most easily becomes acquainted with himself' (1825, 140). But this needs to be kept in a balance in order to obtain 'the solitude of adversity without its melancholy, its instructions without its censures, and its sensibility without its perturbations' (1825, 140).

The Philosophers

Descartes (1596–1650)

Even though philosophy remained 'ashamed' (Hegel, 1990, 112) of mediating truth by individual experience, it was this experience of the universal laws of experience that enabled philosophy to advance beyond its ancient shape. This new principle of inwardness is initiated by Descartes. What we have here, says Hegel, is 'an entirely new territory' (1990, 135). The *cogito* becomes a new beginning, a new shape of KT as a principle containing its own unconditioned necessity. To KT is to know that I am, because I think. '[T]hinking and being are thus inseparably bound together' (1990, 139), a unity requiring no mediation by a third term.[16]

The *cogito* is the beginning of the modern phase of KT in that the I is thought and thinking is the universality of being. The supreme being is the perfection of the unity of being and thinking. That God is the name thought gives to its own perfect being expresses Hegel's observation that 'the idea which a man has of God corresponds to that which he has of his freedom' (Hegel, 2013, 79). If Hegel's argument is interpreted in the idealist strain that God is only whatever he is thought to be, then Descartes takes against this. To the contrary, in the *Principles of Philosophy* Descartes says,

> the idea of a supremely perfect being is not an idea which was invented by the mind, or which represents some chimera, but . . . represents a true and immutable nature which cannot but exist since necessary existence is contained within it. (Descartes, 1985, 198)

He distinguishes this from the habit of more general thinking in which essence and existence are separated.

His case for God is a logical one, carried by the logic inherent in necessity. This logic of necessity posits that the *cogito*, although the unity of thought being itself, is not perfect. It is not perfect because it is *this cogito*, and *this* being, and not *all* thinking being. What Descartes does here is posit that the true God is the unity of thought and being, or NN, and that although this is the condition for the possibility of the *cogito* knowing itself, the latter remains an imperfect representation of this unity. He supports this ancient logic of the necessity of the ineffable NN by arguing that 'what is more perfect cannot be produced by—that is, cannot have has its efficient and total cause—what is less perfect' (1985, 199). This is the same logic that locates perfection in the simple and error in the compound: 'since the supreme perfections of which we have an idea are in no way to be found in us, we rightly conclude that they reside in something distinct from ourselves, namely God' (1985, 199). It is part of this same logic of necessity that, since infinite regression is logically impossible, it is necessary that one's thinking 'must reach a primary idea' (Descartes, 1984, 29).[17]

Locke (1632–1704)

In *An Essay Concerning Human Understanding* (1690) Locke takes the view that a 'person' is the idea in which one will find the *principium individuationis*, the principle of the identity of an individual. This person has continuity of identity in the fact that he is conscious of his own thinking. Locke begins by defining identity as that which has a unique beginning, and which resists sharing space or time with anything else. What distinguishes the person from the man and from substance is his consciousness and his consciousness of this consciousness, or self-consciousness.

In Locke, this is the way in which we might surmise that one can KT. A person, here, is 'a thinking intelligent being, that has reason and reflection, and can consider itself as itself' (Locke, 2004, 302) by means of a consciousness that is inseparable from thinking. Knowing that we think or perceive or feel is that by which a person can be a 'self' (2004, 302). In distinguishing this self from all others, one knows oneself as this personal identity. Loss of this awareness, or self-forgetfulness, are not arguments against this notion of personal identity. These episodes do not undermine personal identity, for the continuity of each individual life holds this identity to itself regardless of changes in its substantial or physical constitution. 'For it being the same consciousness that makes a man be himself to himself, *personal identity* depends on that only' (2004, 303). Regardless of the time between this awareness of self-consciousness, or of actions now considered but carried out in the past, 'it is by the consciousness it has of its present thoughts and actions, that it is a *self* to *itself* now' (2004, 303), and that will make it 'the same *self*' (2004, 303).

He concludes, self is that conscious thinking thing capable of pleasure and pain, or happiness or misery. As such, identity for Locke is not 'in the identity of substance, but . . . in the identity of consciousness' (2004, 310). Where there is substance but no consciousness, 'there is no person' (2004, 310). An immaterial substance that one cannot recollect is not the self, but Locke does add cautiously that it is more likely than not that 'consciousness is annexed to, and the affection of one individual immaterial substance' (2004, 311). Finite identities belong to a unique time and place. God alone has identity in the eternal and is 'without beginning' (2004, 296). Again here KT and NN remain separated by the finitude of individual experience and the unchangeable essence.

Vico (1668–1744)

Speaking to students at the beginning of the academic year in 1699, Vico states that man is born with an insatiable desire for learning. If he is prepared to struggle with the difficulties and shun the facile and easy, then his rewards can be both knowledge of the liberal arts and sciences, which supply the fruits of a peaceful society, and a flight upward to the heavens and to the divine. The key to this education is KT, for to know one's mind, or spirit, is to know God. In his first oration, Vico paraphrases the Cartesian argument that in doubt, or thought, there is also an awareness of the infinite God. Socrates, in pursuing KT, has not so much brought philosophy down from the heavens[18] as raised man to the heavens.

Combining thoughts now from the other Orations, Vico argues that the free will is the greatest gift but also the cause of evil and ruin. The fall here is turning one's back on wisdom and natural law, and surrendering to the tyranny of passions and darkness, or away from the truth of oneself to ignorance. The antidote to the fall is first to follow natural law in which will be found the laws of common association and the stock of common knowledge; and second that philosophers and those learned in literary studies should remember the *docta ignorantia* of Socrates and Nicolas Cusanus, and never claim to know what they do not know. The common person might claim to know, but the learned man, in knowing himself, will know that he does not know.

In Oration VI he argues that 'Wise judgement concerning human affairs follows the acquisition of the perfect knowledge of things divine' (Vico, 1993, 137). The order here is instructive. One arrives at divine knowledge from doing the good, for the good 'cultivates the divinity of the mind, and by means of the mind, reaches God' (1993, 138). Learning of God in religious feelings is where the spirit 'has known itself' (1993, 45). For each student, 'the mind is to you your own god . . . To see, to hear, to discover, to compare, to infer, to recollect, are divine' (1993, 48). Men who do not know themselves 'neglect the divine power of the spirit' (1993, 49). In sum, Vico is able to offer a view of KT in which the knowledge gained in physics, metaphysics and theology enacts the duty of virtue and good behavior to the glory of the Commonwealth and of God. KT here is both religious and civil, where God and the state are united in the true.

The Earl of Shaftesbury (1671–1713)

According to Laurence Klein's Introduction to Shaftesbury's *Characteristics of Men, Manners, Opinions, Times* (1711) philosophy for Shaftesbury was a worldly activity embracing self-knowing and self-transformation, following Socrates and the maxim KT. For Shaftesbury this involved an inner conversation or self-fashioning in which the self was its own author. This was a programme of *paideia*, 'of intellectual and aesthetic as well as ethical cultivation' (Shaftesbury, 1999, ix). Its political aspect concerned one's orientation to the public, aiming 'to cultivate political subjectivities appropriate to civil society' (1999, ix). On pedagogy, Shaftesbury criticized the pulpit as magisterial, preferring discursive practices that were inherently more polite. The challenge for all who could teach was how 'to create and encourage, and not to undermine, the autonomy of the subject' (1999, xiv). He supported 'the open-ended quest for truth and the benefits to be derived from free exchange' (1999, xiv).

In his *Letter concerning Enthusiasm* (1707) Shaftesbury offers KT as an antidote to the religious excesses of prophecy and inspiration. Before ascending to the heavenly heights, man is reminded to descend into himself. His essay to authors, *Soliloquy* (1710), describes KT variously as an inner conversation, a self-division, a self-conversation, an inward rhetoric, summed up as the 'practice of soliloquy' (1999, 128). Authors can be the nation-builders, the modern rhetoricians, but without self-knowledge 'the historian's judgement will be very defective, the politician's views very narrow and chimerical . . . [for] he who deals in character must of necessity know his own, or he will know nothing' (1999, 85). This inner conversation was seen in Socrates *daemon*, the struggle between noble and base parts that offered a path to morals and wisdom. Shaftesbury reads the Delphic inscription as divide yourself or be two, or as a 'home-dialect of soliloquy' (1999, 77). Wise men, in this sense, are 'never less alone than when by themselves' (1999, 77).[19] Shaftesbury sees the need for this soliloquy to be inquisitorial. The home of this practice is philosophy, although not the metaphysical system-builders whose understanding of 'the machine' (1999, 130) closes the door to self-knowing, and 'concerns not the man' (1999, 134). It is in KT that man can learn to pursue the better character, and therein to form the character of that 'modesty, condescension and just humanity which is essential to the success of all friendly counsel and admonition. An honest home-philosophy must teach us the wholesome practice within ourselves' (1999, 162).

This is brought together in his *Enquiry concerning Virtue or Merit* around the liberal arts. It is this education that is advantageous to virtue, and where the individual can be drawn to 'the love of order and beauty in society' (1999, 191). But equally, this is an education regarding both the divine order and the need of a God for the perfection that is virtue. Again here, KT offers the reasons for man to know God in a perfection both religious and civil/political.

In *Miscellany IV* Shaftesbury discusses Descartes' *Fourth Discourse*. It is clear that there is something that is thinking, but that this enjoys a continuous identity is much less clear. In the *cogito* of Descartes, what is it that is the I which thinks? Shaftesbury says here 'I take my being upon trust' (1999, 421); trust in the affections of grief and joy, and desire or aversion. Knowing one's self in this way opens up the need for inner work,

> it becomes him, by working upon his own mind, to withdraw the fancy or opinion of good or ill from that to which justly and by necessity it is not joined, and apply it with the strongest resolution to that with which it naturally agrees. (1999, 423)

He is able to conclude here that the more the inner conversation learns of those opinions which are wrongly conceived, the more the self forms its own natural liberty. 'Thus, at last a mind, by knowing itself and its own proper powers and virtues, becomes free and independent' (1999, 425). In sum:

> Men must acquire a very peculiar and strong habit of turning their eye inwards in order to explore the interior regions and recesses of the mind, the hollow caverns of deep thought, the private seats of fancy, and the wastes and wildernesses as well as the more fruitful and cultivated tracts of the obscure climate. (1999, 427)

Hume (1711–76)

In *A Treatise of Human Nature* (1739–40) Hume retrieves something of the doubts expressed by Socrates in the *Phaedrus* that it is perhaps impossible to KT. For Hume, this is partly due to a relativism that accompanies each perception of what is claimed as truth, or certainty, or identity. This is the skepticism that nothing in philosophy, not the *a priori*, nor eternal substances, can be proved 'beyond experience' (Hume, 1984, 45). If all ideas are derived from impressions, then all notions of perfect knowing, of perfection, are herein compromised. We can know of relations between different impressions, but we cannot find any standard by which to decide the time wherein something forces or acquires 'a title to the name of identity' (1984, 310). Beyond experience, questions of causes or truths are unintelligible.

Unlike Locke, therefore, who argues for a continuity of personal identity or selfhood, for Hume there exists only related impressions or perceptions, and getting behind these to view the self as the essence of these perceptions is impossible. His skepticism here refuses to 'confound identity with relation' (1984, 302). To KT then, means to know that the identity which we 'ascribed to the mind of man, is only a fictitious one' (1984, 306). Hume's skepticism exposes what the tradition had long known, that is, to transform the many into the one, or many perceptions into one *a priori* truth, is to 'make them lose their characters of distinction and difference, which are essential to them' (1984, 307). This is the same aporia we have thus far been following between the compound work of KT and the simple work of NN.

Rousseau (1712–78)

In the Preface to the *Discourse on the Origin of Inequality* (published in 1754) Rousseau says of the Delphic inscription that 'it contained a precept more difficult and more important than is to be found in all the huge volumes that moralists have ever written' (Rousseau, 1973, 43). If his *Confessions* and *Reveries of a Solitary Walker* reveal a man intent on gaining self-knowledge, his more political works, the *Discourses*, *The Social Contract*, and *Emile* take up this same quest on behalf of humankind as a whole.

Illustrative of the relationship between these two forms of KT is his second letter to Malesherbes of 1762. After 40 years of a life dissatisfied with himself, he describes an epiphany in which the whole was laid before him in a 30-minute revelation. Seeing an essay competition, the title for which concerned the moral effects of the arts and sciences, he describes how in a flash of inspiration accompanied by palpitations and tears, he sat down under a tree and let a flood of ideas overwhelm him.

> If I had ever been able to write a quarter of what I saw and felt under that tree, with what clarity I would have revealed all the contradictions of the social system, with what force I would have exposed the abuse of our institutions, with what simplicity I would have shown that man is naturally good and that it is only through these institutions alone that men become wicked. (Rousseau, 1979, 24)

All that he learned in that time sitting beneath the tree is, he says, scattered in his three main works: the first two *Discourses* and *Emile*. It is precisely because they conjoin self-knowing of the individual and of the human race as one project that these books 'are inseparable and together form a complete whole' (1979, 24). This is again stated in the Preface to the *Second Discourse*. 'For how shall we know the source of inequality between men, if we do not begin by knowing mankind?' (Rousseau, 1973, 43). No doubt contrary to the intentions of those who set the title of the essay competition, he states that 'as every advance made by the human species removes it still farther from its primitive state, the more discoveries we make, the more we deprive ourselves of the means of [knowing ourselves]' (1973, 43).

KT in Rousseau's thinking unveils the way that social fashions and private property especially have distorted the true human self. Left to his own devices, natural man has compassion for suffering and *amour-de-soi*, or the love that looks to self-preservation. Together these are the root of individual virtue and a collective sense of humanity. This becomes compromised by *amour-propre*. When natural man is able to fulfil his simple needs independently, then his relations with others are natural and uncompromised. But when collective life and production lead to surpluses, of both materials and leisure time, comparisons of one individual against another begin, and natural man's independent *amour-de-soi* is distorted into social man's *amour-propre*. In this love of self man enslaves himself to others, with the masters commanding private property as the legal recognition of the inequality that comes from dependence. Greed and the pursuit of false needs and appetites are the bedrock of this civil society, and the arts and the sciences, which appear to be the flourishing of humanity, in fact only 'fling garlands of flowers over the chains' (1973, 5) that man, through private property, has run headlong into.

> What a train of vices must attend this uncertainty! Sincere friendship, real esteem, and perfect confidence are banished from among men. Jealousy, suspicion, fear, coldness, reserve, hate, and fraud lie constantly concealed under that uniform and deceitful veil of politeness. (1973, 7)

From this knowledge of the self and of humanity, forged through dependent relations that breed competition and greed, Rousseau offers the education of Emile as an antidote. He does not seek a return to a natural man who may have roamed the forest slaking his thirst at the first stream he came to. Instead Rousseau tries to develop an education of the modern self in modern social relations, one that has to take into account the need for social life. This is a compromise, but also *realpolitik*. Emile will, as much as is possible, learn about himself and the world not from teachers or books or other students, but from his own experiences, which Rousseau as his tutor carefully crafts to ensure that they are as little compromised by social evil as possible. Growing up protected from the influence of false needs, Emile will KT in as true a fashion as he can. This will ground his relations to others in independence and compassion from which comes a sense of justice, openness, and a character grounded in true, not artificially constructed needs. It is well known that for his partner, Sophie, Rousseau will suggest an education in *amour propre* as a way of giving a woman social power over a man in lieu of the physical mastery she lacks. For all its outdatedness now, for Rousseau this is a way of empowering women in their unequal physical relations with men.

Even this brief account of Rousseau reveals how firmly in the tradition of KT his thinking is. KT here is the path to knowing humanity, and to reforming individual character and unjust social relations. But what of KT in Rousseau regarding God and man. The tutor of Emile asks what religion, if any, should be taught to Emile. The answer is: 'We will not attach him to any sect, but we will give him the means to choose for himself according to the right use of his own reason' (Rousseau, 1993, 267). To this end Rousseau speaks of a meeting with the Savoyard priest who opens his heart to Rousseau so that Rousseau can see the priest 'at least as I [the priest] seem to myself' (1993, 273).

In a state of doubt, uncertainty, darkness, and contradiction, the holy man sought first principles on which to base his life. The philosophers offered no help in regard of the weakness of the rational intellect, for

> we have no means of measuring this vast machine, we are unable to calculate its workings; we know neither its guiding principles nor its final

purpose; we do not know ourselves, we know neither our nature nor the spirit that moves us. (1993, 276)

Instead of following the philosophers, he decided to follow his inner light, as he calls it, to turn his eyes upon himself and attest as true only that which is incontrovertible. Passing the test (and similar here to Hayy Ibn Yaqzan) are the evidence of self, external objects, the faculties of mind and sensation, the perception of motion, the laws of nature, and the necessity of a first cause. In addition, he reasons that there is no action or motion without will, and no fixed laws without a supreme intelligence that can be called God. The priest also describes kindness as an inherent quality. But what God is, that says the priest, he cannot know.

Convinced now of the necessity of God, the priest returned to examine himself, to discover his own place in the created order of things. He found a species whose will is controlled by an intelligence lacking in the beasts, and for whom there is a feeling of a common existence. In addition, this 'first return to self has given birth to a feeling of gratitude and thankfulness to the author of my species, and this feeling calls forth my first homage to the beneficent Godhead' (1993, 288).

Amid the order of nature and the chaos of humanity, the priest learned of the existence of the soul. Humanity is divided by two opposing principles, the higher truths sought by the intellect, and the base satisfactions sought by the senses and appetites. 'I feel myself at once a slave and a free man' (1993, 289); 'a slave in my vices, a free man in my remorse' (1993, 291). In the free man intelligence and the power of judgment are the causes that determine the will. In keeping with Rousseau's views, the priest identified with *amour-de-soi*—that man is not free to ignore his own welfare or to desire his own hurt. 'Has not nature made us feel our needs as a means to our preservation?' (1993, 292) Our first duty therefore 'is towards ourself' (1993, 298). The motive power of his actions is an 'original impulse' (1993, 291), an 'immaterial substance' (1993, 291), a soul that will survive death. Reflecting Rousseau's views in the *Second Discourse*, the priest says 'It is the abuse of our powers that makes us unhappy and wicked. Our cares, our sorrows, our sufferings are of our own making' (1993, 292).[20] 'How few sufferings are felt by the man living in a state of primitive simplicity' (1993, 292).

The priest suggests that if humanity knew itself better, understood itself as it really is and not as false social desires have distorted it, then 'if we were content to be ourselves we should have no cause to complain of our lot' (1993, 292). Our unhappiness lies in 'blaming nature for the evils we have inflicted on ourselves by our neglect of the laws' (1993, 293). The central telos of self-knowing here, is 'seek no further for the author of evil, thou art he' (1993, 293). Study yourself and see that to be just is to be happy. Lacking self-knowledge, it is the wicked who thrive through the oppression of the righteous. Included in this self-knowing are how the good lies deep in one's heart, how one takes pleasure in the joys of others, how we are consoled by friendship and humanity, how we shed tears of sympathy, how we delight in protection of the innocent, how we are moved to help the oppressed, how we are inspired by mercy and generosity and above all, how we suffer when we see the sufferings of others. To KT in this way is to know the just man. The wicked man flees from such education. Prior to this conversation, Rousseau accuses the outlook of the priest—that the things we value most in life are mere illusions, feeding illusory and false needs—of being a gloomy denial and disavowal of everything. When asked, who could possibly be happy under such a philosophy, the priest answers 'I am' (1993, 273). At the end of this longer meeting, the priest says the just man finds peace within himself, joy in his heart, and the cheerfulness that is not dependent upon others. This is the reward due to the person who knows himself. Moreover, there is no one alive, even in the midst of such artificial civility, that has 'never yielded to the temptation' (1993, 305) of doing good.

Self-examination has taught the priest that KT is an education that reveals where the good and the just are to be found, and the divine will that has placed them within the reach of such self-examination. 'Has he not given me conscience that I might love the right, reason that I may perceive it, and freedom that I may choose it?' (1993, 308).

At the end of his speaking, the priest is able to sum up the life that KT commends:

> be honest and be humble, learn how to be ignorant, then you will never deceive yourself or others. If ever your talents are so far cultivated as to enable you to speak to other men, always speak according to your conscience, without caring for their applause. The abuse of knowledge causes incredulity. The learned always despise the opinions of the crowd; each of them must have his own opinion. A haughty philosophy leads to atheism just as blind devotion leads to fanaticism. Avoid these extremes; keep steadfastly to the path of truth, or what seems to you truth, in simplicity of heart, and never let yourself be turned aside by pride or weakness. Dare to confess God before the philosophers; dare to preach humanity to the intolerant. It may be you will stand alone, but you will bear within you a witness which will make the witness of men of no account with you. Let them love or hate, let them read your writings or despise them; no matter. Speak the truth and do the right; the one thing that really matters is to do one's duty in this world; and when we forget ourselves we are really working for ourselves. My child, self-interest misleads us; the hope of the just is the only sure guide. (1993, 331–2)

J. G. Hamann (1730–88)

In his own words, Hamann speaks of 'an inner unrest with which I was ailing for a very long period of my life—the discontent and the inability to bear myself' (Hegel, 2008, 6).[21] It was at once a depression, an obstacle to social relations, and a self-immersion which, according to Hegel, he lived out as a 'deep particularity [incapable of] any form of universality' (2008, 6). However, a more recent commentator, James O'Flaherty, sees in Hamann a Humean-inspired critique of enlightenment rationality, an example of Cusanian-type Socratic learned ignorance, and a man able to bring Hellenism and Christianity together. We will set these two views together around the idea of *Knechtsgestalt* in O'Flaherty and the master and slave in Hegel's beautiful soul. Both are shapes that KT takes in its early forays into the totality of enlightenment rationality.

There is one part of Hamann's life that brings these themes to light. In a state of desperation at his depression and inner turmoil, and unable to make friends in any way that can give voice to this self-examination, he read the Bible and came to see himself as the murderer of God's only son. He falls out with the Beren's family, who had funded his traveling around Europe after the death of his mother, when the family read his autobiographical writings: it was with 'disgust' (2008, 14) that they read of his pretensions to piety (in which he said he excelled his friends), and his desire that, in recognising his Socratically-inspired genius, 'they recognise him as their master and apostle' (2008, 14). We will see in a moment that for Hamann such claims perhaps have a pedagogical *telos*, hoping to serve KT in both the author and the reader.

Kant encouraged Hamann to rethink this new-found faith. Hamman responded by asking Kant to raise himself to Hamann's pride else Hamman will have to descend to Kant's vanity. He demands from his friends penance and conversion, inspired by his own Lutheran inwardness, and a calling from God to lead his friends to self-knowledge. He sees it as his fate to be a despised and persecuted prophet. As Hegel notes, such confidence could only be experienced by his friends as pride. Kant refused further contact with him, and Hamann restricted his interventions to publications, beginning with the *Socratic Memorabilia (1759)*. In a letter to Kant, Hamann says that he intends only to disturb the thinking of others, and that Kant had refused this kind of Socratic examination. Hamann's intention in his engagement with Kant, says Hegel, was 'with the purpose of bringing his friend to self-knowledge. The *Socratic Memorabilia* are the execution and explicit exposition of the position he wishes to take: that of Socrates, who had been unknowing and had exposed his ignorance in order to draw his fellow citizens in and to lead them to self-knowledge and to a wisdom which lies hidden' (Hegel, 2008, 19). Kant did not respond to the *Memorabilia* either.

O'Flaherty is able to take a more generous view of Hamann's character and pedagogy. *Socratic Memorabilia* has the source of its creativity, its aesthetic sensibility, in the experience of oppositions. Socrates carried such opposition in his somewhat ugly appearance and the beauty of his teaching and its 'ultimate meaning' (Hamann, 1967, 10). The opposition of subject and object is seen by Hamann to have an essence that transcends it. This essence is God, and, in a more limited form, it is man's relation to God (as to nature). Hamann's skepticism towards any kind of sufficient identity of either subject or object comes from being 'full of Hume' (1967, 41), such that existence cannot be known, only believed. If, as Hamann says, *Socratic Memorabilia* is a microcosm, it is so only because it cannot adequately represent the macrocosm. To know such limitations—of existence in relation to truth—is to have something of Cusanus' learned ignorance.

As Socrates confessed to knowing nothing, so Hamann sees this imperfection as the true microcosm of the truth it cannot have. But in the failure of knowing there lies a greater reality. This is the *Knechtsgestalt*. It is where the form of the servant carries with it the sensibility needed to receive the highest order of truth. O'Flaherty says here that it is a basic principle of Hamann's thought that 'a given reality should always exceed its phenomenal appearance' (1967, 83). As Socrates brought the heavens down to man, so Hamann has profaned boastful prophets on Earth so as to open up the path between the true and the most lowly. To achieve this Hamann uses various techniques including *metaschematization* in which objective and subjective or universal and particular can represent each other. This requires direct personal involvement of the subject, and here Hamann identifies himself with Socrates, and also invokes indirect communication in order to follow 'the divine example of transforming that which is of low degree into an emblem of truth' (1967, 124) through KT.

For O'Flaherty *Socratic Memorabilia* is a work of art, a representation pointing to something greater than itself, and in this sense, is *in forma servi*, in the form of a servant. Faith is always required here precisely because the representation is never complete or exhaustive. Socrates was in this sense a man of faith possessed by the genius of his daimon which, says O'Flaherty, for Hamann was 'a prototype of the Holy Spirit' (1967, 127). In this way, Hamann is able to hold onto the genius and heroism of Greece in his view of Christianity.

This pedagogy of self-knowing and its art of indirect communication involves artifice. Behind this artifice remains the self-confidence that Hamann excelled both Berens and Kant in wisdom, because 'he had advanced further in self-knowledge than they, and knew that he knew nothing' (1967, 163). From the Humean idea that the existence of all things can only be believed, never known, so he lauds such faith as above attack by reason. Pauline doubt is quoted in support here: 'If anyone imagines he knows something, he does not yet know as he ought to know. But if one loves God, one is known by him' (1 Cor. 8:2–3).

Of the present age Hamann notes that modern Socratics, 'the canonical teachers of the public' (1967, 173), sadly 'deviate infinitely from the charter of his ignorance' (1967, 173). Hegel concludes here that Hamann's text is intensely personal, and that faith—being here the sense certainty of all things external—is subjectivity made universal. Where Hamann (in the later essay *Golgotha and Sheblimini*) declares war on the objectivity of divine spirit (NN) in the actual world, seeking its separation from the true religion which is found in the heart, Hegel urges instead that the living reality of divine spirit is precisely to be actual in its finitude, a fact which has 'completely escaped' (2008, 34) Hamann.

This is not just a criticism by Hegel of the way that KT can become a fetishism of the inner world, devoid of actual or objective significance and existence. It also speaks of the way KT becomes trapped within the beautiful soul, a spiritual inwardness conceived in Germany in the 18th-19th centuries. Lisa Marie Anderson says of this spirituality that its ideal is an inner beauty found in the heart, an 'intensely personal Christianity' (Hegel, 2008, xxxix). Here KT has a very distinctive but unsatisfactory form. It communicates with itself, and knows that it needs to externalize itself and become actual in the world. But this remains only an empty yearning, for it lacks the courage to give up this inner satisfaction for a unity with another. It cuts itself off from precisely that which it yearns for: a concrete spiritual existence in the real world. Instead of uniting with others, the beautiful soul is consistently and repetitively estranged from others.

The KT of Hamann here makes 'friends incommunicable to themselves and to each other' (2008, xxxix). It is just such an individual, seeking to be the teacher of KT to others, that can be received only as overbearing, self-immersed and, in not seeing how he or she is seen by others, as lacking precisely the self-knowledge preached for others. In the *Phenomenology Of Spirit* Hegel says of this shape of KT as the beautiful soul that it is 'entangled in the contradiction between its pure self and the necessity of that self to externalise itself and change itself into an actual existence' (Hegel, 1977, 406).[22] Knowing that it leaves this unreconciled and un-reconcilable contradiction within it, KT here 'is disordered to the point of madness, wastes itself away in yearning and pines away in consumption' (Hegel, 1977, 407).[23]

At stake between O'Flaherty's *Knechtsgestalt* and Hegel's beautiful soul is the question of how to understand the slave, and his relation to the master in this period of the European Enlightenment. For O'Flaherty Hamann, like Socrates, is the slave who carries the integrity of the divinely inspired mission of KT. He is slave to the mission, to its pedagogical requirements, and cannot be master because he possesses no knowledge of his own. He is only perceived as master by his masterful critics because of their ignorance, and he is willing to suffer at their hands. The greater the suffering, the more evidence of being the true Socratic slave to truth. For Hegel, however, it is a form of mastery in the beautiful soul that refuses to risk an actual objective existence that leaves it merely inward, and lacking any objective recognition in the world.

Kant (1724–1804)

Before looking at Hegel on KT specifically, we turn to Kant, to illustrate KT in the doctrine of virtue from the *Metaphysics of Morals* (first published in 1797). The first duty of a human being, though not the principal duty, is self-preservation. But as a moral being the greatest violation of a human being's duty to himself is 'lying' (Kant, 1996, 182), for he 'violates the dignity of humanity in his own person' (1996, 182). Yet to deceive oneself intentionally 'seems to contain a contradiction' (1996, 183).

This inner struggle is the modern courtroom of KT. 'Consciousness of an *internal court* in man . . . is conscience' (1996, 189). But to avoid the contradiction here that this court is all one person, Kant distinguishes between the subjectivity of the court and its objectivity in the moral law and the concept and duty of freedom. The duty of one's conscience is to 'have to think of someone other than himself' (1996, 189).[24] It is conscience that has the power of pronouncing the sentence of happiness or misery depending upon the judgment made of the action. Such a person is 'a scrutinizer of hearts' (1996, 190) in relation to the objective moral commands. As such, conscience 'must be thought of as the subjective principle of being accountable to God for all one's deeds' (1996, 190). Conscience is the subjectivity of knowing one's self obliged to submit freely to the truth of the laws of practical reason, or to God as the omnipotent moral being. Religion here is 'a duty of the human being to himself' (1996, 193).

Therefore, this internal court of morality requires that the first command of all duties to oneself is KT, that is, to know one's heart, to know where one finds oneself in the relation between heart and duty. Kant says,

> Moral cognition of oneself, which seeks to penetrate into the depths (the abyss) of one's heart which are quite difficult to fathom, is the beginning of all human wisdom. For in the case of a human being, the ultimate wisdom, which consists in the harmony of a human being's will with its final end, requires him first to remove the obstacle within (an evil will actually present in him) and then to develop the original predisposition to a good will within him, which can never be lost. (1996, 191)

Kant adds here on KT that 'Only the descent into the hell of self-cognition can pave the way to godliness' (1996, 191). Kant is much more concerned here with this hell of KT in relation to the theory and practice of practical reason than in the earlier *Critique of Practical Reason* (first published in 1788), although he did draw attention to the aporias of theory and practice in his 1793 piece 'On the common saying: "This may be True in Theory but it does not Apply in Practice."' He also says in the *Metaphysics of Morals* that inner and outer perfection is true objectively but never subjectively. 'All duties to oneself regarding the end of humanity in our own person are, therefore, only imperfect duties' (1996, 197).

In this hell of KT one learns the good of the inquiry against the evil of the self, for one learns the predisposition to the good in finding the gap between heart and duty. Impartiality and sincerity are demanded as duties to oneself in the command to KT. The duties of morality have to be learned, even against one's own inclinations, and judged by the power of conscience.

All of this has its condition of possibility only in the duty that the human being has to KT. Without the active conscience, the descent into the hell of self-knowing, there would only be a kind of automatic conformity to duty. This Kant clearly warns against at the end of the *Critique of Practical Reason*, arguing that without the conflict which 'the moral disposition has to wage with inclinations' (Kant, 1956, 152) duties could not be performed freely but from fear, and from heteronomy not autonomy, leaving moral action as a 'mere mechanism, where, as in a puppet show, everything would gesticulate well but no life would be found in the figures' (1956, 153).

Hegel (1770–1831)

Hegel begins his *Philosophy of Mind (Geist)* with the claim that KT refers not to the single self but to the whole of humankind. In contrast to Kant and conscience, he says that KT does not aim at the 'recesses of the human heart' (Hegel, 1971, 1)[25], for this does not get to the essence of all life, that is, *Geist*. Nor is KT to be seen as an external imposition for 'the God who impels to self-knowledge is none other than the absolute law of mind itself' (1971, 1).[26] The Greeks, he observes, were the first to see the divine not as merely an external other, but as intellect. Christianity then enabled intellect to have a free relationship to itself, to know itself incarnate. Philosophy proper here is *spirit: know thyself*. It has little time for psychology, which eschews metaphysics.

As such, says Hegel, Aristotle's works on the soul remain the most admirable works of philosophical value on intellect learning of the divine within it, and indeed, of intellect as the divine. The sophistication of Aristotle and Hegel here lies in the difficult notion of actuality, for spirit is 'not an essence that is already finished and complete before its manifestation . . . but an essence which is truly actual only through the specific forms of its necessary self-manifestation' (1971, 3).[27] It is this actuality that, in knowing itself as the knower and as what is known, is the modern version of mind or intellect or spirit knowing its own truth. Thus Hegel says, 'Only when we contemplate mind in this process of the self-actualisation of its Notion, do we know its truth . . . [and] the entire development of mind is nothing else but [this] raising of itself to its truth' (1971, 6).[28]

KT features most prominently in various parts of Hegel's *History of Philosophy*. In the Introduction of 1820 he says that while nature can reproduce itself in its actions, the actions of spirit are qualitatively different: the act of spirit is 'self-knowledge' (Hegel, 1985, 24). As such, as spirit, 'I am only insofar as I know myself' (1985, 24), and here spirit is actual as time, as the history of the world in its different manifestations and shapes. Hegel argues that it was Socrates who obeyed the Delphic Oracle's command to KT, seeing it as the law of spirit (1971, 502), and bringing to the Greeks the idea that truth is to be looked for within the individual, and it is Socrates who, in embodying the spirit's self-actualization out of nature, added ethics to philosophy. His principle is that man must find the truth through himself, unlike for Antigone, who knew not where the eternal law of the gods came from.[29] He lived his philosophy as his life, and in his dialectical activity he showed how, in thought contradicting itself, what is thought to be known refutes itself. The missing eternal law is now to be found in thought, in thinking. As such the good is no longer merely abstract, as the νους of Anaxagoras; now it is the self-determining universal as the individual and the world. Here spirit embarks on its journey to KT, or, the same, God is actual in human form, a living consciousness.[30]

Christianity is the development of spirit as it seeks to KT. In Hegel's philosophical history, God becomes incarnate and known to itself in human form. In Christianity 'God is grasped as self-differentiating' (Hegel, 1990, 21), *known* as an idea that is known to itself in differentiating itself. History is now conceived of as 'the process of spirit . . . raising itself to this standpoint of its own self-consciousness' (1990, 22). In this, its freedom with regard to itself, it fulfils its own imperative: *know thyself.*

* * * *

The advantage of following through the Western intellectual tradition of God and man, or of substance and subject, or of universal and individual, as KT and NN, has been to illustrate that the relation is always a shape of education. How man knows himself, his freedom, is also how man conceives truth and God. NN is perfect education, KT is imperfect education learning of its imperfection against the model of perfection. The criterion for judging, as we saw, was the political definition of freedom in the ancient societies of masters and slaves. But by following this relation as education, as KT and NN, we have been able to keep in view not only the ways education sees itself to be the solution to its own problems, but also how God and individual are not a duality, but a trinity of educating relations—God as NN, man as KT, and the educative relation of each to the other.

We have also been able to reconstruct the philosophy of the history of the thinking of God and man rather than present merely a history of the thinking of God and man. The philosophy of history is not, as is so often claimed, some kind of predetermined teleological progression of truth displaying itself independently of its actors and their ideas. Instead, the philosophy of history is the most deeply contingent view of Western development, one that explains this history only from within the difficulty—a difficulty that cannot be wished away—that the idea of God and of man's freedom are somehow determinative of each other. This difficulty is kept open and very much alive when the earthly realm of self, subjectivity, and freedom, or the compound, is seen as the work of KT, and when the divine realm of substance, necessity, and God, or the simple, is seen as the identity of NN. The ancient logic of mastery sustains their separation by means of the intractable aporia. As we will now see, a different logic, a modern metaphysical logic, both sustains and negates their separation by means of a different understanding of aporia. This is a new understanding of God, and of man, and it is one that has education about mastery, not mastery in-itself, as its own logic.

If we were to proceed with a historical sweep of the relation between KT and NN from 1831, Hegel's death, to the present day, we would trace the continuing struggle of subjective substance, of aporia, and of educational logic, to speak itself against the still-dominant prejudices that suppress it and silence it. Each contribution to Western philosophy could be explored for the ways in which education is lost in the continuing scholasticism wherein thought must still be made to save the appearance of the old system of logic.[31] But Part 2 now does not make such an historical sweep of philosophy from Marx to Derrida. Rather it pursues the modern metaphysical development of subjective substance in ways in which education is able to speak of and for itself in its own voice.

Notes

1. His editor notes that no date was attached to it and, although the handwriting only looked similar to Swift's, the sermon was included among his works in volume 8 in 1746.
2. 2 Kings 8:9–12.
3. I.i
4. III.i
5. I.iv
6. II.ii
7. I.x; see also 73, IV.v; & 79, IV.vii
8. IV.ii
9. II.v
10. II.v
11. IV.vii
12. If this sermon by Sterne is derivative of Swift, and of Butler's *Upon Self-Deceit*, this is appropriate for Sterne recollecting his early clerical career as someone who churned out homilies somewhat like Homenas [in Sterne's *Extract in the Manner of Rabelais*] who would often borrow the sermons of others. Yorick, Sterne's other clerical alter-ego, is altogether 'a more original thinker' (Marjorie David, Introduction, Sterne, 1973, 7).
13. nos. 24 (June 9th) 1750, and 28 (June 23rd) 1750.
14. See James Boswell, 1831, *The Life of Samuel Johnson vol. 3*, London, J. Murray, 159n.
15. From *Thyestes*, 401–3 in Seneca (1961); also Johnson (1825, 129).
16. For Hegel, being is merely 'posited' (1990, 142) here.
17. From the *Third Meditation*.
18. See Cicero, *Tusculan Disputations*, V iv 10.
19. Italics removed
20. *The Social Contract*, of course, begins with 'Man is born free; and everywhere he is in chains' (Rousseau, 1973, 181).
21. From Hegel's first essay on Hamann.
22. §668.

23. §668.
24. Italics removed.
25. §377.
26. §377 *zusatz*.
27. §378, *zusatz*.
28. §379, *zusatz*.
29. See Hegel (1986, 443).
30. See Hegel (1971, 469).
31. I have tried to illustrate this in Tubbs (2008, 2009).

Intermezzo

What is God? For Aristotle and Neoplatonism after him, it was a logical category fulfilling a logical necessity. This logical necessity was that truth lay at the end of a process of reduction to the most simple. The most simple was true because it was the condition of its own possibility or was its own beginning. Anything that could be reduced to something more simple failed to have its condition of possibility within it. Already here, truth is deemed independent and in-itself, and untruth deemed mere contingency, or that for which truth is other, to which it can be reduced, and upon which it depends for its foundation. This broadly remains the logical template of God in Western culture and in the Abrahamic monotheistic faiths: truth in relation to error, and the simple in relation to the compound.

This template of the logic of God is complemented by a template of the being of God. How could something whose truth is in-itself live as this in-itself, and how could the untruth of the contingent live as this untruth? The answer is provided by the template of being as immediacy and mediation. God could be itself only immediately and as an unbroken continuity. If it was divided, it would cease to be the most simple. In turn, that which was contingent or error could be itself only as mediated, or as something compromised by existing only in relation to the true and not immediately on its own terms. The immediate could never be mediated by untruth, for then it would only be contingent upon such mediation and no longer in-itself or its own condition of possibility. Logically the mediated could never exist immediately, for immediacy is lost in mediation and is impossible for mediation.

It is possible to trace the development of these templates of logic and being together in European thinking as the culture of aporia. This culture presents itself in three phases. The first is the triad of Socrates, Plato, and Aristotle. Socrates heralds the relation of individual intellect and its objects and therein relativizes the identity or the in-itself of every object as being *for* thought, or as being dependent upon or mediated by (and therefore changed by) the thought that thinks it. Plato makes this relation conceptual. He abstracts thinking from every material object, deems this abstraction a universality of thought, and calls it the Form. But to call this merely an abstraction is not correct, for Plato neither sets the Forms completely adrift from the mind that knows them, nor defines them completely within the logic of mastery. He does not posit a total separation between immediacy and mediation. Instead, in the simile of the sun,[1] the Form is not a detached immediacy, but is rather the cause by which it can then be mediated by and known to individual consciousness. The issue here is whether the light that is produced by the sun so that it can be seen, or the thought that is produced by the Form so that it can be known, is a continuity without interruption, or whether it falls into the dialectical relation of the Form as an object for consciousness. As we saw in Part 1, this difficulty was partly accepted by Aristotle when he confessed the aporia of universal and particular, and of eternal forms and actual and individual forms. But it is also partly refused by Aristotle in his adherence to the logic of mastery in holding the in-itself as that which is simple and cannot be other than it is, or is unchangeable and as others would emphasize, therefore ineffable. Post-Aristotelian philosophy mostly took to the logic of the in-itself and rejected the aporetic Aristotle.

Within this ambivalence, the Aristotelian concept of actuality is a culture of aporia. Actuality heralds the mediation of matter or potential where the latter is nothing without its being the form of something real. But this only reemphasizes the aporia. For actuality to be true, the prime mover would have to be an immediate actuality, uncaused by anything else and eternally actual. But 'immediate actuality' and 'eternally actual' are something of an oxymoron here. In the logic of mastery, if something is eternal then it is only ever an immediacy and never becomes a form. But if it is actual, it is an individually existing form and not eternal and unchanging. The idea of *anima mundi* is one attempt to embrace the universe as the immediacy of God's actuality, an existence mediated, as it were, only internally with itself. This same immediacy of mediation underpins the model of emanation, and as we saw above, Cory argued for just such an idea of 'immediacy of actuality' (Cory, 2014, 109) in interpreting Aquinas's view of KT.

The second distinctive phase of the culture of aporia is Kantian. Kant takes the unavoidability of the aporia seriously and enacts his Copernican revolution wherein thought no longer has to conform to the object but instead the object has to accept its dependence upon being thought. Within the logic of mastery and identity, the implications for truth here are profound. An infinite regression appears in which truth is ever changing, always compound, always composite, and never able to rest in-itself as its own first principle. The role of the *a priori* in the *Critique of Pure Reason* protects truth, and God, from the abysmal fate of being only a thought of a thought of a thought . . . In the *Critique of Practical Reason* it is the will that is granted priority, in which objective morality is protected from mediation by personal interest by the categorical imperative. In the *Critique of Judgement* Kant seeks to protect beauty and nature even from the *a priori* by granting to imagination, to feeling, and to a natural accord a subjective notion of truth in the realms of aesthetics and nature.

The third phase is Hegelian. Hegel accepts the aporetic Kant but rejects the positing of truth as the *a priori*, the pure will, and the pure natural accord. This allows aporia to have its own truth, and even to *be* truth, to be the absolute. This logic of aporia makes no sense to the logic of mastery that has dominated the tradition for two thousand years. But Hegel notes that 'logic has not undergone any change since Aristotle' (Hegel, 1969, 51) and states that as such 'it is all the more in need of a total reconstruction' (1969, 51). This reconstruction involves the logic of aporia, which, as Booth demonstrated, has been mostly suppressed by the dominant logic of mastery and identity. It is a reconstruction in which aporia, as difficulty, is the logic of the presupposition of its own condition of possibility.

In the ancient templates of the logic and being of truth and untruth immediacy is the One and mediation is self-consciousness. Philosophy, religion, and art are cultures of the irreconcilable relation, or aporetic relation, between the individual and truth, God, and beauty. We have traced this culture of aporia in Part 1 against and within the template of NN as immediacy and KT as mediation. For some, this struggle is resolved when the individual is successfully absorbed into the immediacy of the One, negating the individual and preserving only the One. Plotinus goes furthest here in believing that the One cannot have any self-knowledge because that would introduce contingency into immediacy.

Nevertheless, as we saw in Part 1, the 'doctrinaire clarity' (Booth, 1983, 94) demanded by the logic of mastery continued in full awareness of the danger of aporia. Avicenna, for example, seeks to avoid the culture of aporia by means of the continuity of emanation layered only by sadness and darkness. Through the angelic pedagogy, divine consciousness never detaches from itself in such a way that would mean its self-continuity is broken. For Ibn Arabi the imagination and Khidr are also this continuity with the One implicit within the KT of the individual. Aquinas and Averroes fought out the implications of this culture of aporia. If there was a universal intellect but no unique personal intellect, this prioritized immediacy over individual KT, but if there was a personal intellect unrelated to a separate pure intellect then individual KT seemed to have no direct path to the immediacy of the One. Cusanus and Hamann tried to find immediacy in the negative and mediating work of KT that conformed to Socratic learned ignorance. Cassirer names this culture a 'dialectical antinomy' (Cassirer, 2000, 191) while Pascal calls it a civil war of internal conflicts, and Kant calls it the hell of self-cognition. In each case, as we saw, the culture of aporia is the work of KT trying to reconcile itself with the immediacy of NN.

Modern metaphysics is a reconstruction of logic within this culture of aporia, challenging this culture and its logic to undertake the work of self-knowing, or of *aporia: KT*. What it learns is the life and logic of its own work as difficulty. We will explore this now in Part 2. We will see that this is a much more difficult way to understand the templates of logic and being, but it is a difficulty that commends itself in and to modern thinking.

To the templates of logic and being, of the in-and-for-itself, and of imme-diacy and mediation, is joined the template of social relations. If the One is held to be master in the logic of the in-itself, then mediation is the slave, for mediation and the slave are compound and without their own truth. In this sense the templates of logic and of being are also the template of indepen-dence and dependence, or of master and slave. This is the template of social relations. However, as we have seen, the aporia of mastery, its inability to avoid mediation, is never completely overcome. In fact, it is repeated every time the master claims to have overcome the aporia of his own mastery. In time, the truth of this aporia overwhelms mastery and betokens a social revolution where mediation is recognized as the power of *rational thinking*. This is the revolution of enlightenment reason. What the difficulty of medi-ation learns in the Enlightenment—indeed, what the Enlightenment is—is that it is and always has been the work of *reason*. As such, the templates of logic and being come to see themselves in the template of rational experi-ence. But as we will now see, this too enacts the culture of aporia.

At first the rational experience of mediation claims this experience as its self-determination, its freedom. Here it tries to claim that its authority is different to that belonging to the ancient logic of mastery. What it learns, however, is that this enlightenment is not as straightforward as it at first appears, for it now has to face up to the presuppositions upon which it—that is, enlightenment reason—is grounded. It is invited to learn that its victory is still masterful and still prone to the aporias of such mastery. In this education reason learns of a template even behind the templates of the logic and being of mastery, behind the templates of social relations and rational understanding. This is the template of education enacted within the strange logic of presupposition. It is in this question of presupposition, or of posit-ing, that the modern logic of a modern metaphysics is to be found.

The education that grounds enlightenment reason is of the truth of itself as mediation. Ancient logic prejudges immediacy as the One, and its ineffa-bility to that which can only approach it through mediation. But the positing of ineffability here is already a mediation of immediacy. Both immediacy and mediation are pre-judged and employed to resolve a problem that is of their own making. The judgment of the being of the One as immediate and of the compound as mediated is grounded in prejudging the logic of imme-diacy as identity in-itself and the mediated as only for-another. Similarly, the judgment that the logic of the in-itself is true and the logic of the compound is error is grounded in prejudging the truth of being as immediacy and the error of being as mediation. Each template of logic and being presupposes the other. Both repeat the culture of aporia but appear to resolve the aporia by recourse to each other.

Enlightenment reason now beholds itself as being aware of such presup-positions. Not only are they unavoidable, but they are also desirable, for this awareness of the universality of mediation is now *the universality of modern reason*. It is heralded as the victory of mediation, the victory of the recognition of the universality of reason. Now it is clear to reason that it is mediation and not immediacy that has been shaping the development of Western thinking. In the Enlightenment, *truth as rational mediation* is the radical and revolutionary weapon employed against dogma, superstition, abstraction, and any tyranny of the One, be it political or religious, with its attendant abuses of power. Mediation was only ever slave to its master until mediation at last claimed the high ground as the rationality of enlightenment thinking. Here the tables appeared to be turned. The divine right of immediacy was overthrown by the rationality of mediation—think for yourself, suffer no tutelage, accept no false gods—allowing mediation to have its own truth as the self-determination of universal reason. Nothing now comes to truth except through its mediation in and by reason. Rationality is now the mediation of all claims to truth, and truth-claims will only be true when they are rational, and will only be rational when mediated by each individual thinking self-consciousness. In logical terms, it is when the for-another (mediation) becomes for-itself, and takes this education to be its self-determination.

But even here, in reason's own self-enlightenment, the logic and being of mastery dominate, this time suppressing the aporia of reason's presupposition of its own logic and being. When mediation (reason) *asserts* its truth, it does so by employing the ancient logic of mastery. In turn this abstracts reason (mediation) from mediation in becoming the identity or mastery of mediation in-itself. The modern experience of this is of reason abstracted from the very thing it claims to be—mediation. As such, rational universal concepts are compromised by the logic of mastery that reason presupposes for itself. Notions of equality and property, of universal law, of the rational and free individual, and of God and the death of God, are all framed within this logic of mastery, and are all part of the modern culture of aporia that accompanies this mastery.

Alongside these universal concepts, the *being* of enlightenment reason (or of universal mediation) within the logic of mastery becomes cold, hard, unfeeling, and instrumental logic. Hence instrumentalism now dominates, and immediacy is clung to as the home of all things 'human' in distinction to all things 'rational', that is, clung to as the spontaneity of feeling and emotion, of empathy, of the truth of art and the aesthetic. These judgments are commonplace and are easy in the sense that they (appear to) absolve themselves from the difficulty of prejudgment or presupposition. But it is here, in the easy judgment of the distinction between the objective and the subjective, that the culture of aporia returns in its modern form, not least in this easy distinction between the logical/rational and the human.

We experience the modern culture of aporia as the inability of abstract reason (abstract mediation) to establish itself as a principle without turning itself into a tyranny, standing aloof and immune from the truth of mediation that gives it its power over everything else. Mediation (reason) establishes itself according to the same logic of mastery that it claims to have overthrown. It overthrows any mastery that refuses mediation but refuses to mediate its own mastery (to interrogate its own prejudgments) and therefore becomes the master again.

But something else is also going on here. The logic of mastery has always been, and continues to be, accompanied by its own culture of aporia. Within the logic of mastery, any aporia is untenable and has to be overcome. But we recall now the difficulty that arises when we see that the logic of being and the being of logic presuppose each other. In this experience we learn that they are grounded in a different logic altogether—an educational logic of presupposition. Indeed, they are the result of this logic, which works unseen beforehand, and emerges only as the aporia of the in-itself of immediacy and the for-another of mediation. It is the aporia that brings the separated elements into relation with each other. This has astonishing significance. As we will see now in Part 2, in this relation we are able to feel truth and know the truth of feelings in a logic of tears; we are able to teach truth within the truth of teaching; and (most tentatively) we are able to find a logic of monotheism that relates the three Abrahamic religions together in and as education.

So what is this different logic? It is the logic that inheres in *difficulty*, and as such is a logic of education or learning. Its story (the philosophy of history) is the work of critical thinking mediating its object—this is Socrates. It is this work experienced conceptually—this is Plato. It is this concept experienced again, actually—this is Aristotle. It is the necessity of presupposition within this experience known as the condition of the possibility of experience—this is Kant. It is this necessity of presupposition as its own logic of experience—this is Hegel. It is this necessity of presupposition as the question of living according to what one understands—this is Kierkegaard. And it is this necessity of presupposition as its own educational logic—this is modern metaphysics. Here the necessity is that the culture of aporia knows itself as having its own kind of truth. This necessity is god and freedom.

Educational logic does what the logic of mastery can never do. Where the logic of mastery is true only in overcoming error or in being protected from error, the logic of education has its truth in negation and preservation, in error, and in the preservation of error as learning. Negation and preservation are the KT of modern rational experience as learning and education. The logic of education is the logic of KT wherein that which is true to itself is that which preserves itself while negating itself. This is precisely what learning is and does.

Of course it has long been observed that religion (and philosophy) begins with the awareness of the necessity of presupposition, or that we are not the creators of our universe. Within the logic of mastery, this is played out as the culture of aporia, and we have traced it in Part 1 in the incommensurability of NN and KT. Within educational logic, however, what is posited here in religion, and what learns of itself as posited, is education, and in such a way that because we learn, because there *is* religion, education is presupposed. If education is the condition of the possibility of religion, if education is the condition of the possibility of knowing the question of creation, then it is education presupposed *as* this question that is the actuality, the negation and preservation, of creator and created. If this is now the god of Part 2, is it the same God as in Part 1 above? The God of Part 1 was never the same as itself within the logic of mastery that tried and failed to define it. What this God was not, and now what the God of Part 2 is, are both the educational logic of modern metaphysics. They are both the one God as the logic of KT. We do not have to accept this of course. But the culture of aporia is always present to make us aware, should we neglect it, that there is an educational necessity and logic even in the presuppositions upon which such refusals depend.

Note

1. *The Republic*, 508–9.

Part 2
Know Thyself
Modern Metaphysics

7   The Logic of Tears

Could there be a coupling more likely to arouse the indignity of those whose colors are nailed firmly to one side or the other of the pairing of logic and tears? Logic: the arctic regions of human thinking, cold, impersonal, and hostile to life; the arid methodology that tyrannizes freedom, imagination, and emotion; the rule of system which is 'bloodless and barren' (Haskins, 1957, 42),[1] which neither cries nor laughs, but draws everything remorselessly into its icy web, holding all things accountable to it for their sense, their cohesion, and their truth. Tears: the antithesis of logic; warm, salty, and spontaneous; flowing from within the deepest emotional recesses of the heart; undefinable by systems; uncontrollable by administration; unaccountable to audit; expressing a freedom and a human universal exceeding rationality or method or rule.

Into this most intractable and obdurate of oppositions, we offer a logic of tears as an expression of KT underpinned by modern metaphysics and its logic of education. Here, tears bear the logic of educational necessity. They make inner education explicit to itself, negating this inner work and preserving it at the same time. They carry the work in which the individual gains universal significance, and the universal gains individual significance. Within the logic of mastery, the necessity is to overcome such oppositions. But within the logic of education, and now in the logic of tears, this work has religious and political import; tears cry god, and they cry freedom.

We will begin by looking at the place of tears in the macrocosm and microcosm, but the distinction here is not a decisive one, for tears are of the individual in the universal (macrocosm) and of the universal in the individual (microcosm). Modern metaphysics takes up the challenge of finding the educational logic of this duality.

Ancient Tears in the Macrocosm

'There are tears at the very heart of things'

The 'finest verse in Latin poetry' (Keith, 1922, 398) is found in Virgil's *Aeneid* (I.462) which states that there are tears at the very heart of things.[2] Aeneas and Achates arrive at Carthage and come upon Juno's temple. In it there is a frieze showing the fall of Troy, and with it the death of Aeneas's family and friends, along with other Trojan heroes. At this point Aeneas speaks: *sunt lacrimae rerum et mentem mortalia tangunt.*[3] Does Aeneas mean there are tears *for* things, or tears *of* things? Tears for things are for things endured, tears 'for man's adversities and mortal affairs that touch the heart' (1922, 398). This extends the meaning of the line from tears for particular things to tears as a shared human sympathy for adversity and suffering in mortal life. In this regard James Henry says it is as if Aeneas had said to Achates that, even here, far from home, 'the misfortunes of the brave meet with sympathy, for sympathy is a part of human nature' (Henry, 1873, 706).

If the line is translated not as tears for things but tears of things, this suggests that the universe as a whole, including inanimate objects, shares a mind and a sympathy with man in his adversities. This would in turn suggest an *anima mundi*. Indeed, the *Aeneid* contains just such an idea:

> First, the sky and the earth and the streaming fields of the sea,
> The moon's bright ball and the mighty sun and the stars
> Are maintained by a spirit within, and Mind, which flows
> Through each of its members, mingles with all that substance
> And keeps the whole mass moving.
> (Virgil, 2002, 143)[4]

This is a sympathy found also in Montaigne:

> There is a kind of respect and a duty in man as a genus which link us not merely to the beasts, which have life and feelings, but even to trees and plants. We owe justice to men: and to the other creatures who are able to receive them we owe gentleness and kindness. Between them and us there is some sort of intercourse and a degree of mutual obligation. (Montaigne, 2003a, 488)[5]

Here, then, tears of things make sorrow 'the essence of the universe. Tears and the sorrow they express are the ultimate realities, and, conversely, the material objects of the universe have a spiritual significance expressed in terms of suffering' (Keith, 1922, 402). James Henry agrees. By no means can the phrase stand for tears for the microcosm of misfortunes, 'but must signify tears of the world' (Henry, 1873, 705). His understanding of the line, then, is 'Tears are universal (*rerum*), [and] belong to the constitution of nature, and the evils of mortality (*mortalia*) move the human heart' (Henry, 1873, 705).[6] This is very close to the translation that Doering gives the verse in his piece on Maritain and Rouault. The 27th plate of Rouault's 58 engravings that make up his *Miserere* has the words beneath it: *Sunt lacrimae rerum*, which Doering expands into 'There are tears at the very heart of things, and the mortal nature of these things troubles the mind of man'

(Doering, 2004, 207). This rendering unites the tears of the microcosm with the universal nature of the macrocosm.

Tennyson's 'Tears, Idle Tears' is a term that Virgil also uses in the Aeneid[7] (*lacrimae inanes*). These are tears perhaps shed by Dido in vain for Aeneas or shed by Aeneas himself. 'By a calculated ambiguity, the final phrase allows the inference that he has been moved to tears at last' (Quinn, 1999, 103).[8] When Tennyson says, 'Tears, idle tears, I know not what they mean/Tears from the depths of some divine despair,' these idle tears might be for a love lost by Violet, or inspired by Tintern Abbey, for a convent full of bygone memories, a passion for the past, and suggestive of abiding in the transient as 'Death in life, the days that are no more.' James Knowles reported being told by Tennyson that the poem spoke of mystical depths like those of St. Paul (Romans, 8:26) who, in not knowing how to pray as he ought, saw the spirit intercede 'with groanings too deep for words' (Kozicki, 1986, 100). Kozicki suggests that the general conclusion of the modern view (begun in the 1890s) was that the idle tears expressed 'a grievous sorrow precisely because Tennyson had no thought or objective correlative to go with it' (1986, 99). As such, idle tears are idle because they are shed in vain over that which is ineffable, not least NN, the universal mind, or the ways of God.

There are also tears at the heart of the macrocosm in relation to creation and to the stages of the creature's development. In the 14th canto of Dante's *Inferno*, Virgil and the Pilgrim come to the Wood of Suicides, through which flows a stream of boiling blood. Intrigued by Virgil's description of the stream as the most remarkable sight in Hell so far, the pilgrim learns that within Mount Ida on Crete there is the statue of the Old Man of Crete gazing toward Rome. Its golden head represents the golden age of man before the Fall. This is the only part of the statue that is not cracked. Through the fissures of the silver arms and breast, the trunk of brass, the legs of iron and the clay foot flow the Old Man's tears of sadness for man's sins. These tears are the source of the three rivers of Hell, the Acheron, the Styx, and the Phlegethon, which, together with Satan's tears, form the frozen lake of Cocytus in the lowest circle of the underworld. As the Aeneid had claimed that there are tears at the very heart of things, so too there are frozen tears at the very heart of Hell.[9]

God's Secret Is Sadness

Dante's evocation of the fall of man has tears at the heart of things above and below the ground. But perhaps even more dramatic is the interpretation of sadness as the animation of the construction of the cosmos—the macrocosm—and the individual—the microcosm—found in Corbin's reading of Avicenna and Ibn Arabi.

In Avicenna's model of emanation from a divine unity there proceeds 'a First Intelligence, or a First Archangel-Cherub, whose being already contains a duality, since its own being is distinct from its necessity for being' (Corbin, 1990, 25). There is here a trinity in emanation, the One, the duality, and the principle (νοῦς, *nus*). We saw above in Chapter 3 that this process of self-relation, or of exile and return, was the structure and movement of creation knowing itself. Now we can revisit this model of emanation to recover the sadness that lies at its heart.

In triadic emanation, the first being is the first knowing or intellection of the first principle by itself. Darkness is part of the process because there is a desire in the soul to return to the archangel 'from whom it emanates and of whom it is the thought' (1990, 61). In each case, it is the desire of the soul for the intelligence from which it emanates that creates motion. By its own necessity, the animation of the universe is driven as far away from its origin as it is possible to go, that is, to exile on earth as terrestrial matter. For Corbin the idea of describing this as a 'fallen' intellect is not an appropriate way of describing emanation. In contrast to a universe marked by a fall from good to evil, the Avicennan angelic cosmology is one of pathos. 'Each heaven is the thought of an Archangel, not of an Archangel fallen from his station, but rather an Archangel "saddened" by the limitation of his being' (1990, 26). Where the Athenic and Christian models find negation and separation, Corbin finds in Avicennan philosophy a universe creating and moving itself by pathos and nostalgia. Sadness rather than the fall provides the continuity of the macrocosm and microcosm, if we take microcosm here to mean the stranger-consciousness of each individual who is not at home on the terrestrial plane, but only on the spiritual plane. Sadness is at its peak when the active intellect, the tenth cherub, no longer has the strength to reproduce itself as the trinity of one intellect, one soul, and one heavenly sphere. When this terrestrial sadness reorients itself upward then it can find its way back. Sadness is the animation of the whole process.

Pathos is also the continuity between creator and creature in the philosophy of Ibn Arabi. Corbin argues here for a 'phenomenology of sympathy' (Corbin, 1998, 108) that binds God and man. But he notes too, that such theophanic sympathy brings to our consciousness the idea of God

> whose secret is sadness, nostalgia, aspiration to know Himself in the beings who manifest his Being . . . And this always individually, in an "alone with the alone," which is something very different from universal logic or from a collective participation. (1998, 94)

This is a 'stumbling block to the rational theology of Christianity, Islam and Judaism alike' (1998, 108) because it offers 'a *pathetic* God, that is, a suffering and passionate God . . . a notion of God who is affected by human events and feelings and reacts to them in a very personal way' (1998, 108). It is again a cosmological vision that has tears at the very heart of things.

Moreover, creation here is a sigh of compassion, and pathos is 'the very substance, the "immaterial matter' constitutive of all beings' (1998, 116). It is not a theoretical understanding by God; it is 'a passion lived and shared with the understood object, a com-passion, a sympathy, (1998, 116) and as such 'God describes Himself to us through ourselves' (1998, 117). God's secret love makes him 'dependent on me' (1998, 128); it is necessary—a necessity at the very heart of things—'that beings exist in order that He might be known and know Himself' (1998, 128). In divine pathos the role of knowing truth 'is shared between Him and us' (1998, 129). Lacking this pathetic relation to God, the philosopher and the theologian 'posit a contingent creature, whom they opposed to the Necessary Being, thereby disclosing an inferior knowledge of God (for in it the soul knows itself only as a *mere creature*), a purely negative knowledge which cannot comfort the hurt' (1998, 133). Suffering in this pathetic cosmos is a continuity of relationship, not an irreparable split made into 'metaphysical idolatry' (1998, 133). We might add here that pathos clearly has an educative significance. Not only are tears at the very heart of things, they are at the heart of things educationally. Sadness is the pedagogy of the relationship between God and man. Pathos is the cosmos, and sadness is its own logic of the divine imperative: Being.[10] As such, sadness has a logic that conjoins NN and KT within an angelic cosmos in which sadness is already the logos of the universe. It is a logos of truth aware of itself as the sadness that is witness to its desire to return to itself, a sadness that is the logos of creation, and of the relation between man and God.

Ancient Tears in the Microcosm

> *'I am Janus bifrons; I laugh with one face, I weep with the other'*
> *(Kierkegaard, 1938, 47)*

Socrates

In the *Philebus* Socrates discusses whether the human good is found in knowledge (logic) and pleasure. A life of reason lived without pain and pleasure would be unsatisfactory, while a life of pain and pleasure lived without knowledge, understanding, reason, and memory would be like 'the life of a mollusc' (Plato, 1997, 409).[11] Some combination of opposites seems preferable, a third element, but governed by a fourth element that mixes them in appropriate proportions.

The good, then, is to be sought not in a pure in-itself but in the composite, in the mixture of knowledge and pleasure. Man stands before the fountains of pleasure and intelligence, seeking the perfect mixture. Perfection requires mixing the knowledge of the One and the many with the truest pleasures, those associated with temperance, health, and virtue. The unlimited pleasures lie beyond the mixture in which they are limited by knowledge. This is why the limitation imposed by composition is not the ruination of pleasure, but its 'salvation' (1997, 414).[12] If reason determines the correct proportion by which knowledge and pleasure are mixed, then reason is closer to truth and beauty than pleasure. If god is the mixture of reason (proportion), knowledge (logic), and pleasure, it is because the good has this ordering as its own principle.

This is a remarkable conclusion. It suggests that the good is not the pure form in-itself, but rather a perfectly proportioned combination. It might be tempting to say that reason and logic as the principle of proportion, in fact triumph over pleasure, but Socrates is clear that each is 'lacking in autonomy and in the power of self-sufficiency and perfection' (1997, 456).[13] The proportioned and ordered mixture holding logic and pleasure together is the compound of the single good.

Heraclitus and Democritus

If Socrates prioritized pleasure in relation to knowledge,[14] the two names who have carried the relation of pleasure to pain, or the relation of laughter to weeping, are Heraclitus—the weeping philosopher—and Democritus—the laughing philosopher. Through them we can again explore the question as to whether there are tears at the heart of things.[15]

The laughing philosopher appears first in Cicero's *De oratore* (55BCE) as *Democritus ridens*. From Horace (1st century BCE) we learn that his was not the laughter of everyman but of the serious man living apart from the world and choosing laughter as 'the most adequate response to his view of the human condition' (Gomez, 1984, 2). In Seneca and Lucian Democritus is coupled with Heraclitus. Seneca notes that instead of anger at the human condition one can laugh or cry. 'It is more civilized to laugh at life than to lament over it' (Seneca, 1968, 102). It is Sotion, Seneca's teacher, who gives rise to the idea that 'Among the wise, instead of anger, Heraclitus was overtaken by tears, Democritus by laughter' (Cooper and Procopé, 1995, 50).[16] Seneca, although siding with Democritus, nevertheless returns to his stoicism, saying that a calm acceptance of things is to be preferred to either laughing or weeping. Letters claimed to be between Hippocrates and others, including Democritus, report that Hippocrates was asked by the people of Abdera to cure Democritus, their citizen, but that Hippocrates found him to be in perfect health and indeed, an example of wisdom to all humankind. In Juvenal's *Satire X* laughter is seen to be spontaneous whereas weeping appears rather more deliberate and artificial. Lucian (b. 120CE) sees tears as stupidity and has the two philosophers remaining unsold at an auction conducted by Zeus and Hermes.

Christopher Lüthy (2000) notes that although Chrysostom and Isidore chose tears in imitation of Christ, most Renaissance humanists followed Seneca and sided with the laughing philosopher. Erasmus, for example, compared Thomas More to Democritus as *demo-criticus*, the people's critic. In *Praise of Folly* Erasmus calls on the name of Democritus several times to illustrate 'how much laughter, sport and fun' (Erasmus, 1971, 141) man provides for the gods, thereby associating the laughing philosopher with the gods, and likens Thomas More to Democritus as delighting in jokes, getting on well with all men, yet at the same time having an intelligence penetrating enough to see the follies of man.[17] John Ridewall (c. 1330) sees sorrow and sadness at man's sins as yielding a relation of man to God.

The Greek Anthology, arranged by Constantin Cephalus (c.912–59) included works spanning the period from 7th century BCE to 10th century CE. Two epitaphs in the collection urge the gods of the underworld to receive Democritus as one who laughs. In the same book, Heraclitus is portrayed as arrogant and overbearing, and without reference to his tears, and in another epigraph as one who never laughs.[18]

But in Book IX of the *Anthology* one epigram—the *ton bion* epigram—returns to the significance of their combination and asks how it might be possible to laugh with Democritus *and* to cry with Heraclitus in a world that has deteriorated since they were alive. The epitaph suggests that tears and laughter are both appropriate, but asks how they can occur together. In Latin this epigram became known as '*In vitum humanam*', and it read as follows:

> Weep for life Heraclitus, much more than when thou didst live, for life is now more pitiable. Laugh now, Democritus, at life more than before; the life of all is now more laughable. And I, too, looking at you, am puzzled as to how I am to weep with the one and laugh with the other. (Gomez, 1984, 57)[19]

Ficino seems to have been inspired by the *ton bion,* which fitted well his view of the relationship between the inner and the outer man, and to have found both tears and laughter appropriate to the human condition. In letters to fellow philosophers, he notes that while Democritus laughed at the folly of men, Heraclitus wept at their misery. 'The foolish', he said, 'fail to enjoy what is present, always striving for the new. They feed their body and starve their soul. No wonder they are unhappy, for 'misery is the fruit of [this] foolishness' (Ficino, 1997, 32). Instead, one should have small regard for physical things and nourish the soul with spiritual food so that one can be neither foolish nor miserable. In the second letter, Ficino speaks of the painting in his Academy of a sphere of the world with Democritus laughing on one side and Heraclitus weeping on the other.[20] They laugh and weep together because 'the mass of mankind is a monstrous, mad and miserable animal' (1997, 32). Humanity fights a constant battle between reason and the senses, at war with itself and never able to 'harmonise the parts and movements of the soul' (1997, 33). They know about everyone else, but never know themselves. And in a third letter he asks why do we strive to be masters of others when we are not masters of ourselves, and why seek external treasure when the treasure is within? It is no wonder then that 'we end up falsely happy, and sincerely miserable' (1997, 35). Kristeller makes a similar point. 'Laughter and tears are merely different expressions of the same insight through which the wise man rises above the outward world and above the ordinary people who are bound to it' (Kristeller, 2015, 294). Gomez says that Ficino is able to place laughter in sadness, and this made it possible 'for laughter and tears to mingle freely' (Gomez, 1984, 74).

Gomez also describes the two poems of Antonio Fregoso, the first on Democritus's laughter and the second on Heraclitus's tears, published by 1511. In the first poem, the narrator is reminded by his angelic guide to acquire self-knowledge. He then meets a laughing Democritus, who confirms that laughter is an antidote to madness, and that human madness is best observed from a distance. Democritus explains that he laughs at lust, at hunting, at war, at funerals, at physical prowess, and at ignorance regarding the inner riches of the soul against the fickle fortune of the outer world. When the poet leaves Democritus, he does so with 'moist eyes and a heavy heart' (1984, 78), announcing his intention to seek out Heraclitus but with a tranquil spirit nurtured by his company with Democritus.

A different guide flies the poet to Heraclitus, who lives high in the mountains. He drinks from a spring, and the guide, Dianeo, explains that its bitterness is due to it being mixed with Heraclitus's tears. Inside, the philosopher's books are also damp and rotten from the effect of his tears upon them. Heraclitus explains that he cries from compassion for man's wretched state, for his capacity for evil and other vices that accompany it. The stages of human development toward death also carry their own misery. Infancy is helpless; childhood blighted by teachers; youth wounded by love; manhood burdened with anxieties and corrupted by authority, friendship, and family; marriage wears a chain, and one's children cause pain and anxiety; and old age brings its own pain and discomfort. Within all of this, it is possible for man to know God, but most often remains ignorant of him, choosing worldly fortune instead. 'Man's ingenuity, the instrument of reason, is used in the service of pleasure. Reason is thus enslaved, darkened and entombed' (1984, 81). The poet is grateful to the philosopher and before departing, promises to pass on his doctrine. At the end of the poem the poet reminds us that 'he had both laughed and cried as Nature teaches man to do' (1984, 82).[21]

Gomez says this dialectical conclusion does not side with the one or the other, but is 'a balance of opposites wherein the tension is maintained without any apparent intent to resolve the conflict by the victory of either of the contending parties' (1984, 82), even though the book on Democritus was written independently and had popularity on its own.

In tracing this history Gomez comments that

> the telling point is not that Heraclitus wept over men's miseries and Democritus laughed at the amusing side of life. If the legend had consisted simply in this it would have been no more than a banal, though picturesque, anecdote recounting the obvious. The legend's vitality and appeal lie in the fact that it shows how a similar experience of humanity could give Heraclitus reason for tears and provide Democritus with a cause for his laughter. (1984, 104–5)

For the Greek epigrammatist of the *ton bion* this was the question of how one 'could laugh and cry simultaneously' (1984, 105).

Gomez makes his own view clear at the end of his book;

> as our contemporary world, so richly endowed with achievements that have sprung from the cultivation of human *dignitas*, spins apprehensively towards the abyss of ultimate *miseria*, it is more imperative than ever to recall the laughing Democritus. Perhaps only enhanced awareness of deep-seated folly may be potent enough to avert the final despair of the Heraclitean conflagration that looms so menacingly over the human race. (1984, 278)

Cora Lutz takes a different view. She argues that putting the two together in fact illustrates Heraclitus's own fragment about the harmony of opposites,[22] each element dependent upon the other. She quotes George Santayana for a modern statement of this relation. In his life, sorrow at his failings

> has always been mitigated by the gift of laughter. Laughter helped one both to perceive those defects and to put up with them. Between the laughing and the weeping philosopher there is no opposition; the *same facts* that make one laugh make one weep. No wholehearted man, no sane art, can be limited to either move. (Lutz, 1954, 313)[23]

In comparing Democritus and Heraclitus, and laughter and weeping, Montaigne says he prefers laughing but only because laughter is more condemning and disdainful of humanity, and humanity 'can never be despised enough' (Montaigne, 2003a, 339).[24] Alongside this, and with Petrarch, Montaigne also notes that the mind cloaks every passion 'with its opposite, our faces showing now joy, now sadness' (2003a, 262).[25] Thus, even the 'greatest of our pleasures has an air of groaning and lamentation' (2003a, 764).[26] This duality of laughter and tears is remarked upon by Socrates.

> What a strange thing is that which men call pleasure seems to be, and how astonishing the relation it has with what is thought to be its opposite, namely pain! The man cannot have both at the same time. Yet if he pursues and catches the one, he is almost always bound to catch the other also, like two creatures with one head. (Plato, 1997, 52)[27]

Before moving to a modern logic of tears, we note Pascal's views on the relationship between feeling and principle. Pascal says that first principles, such as space, time, motion, and number, are known and found via the heart, they are not known rationally. The skeptics work to refute first principles but do so by ignoring the obvious. For example, even if we cannot rationally prove it, we know that we are not dreaming. If it cannot be proved rationally, then the weakness lies with reason. In fact, reason is wholly dependent on these first principles, which come to us through feeling and instinct. The heart feels spatial dimensions, and then reason works out propositions concerning them. 'Principles are felt, propositions proved, and both with certainty though by different means' (Pascal, 1966, 58).[28] He laments that nature gives us so little knowledge of this kind and that we need reason at all. Those who have faith in their hearts know God in ways not open to those who only understand faith through reasoning. In terms of a hierarchy here, 'All our reasoning comes down to surrendering to feeling' (1966, 216).[29]

For Pascal then, instinct and reason are 'signs of two natures' (1966, 59).[30] These two natures are in a civil war, and man 'can only be at peace with the one if he is at war with the other. Thus he is always torn by inner divisions and contradictions' (1966, 235).[31]

From Ancient Tears to Modern Tears

We can observe from the evidence presented above that within the logic of mastery the macrocosm is seen to have an advantage over the microcosm in the way it lives its emotions. The macrocosm can express truth in tears in a way the microcosm cannot. Its tears are the heart of all things, be that the heart of humanity or the heart of the whole cosmos. From this point of view, tears are an immediacy, crying the truth of universal pathos, and binding man and animal and cosmos together. For Corbin especially, sadness is the immediate unity of the cosmos, and is the way in which God knows himself through those who know him.

On the other side, but still within the logic of mastery, individual tears shed in the microcosm can only know themselves in privation of and in deficit to the universality of the macrocosm. The microcosm has no access to the purity of universal sadness. Instead, its sadness is compound and is in combination with reason, pleasure, and the principle of proportion (Socrates), and with tears and laughter (Heraclitus and Democritus). Here the follies that lead to tears and laughter are those of man, not of God. This is man at war with himself, never able to harmonize compounds into a pure or simple element, and standing in complete contrast to the Stoic conception of tranquillity in which peace within the soul is just such a purity. The more one knows the self as harboring the follies, the more one laughs and cries. The significance here is in knowing how each is a mediation—an error—of the human in relation to the divine, and perhaps never more so than in Pascal's civil war.

But as ever, the logic of mastery here gives no credence to its own contradictions. Universal tears have to be shed individually, and cannot survive in a merely abstract universal identity immune from this actuality. Similarly, individual tears, actual tears, are not simply arbitrary and without universal import. The charge of 'emotionalism', or of an excess of emotion, is based on just such an accusation of caprice, of an inability to tie emotions to reason or to a principle, of an inability to keep them in proportion, and of an absence of self-control. It is met with the remonstration 'pull yourself together'. But this is just the perspective of mastery. Within the logic of mastery, and perhaps counterintuitively, 'emotionalism' is judged not as the absence of mediation but as the excess of mediation. This excess is the barbarism of the uneducated slave, lacking the purity (the immediacy) of a first principle.

Within educational logic, there is something of a reversal of roles. The educated masters not only refuse excessive emotion (excessive mediation and excessive error), but they also crave a higher state—an immediacy or purity or divinity—for their feelings, which can be paid for as high art. Here it is the craving and its market value that enact mediation. The piety is that barbarian emotion (mediation) is overcome by the masters, who can enjoy (buy) a principle having its own immediacy in-itself. Meanwhile the slaves of emotion, or of mediation, those whose tears seem without universal significance, embody and endure this sadness as their own truth in a way the masters do not and cannot. The masters are as much slaves to emotion as the barbarians, but only the latter understand this and exist in what they understand. No matter how expensive the Box at the Garden, mediation, not purity, is the universal education.

How then does modern metaphysics, or the educational logic of KT, understand differently the way in which tears are at the heart of everything, macrocosm *and* microcosm? As we saw in the *Intermezzo*, and as we rehearse now in Part 2, in the templates of the being and logic of education, existing as mediation is not merely error, and existing as immediacy is not merely truth. Instead, mediation and immediacy are negated and preserved in the experience that is learning. Learning is its own truth because it preserves itself in negating itself. Negation presupposes what is immediately lost to mediation, and mediation preserves this immediacy as *being* learned. In Chapter 7 we will see this logic of being and being of logic as recollection, repetition, and presupposition. Before that, in this chapter, we will see this education negated and preserved in and as the logic of tears. Tears preserve for us the loss that sadness bears. Tears carry this sadness as our education because they put learning into the world and enable its meaningful retrieval. As such, the truth of the logic of tears has both political and religious significance. As learning, tears cry freedom and god.

We will now attempt to find this logic of tears as it commends itself in Hegel, Van Gogh, Weber, and Adorno. In each case sadness reeducates joy to see itself not as the opposite of sadness but as the truth of sadness. Joy accompanies sadness when sadness is comprehended in its universal and individual—logical—significance as education and learning.

Hegel

For Hegel freedom requires the process of something becoming an object of thought, and of this thought returning to itself changed or educated by its experience. This is the modern metaphysical notion of NN and is how the absolute is able to be thought, by itself, in what is actual. The fact that truth returns changed or educated is the difference between ancient NN and modern NN. The fact that truth knows itself changed and educated means it is no longer served solely by a logic of mastery but also by a logic of KT.

For Hegel, freedom as art sees emotion and feeling put into the external world, able then to return as emotion and feeling now carrying universal import. Tears for Hegel make what is implicit within an individual 'explicit to himself' (Hegel, 1998, 32). They make external the most intimate subjective inner world and betray those feelings. But in betraying inner emotions, in negating them, it gives them life, life in the external. Once made external, they are then that from which the inner emotions learn of themselves. This negation and return is the work of emotion as the truth of freedom and the freedom of truth, giving itself life, and learning of itself from doing so. If art is the discipline of this work of betraying our emotions, then tears are an art of freedom and an art of religion. This art has its truth in the educational logic of negation and preservation, specifically here externalization and return, and also in the logic of KT. This education is the logic of tears, a logic able to cry freedom and god.

But what does Hegel mean when he suggests that the shedding of tears can alleviate or overcome grief? In the *Philosophy of Right* education is 'liberation' (Hegel, 1967, 125)[32] from the uncultured passions. In the tutoring of the emotions, one is taught to grow out of overwrought outpouring and unseemly excess. But if this liberation is taken as mastery or as overcoming in accord with the ancient logic, then what is overcome is the betrayal of emotion, or its becoming an act of freedom. Such overcoming, such mastery of sentiment, often portrays itself as a mastery over naiveté or romanticism, and expresses this mastery as superiority, often by means of cynicism, sarcasm, irony, and biting and disparaging humor against the barbarian emotions.

But this mastery knows little of freedom's own tears, and it is not what Hegel means by liberation here. As an artist can mitigate the intensity of her feelings by representing them as art, so tears enable a similar freedom; 'at first entirely sunk and concentrated in grief, a man may then in this direct way [through tears] utter this purely inward feeling' (1998, 49).[33] To make conscious one's emotions in this way, to betray one's inner feelings, is for tears to be the very heart of things, that is, of self-consciousness and of freedom.

> And so to cry one's eyes out and to speak out has ever been regarded as a means of freeing oneself from the oppressive burden of care or at least of relieving the heart. The mitigation of the power of the passions therefore has its universal ground in the fact that man is released from his immediate imprisonment in a feeling and becomes conscious of it as something external to him, to which he must now relate himself in an ideal way. (1998, 49)

In tears one has part of oneself as one's own object, which is an educational prerequisite for the notion of modern rational/educational freedom.

The education carried in logic of tears can also be the expression of the emotion of philosophical understanding. Hegel states, 'the final purpose of education' (1967, 125)[34] is this struggle for philosophy to KT in the shapes it takes in the world. Thought does not overcome itself by knowing itself. Rather it knows itself to be the hard work of this continual education. This struggle, this hard work, is how education is 'immanent in the Absolute' (1967, 126).[35] This is the joy in the sadness of such education.

There is another equally difficult way in which modern metaphysics understands the logic of tears. In the way that truth in modern metaphysics negates and preserves itself, so also it lives its freedom in resistance and acceptance. For this we turn to Hegel on pathos.[36]

Pathos in ancient Greece is the power of the gods made individual, or the universal present in man's inner spirit. It is the universal in the heart of individual action. It is, in sum, human character and is a battlefield of conflicting passions. This conflict is the richness of the inner life, sought by playwrights in characters strong enough to bear them. As the struggle between passions, pathos has its own educational logic, lived by the strength of character that in its many-sidedness resists itself, yet accepts itself as this character at the same time.[37]

Here Hegel is clear that a different logic is required for the truth of this contradiction of the strong character.

> Considered by the *Understanding*, such many-sidedness within a dominant determining pathos may, it is true, appear to be illogical . . . The Understanding, that is, will emphasise abstractly only one side of the character and stamp it on the whole man as what alone rules him. What is opposed to such dominance of a one-sidedness appears to the Understanding as simply illogical. But in the light of the rationality[38] of what is inherently total and therefore living, this illogicality is precisely what is logical and right. For man is this: not only the bearer of the contradiction of this multiple nature but the sustainer of it, remaining therein equal and true to himself. (1998, 240)

This is one of those occasions where Hegel spells out his modern metaphysics. Pathos is the contradiction of universal and individual, of reason and passion, of head and heart, of god(s) and man. They meet in the character of the individual. To the ancient logic this character requires to be defined as one dominating passion to be a consistent self. But Hegel makes clear that there is a different notion of rationality in play here, one where 'totality' is not abstracted from contradiction but lives in contradiction with itself. In modern metaphysics, it is the illogic that is logical and irrationality that is rational. Man is not only the bearer of this battlefield of pathos, but he is its actuality, its living form, or as we have been expressing it, pathos is both acceptance and resistance. In modern metaphysics, the character of pathos is 'true to itself' (1998, 240) as the KT of NN.

Van Gogh

There is a logic of tears in the work and writing of Vincent van Gogh. For those who are offended by logic attached to art, perhaps there will be no greater affront than that this term should be applied to such a creative spirit as Vincent.

As a young man, Vincent gave up his training as a clergyman to become a lay preacher to the coal miners of the Belgian Borinage. He speaks of homesickness at this time, but says 'instead of giving in to despair I chose active melancholy . . . the kind of melancholy that hopes, that strives and that seeks, in preference to the melancholy that despairs numbly and in distress' (Van Gogh, 1996, 66). This active melancholy worked in the teeth of Vincent's poverty, but is aided by self-education. 'If I do nothing, if I study nothing, if I cease searching, then, woe is me, I am lost. That is how I look at it—keep going, keep going come what may' (1996, 68). What is the endpoint of this vocation of learning and study? The end will emerge 'slowly but surely, much as the draft turns into a sketch and the sketch into the painting through the serious work done on it' (1996, 68). But at this moment it is not at all clear to him just how his love of books and immersion in pictures is going to be of use or of public service. As a result, he says, 'one cannot rid oneself of melancholy, one feels emptiness where there might have been friendship and sublime and genuine affection, and one feels dreadful disappointment gnawing at one's spiritual energy' (1996, 70). The educational logic of his melancholy is active here as KT. 'There is something inside me, but what can it be?' (1996, 73).

The logic of tears is movingly recounted in a sermon that Vincent wrote in 1876. In August of that year he had written to Theo, his brother, of his need to be bound to Christ as 'sorrowful yet always rejoicing' (1996, 24). These are the words of St. Paul (2 Cor. 6:10), who brings a number of oppositions together here. Vincent rehearses this theme in his sermon. There is, he says, great sorrow and great joy in the hour when someone is born into the world. Equally there is great sorrow and joy in the hour of one's death. But, says Vincent, 'Sorrow is better than joy—even in mirth the heart is sad and it is better to go to the house of mourning than to the house of feasts, for by the sadness of the countenance the heart is made better' (1996, 28). Here is a logic of tears. Sadness enacts the logic of education, of KT. In sadness is truth learned, and in tears is learning expressing itself. In this learning, in these tears, is the joy of understanding the truth of sadness. So 'let us rather cling to the seasons of difficulty . . . Weeping may endure for a night, but joy cometh in the morning' (1996, 31).

The spirit of Bunyan's *Pilgrims Progress* is infused through this sermon. It was Vincent's favorite book at this time. He speaks of a painting he saw (by George Henry Broughton) in which a pilgrim meets an angel of God, and which for Vincent speaks of being sorrowful yet always rejoicing. In a letter to Theo four months after the sermon, he interprets St. Paul's maxim as melancholy consisting of woe and courage, noting that St. Paul included as another opposition the pairing of known yet unknown. Living in these oppositions, Vincent is living the education of God and man. Two years later he is explicit about the struggle and the significance of this life. 'Anyone who leads an upright life and experiences real difficulty and disappointment and yet is not crushed by them is worth more than one for whom everything has been plain sailing and who has known nothing but relative prosperity' (1996, 52). He reminds Theo that melancholy 'may be a good experience' (1996, 52) providing one sees it as the mediation of woe and courage by each other. And in thoughts that resonate with the art that still lies before him, he says 'it is good to go on believing that everything is more miraculous than one can ever begin to understand, for that is the truth' (1996, 54).

Religion was always present in his life. In his early sermon of 1876, he says that belief in Jesus Christ provides not despair at death but sorrow and hope. By 1881 he writes that

> for me that God of the clergy is as dead as a doornail. But does that make me an atheist? Clergyman consider me one—but you see, I love, and how could I feel love if I were not alive myself or if others were not alive, and if we are alive there is something wondrous about it. Now call that God or human nature or whatever you like, but there is a certain something I cannot define systematically, although it is very much alive and real, and you see, for me that something is God or as good as God. (1996, 124–5)

What is alive and wondrous is expressed in his art, specifically in the ways in which he uses color not to express reality, but to express outer beauty and suffering to the inner world, to express not what is objectively verifiable but only what is 'subjectively understandable' (Walther, 2000, 34). For Vincent this means god and nature at times expressed in the beauty and sorrow that returns to the soul through the use of color, and using color to express 'struggle and antitheses' (2000, 41) and at times 'terrible human suffering' (2000, 41).

In Vincent's life and work, then, the logic of tears expresses itself as an art of freedom. In Hegel this was the divine in the individual needing to be expressed in more than the empirical reality of nature or the external. For Vincent the 'something' that is inside him is, in Hegel's terms, 'the universal need for art . . . [a] rational need to lift the inner and outer world into his spiritual consciousness as an object in which he recognizes again his own self' (Hegel, 1998, 31). This is not objectification because the logic of tears is not wholly reducible to the universal scale of things—and how poignant it is that Vincent sold perhaps only one painting in his lifetime, and now of the 31 most expensive paintings ever sold six are by him. The logic of tears speaks of Vincent's art because it does not posit god and man as unknowable to each other, but rather expresses that relationship in some of the most self-educative artwork in the tradition. What is posited as beyond and ineffable in the logic of mastery, Vincent sees in nature and in labour, and in the most ordinary examples of both—trees and flowers, peasants and miners. If the ancient logic exiled truth to the ineffable, Vincent returns it to a logic of tears, knowable and present.

Vincent's art and life are this logic of tears, the outward expression of feelings in which the educational relationship of god and man is known. The sadness of his life, his torments, and his suffering are cause enough for tears, but to find ways in which to express the joy of this sadness, to paint the KT of NN, is a joy to accompany all human sadness. 'Truth would not be truth if it did not show itself and appear, if it were not true *for* someone and *for* itself' (Hegel, 1998, 8). That it should have been for Vincent in the way he knew, felt, and understood it, and that he should have the spirit and talents to express this melancholy in the ways he did *for us*, is to have a logic of tears that, in a realm so thoroughly occupied by the pretentiousness of art criticism, offers an expression of the logic of tears felt universally in the tears of each individual. His logic of tears expressed in this art is the education of god and man, an understanding of feeling expressed in the most educationally beautiful and profound way.

Weber (1864–1920)

Weber's melancholy sociology is well known. It still stands testament to the forms that shape the modern world. For Weber, these were the spiritless work ethic, accountability to abstract rationality and calculation, organization of human beings mechanically and bureaucratically, and a disenchantment of the human soul, lacking any inner devotion or struggle for integrity in the face of the relativism of warring gods. When asked why he pursued his scholarly research, he replied, 'I want to see how much of it I can stand' (Bendix, 1977, 9). Nevertheless, in turning to education in response to this sadness, Weber commends us to see if there is a logic to the tears shed in and for modern sociological existence.

His analysis of modernity encapsulates the fate of the inner world in the ever-increasing abstract rationality of the external world. In his masterpiece *The Protestant Ethic And The Spirit Of Capitalism* (1904–5), he describes the Protestant ethic in which those elected by God demonstrate their election by the ascetic life of hard work for the glory of God alone. 'Waste of time is thus the first and in principle the deadliest sin' (Weber, 1930, 157). Religious devotion is to be measured by restless labor and the resultant acquisition of goods and property. In working hard for God, if material reward accrued, so be it. This combination of work, asceticism and faith must have been 'the most powerful conceivable lever for the expansion of . . . the spirit of capitalism' (1930, 172). Thus, his melancholic conclusion to the great study of capitalism and Protestantism; religious asceticism is now the 'iron cage' (1930, 181) of the modern economic order.

Alongside this, the disenchantment of the world reveals that all things are being mastered by rational calculation and administration, reducing 'every worker to a cog in this bureaucratic machine' (Weber, 1978, lix). It is a 'passion for bureaucracy that drives us to despair' (1978, lix). The work ethic strengthened by mechanization provides only 'a polar night of icy darkness' (Weber, 1970, 128). His question in the face of all this was how to keep a portion of mankind free from this 'supreme mastery of the bureaucratic way of life?' (Mayer, 1944, 128).

This melancholy extends to the condition of research and scholarship in higher education. In his famous essay 'Science as a Vocation' (1918),[39] he observes that science is gaining the reputation of becoming mere calculation, no longer compelling the inner world of 'one's heart and soul' (Weber, 1970, 135). Higher education is unhelpful in countering the disenchantment issuing from this separation of the inner and outer life. What is missing in the increasing specialization of academic work is any vision of the bigger picture. Chemistry cannot prove that the universe has meaning. Medical science does not know if the life it presumes is worth living. Aesthetics does not ask whether there should be works of art. Jurisprudence does not answer the question as to whether there should be laws. The cultural and historical sciences give no answer as to whether cultural phenomena are worthwhile. Weber suggests that few now believe that science can offer meaning to the world, and he refers us to Tolstoy's observation that 'Science is meaningless because it gives no answer to our question, the only question important for us: "what shall we do and how shall we live?"' (1970, 143).

But each of these manifestations of disenchantment are encapsulated in the predominant feature of modern life. Values in the world seem to be in 'irreconcilable conflict with each other' (1970, 147). Herein, 'different gods struggle with one another, now and for all times to come' (1970, 148). The lecture room, and therefore science, can describe what one god is in one order, another god in another order, and so on. But this is its limit. It cannot choose between the meanings on offer here. The individual is left to decide 'which is God for him and which is the devil' (1970, 148). Faced with this relativism of the warring gods and the disenchantment it reproduces, Weber offers the idea of science or education as a vocation.

Science as a vocation has several features. It offers control over life by calculating effects. It offers methods of thinking. It helps students gain clarity regarding the appropriate means to ends, and it puts before them the question of whether such means are justified by the ends. It also encourages students 'to recognize "inconvenient" facts' (1970, 147). But it is with regard to the relativity of truly ultimate ends that science can make a telling contribution, by illustrating what it means to have an inner consistency and an integrity regarding such ultimate ends. In adhering to a vision of ultimate ends, one will offend other ultimate ends, but 'if you remain faithful to yourself, you will necessarily come to certain final conclusions that subjectively make sense' (1970, 151).

The vocation of philosophy and of philosophical discussions in other sciences is to help the student 'to give himself an *account of the ultimate meaning of his own conduct*' (1970, 152). This is the morality and responsibility of science. The vocation of science is to serve clarity and integrity in regard to first principles, even if these first principles exist in a relative relation to other first principles, and in a context where they are incommensurable. This search for the integrity of the inner life in a world where the warring gods offer no universal external justifications sets this vocation against the fate of the times characterized by 'rationalism and intellectualisation and, above all, by the "disenchantment of the world"' (1970, 155). Those lacking in the strength for this vocation of science will lack 'the courage to clarify one's own ultimate standpoint' (1970, 155). Some may make the 'intellectual sacrifice in favour of unconditional religious devotion' (1970, 155), which Weber holds in higher esteem. But still he does not theorize science as vocation as a universal value, only according to its subjective value, its integrity, in the disenchanted world.

Can we find a logic of tears in this vocation of science? If we recall that this logic is an art of freedom and religion, in which the inner is made explicit in the world, enabling it to return to itself, then Weber's tears can cry freedom and god in the disenchanted world. The inner vocation becomes external reality as science which therein returns vocation to itself as its own truth. The vocation is the whole. It is sadness and disenchantment made objective and subjective. It is the logic of tears. This modern metaphysical educational logic is not far from Weber at the end of the 'Vocation' essay when, quoting Isaiah, he says 'if ye will enquire, enquire ye: return, come' (21:12). Inquire without by inquiring within and 'we shall set to work and meet "the demands of the day," in human relations as well as in our vocation' (1970, 156). That this is both Socratic and Delphic, that it is the logic of KT, is emphasized in requiring that 'each finds and obeys the demon who holds the fibres of his very life' (1970, 156).

Marianne Weber said of her husband that he was 'moved, above all, by the fact that on its earthly course an idea always and everywhere operates in opposition to its original meaning and thereby destroys itself' (Bottomore and Nisbet, 1978, 362); for example, inner asceticism and devotion become a mechanical work ethic; life lived in the glory of God becomes the spirit of capitalism; and science aiming at truth becomes the battle of waring gods. There is disenchantment and sadness at this self-opposition, but there is also a logic of tears in which learning negates and preserves itself. It operates against itself to return to itself, changed but still present in the experience of this self-opposition. Even though for Weber this is the source of deep sadness, it is also the source of his notion of vocation. The vocation to find inner meaning will oppose itself in its external existence in the disenchanted world. But as learning vocation is able to return to itself, and not just as a vocation but as the truth of this vocation as education. It is in this logic of KT that Weber finds an integrity in the face of relativism. Vocation itself is a value judgment, but by means of its own necessity it sustains an integrity in the value that is education returning to itself. Integrity as logic here is for Weber 'a presupposition of teaching' (1970, 152), something we will explore with Kierkegaard in our next chapter.

Adorno (1903–1969)

Adorno's melancholy sociology is perhaps even more deep-seated than Weber's. Where Weber laments ideas opposing themselves, Adorno (with Horkheimer) extends this to the whole of reason, calling it the dialectic of enlightenment. Here is a seemingly vicious circle: enlightenment overcomes myth, but such overcoming is just another myth requiring to be overcome. Adorno is ambivalent about the educational value of this dialectic. On the one hand, 'Enlightenment is totalitarian' (Adorno and Horkheimer, 1979, 6) and holds power over a 'disenchanted nature' (1979, 4) and over human beings who fear any deviation from facts. Here enlightenment is a 'universal mediation' (1979, 12) reducing everything to objects. On the other hand, even within this totality, which is false, there is educational significance. The Enlightenment, he says, '*must examine itself*' (1979, xv) by means of a dialectic in which non-identity is the only consistent critical process. Here, and unlike abstract reason in the logic of mastery, mediation of the dialectic by the dialectic ensures that it does not come to rest as one of positivism's facts. 'This is its form of hope' (Adorno, 1973, 406).

Adorno's melancholy science expresses how the totality of production has gained sovereignty over life and truth; how the philosophical inquiry into the good life has become neglected because of philosophy becoming method; how life therefore has become appearance; and how the ways in which this sovereignty might be challenged are all being bought up by the commodity market that is the object of such critique. 'Our perspective of life has passed into an ideology which conceals the fact that there is life no longer' (Adorno, 1974, 15). The life that can now be lived is brutal and forces us into calculations that are barbaric. Competition has passed into objectivity, and what is left is merely to 'deny oneself the ideological misuse of one's own existence' (1974, 27) and live quietly and modestly, breathing the air of hell. Courtesy is imposed (have a nice day!), to which there is 'no remedy but steadfast diagnosis of oneself and others' (1974, 33). Tact becomes lying because 'wrong life cannot be lived rightly' (1974, 39). Experience withers under the 'law of pure functionality' (1974, 40). Money extends into even the most tender and the most spiritual experiences. Theory is seen to be impotent; 'the whole is the false' (1974, 50); speculation is crushed; common sense is diseased; and the universal order is sick.

Such oppositions speak of a logic of mastery challenged by dialectical logic. The latter looks 'mad' (1974, 73), but this is only part of the sadness.

The totality will not let the madness of unrest roam free. The totality assimilates such resistance back into the totality so that resistance opposes itself by 'acquiring a coercive character' (1974, 150). Resistance to the logic of mastery and overcoming repeats this same logic of mastery. At the heart of the melancholy science is the dialectician's duty to help the fool's truth 'to attain its own reasons, without which it will certainly succumb to the abyss of the sickness implacably dictated by the healthy common sense of the rest' (1974, 73). Indeed, the truth of this sad foolishness is a joy. 'Contemplation without violence, the source of all the joy of truth, presupposes that he who contemplates does not absorb the object into himself: a distanced nearness' (1974, 89–90). This is what the unreason and madness look like.

Adorno here carries two characteristics of the logic of tears: dialectical thinking works with a different logic to that of mastery and overcoming; and this work has as-yet-undefined educational significance, finding joy and sadness in the negation and preservation of the false totality.

Paragraphs ninety-nine and one hundred of *Minima Moralia* in particular work with the logic of KT and with the logic of tears. The first piece considers the nature of genuineness and the genuineness of nature. Adorno argues here for a very difficult notion of the individual. On the one hand, the KT of the individual is a search for its authenticity.[40] On the other hand, authenticity is ideological. KT is its own aporetic totality here. It encourages one to seek for the authentic self, knowing that only inauthenticity will be the result, and in the process becoming even more a product of the totality that advocated finding authenticity in the first place. All who seek the authentic individual self become ever more the same as everyone else. The richer the inner life in the quest for KT, the stronger grows the hold of the ideology of authenticity. It is, says Adorno, only in the age of industrial mass production, in the age of standardized commodities where each commodity can become one's unique property, that the idea of genuineness as being non-reproducible takes shape. To seek the genuine in the 'truly' original, or the 'truly' non-reproducible, the 'truly' individual, is already to be enmeshed in the fetish of originality that social relations creates as its antithesis. But it is an antithesis that serves the very social relations that it expresses.

In the second piece, the same logic is found in the question of happiness. Asked what a 'truly' emancipated or free society might have as its goal, Adorno suggests that the answer is often given as 'the fulfilment of human possibilities or the richness of life' (1974, 155–6). This, he says, is an Epicurean response, one which is itself only a utopia of 'production as an end in itself' (1974, 156). The 'mad,' 'foolish,' and 'illogical' idea of happiness in a world of private property, and in the totality that is false, is that 'that no one should go hungry any more' (1974, 156). The pleasure dome of uninhibited freedom needs to be confronted with *need*.

The conception of unfettered activity, of uninterrupted procreation, of chubby insatiability, of freedom as frantic bustle, feeds on the bourgeois concept of nature that has always served solely to proclaim social violence as unchangeable, as a piece of healthy eternity. (1974, 156)

Utopia thus becomes defined as 'an unambiguous development towards increased production' (1974, 156). Emancipation perhaps should include within it the need for emancipation from this utopianism of 'uninhibited people' (1974, 156). Of this new freedom he says, 'A mankind which no longer knows want will begin to have an inkling of the delusory, futile nature of all arrangements hitherto made in order to escape want, which used wealth to reproduce want on a larger scale' (1974, 156–7). This would redefine happiness, and most likely sadness with it, for in present social relations enjoyment is 'inseparable from operating, planning, having one's way, subjugating' (1974, 157). 'Life has become the ideology of its own absence' (1974, 190).

Adorno's melancholy science reveals the pernicious nature of the totality that is false. The sadness here is that social relations determine not only the problems of the world, but they also determine the range of possible solutions in their own image. To what extent, then, is this a logic of tears?

Adorno works with two logics: the logic of mastery and the mad illogical dialectical logic. But he also intimates an educational logic in the aporetic relation between them. The condition of the possibility of this aporia is presupposition, and here what is preserved, unavoidably and necessarily, is the (false) totality which now also yields its truth in a logic of tears. The logic of presupposition, in this case, of the false totality, is our education regarding the illusion of beginning. In discussing authenticity Adorno notes that even though the self is deformed, 'there is no substratum beneath such "deformations"' (1974, 229). Indeed, the more 'passionately thought denies its conditionality for the sake of the unconditional, the more unconsciously, and so calamitously, it is delivered up to the world' (1974, 247). KT has no authentic self to discover. Instead, KT in the melancholy science expresses the logic of tears within the aporia of Adorno's dialectic. What can be learned here is that the sadness of negating both the genuine individual and the social relations that reproduce themselves through the illusion of the genuine is also the sadness that preserves their relation. Just as tears bring the inner world into the outer world so that truth can have its objective existence and return to itself from this objectivity as its own experience of itself, so the melancholy science can enact this same educative logic. Individual and society, authentic self and its total contingency, express the dialectic here in and as the logic of sadness, and as we saw, in the joy of this sadness. This is the melancholy science. KT preserves negation and does so specifically as the modern metaphysical logic of education.

Thus, the dialectic is never a dead-end. The dialectic of enlightenment is never just a vicious circle. Instead, the dialectic is its own logic of tears; it is the truth of *dialectic: KT*.

Notes

1. Quoting John of Salisbury here regarding the 'battle of the books', or the battle fought between the *antiqui* and the *moderni* in 12th century Europe. See Tubbs (2014).
2. There is no definitive translation of *sunt lacrimae rerum,* as we will now see.
3. For a list of different interpretations of this verse see Wharton (2008, 258–79).
4. *Aeneid*, VI. 724–8.
5. *Essays*, II.11.
6. Wharton argues that Henry's interpretation would require a different word order: either *lacrimae sunt rerum* or *lacrimae rerum sunt*; see Wharton (2008, 266). Henry's interpretation of *anima mundi* here could be strengthened by making *mentem* refer to the heart of the universe instead of to the heart of man, giving us: 'tears belong to the universe (*rerum*) and mortal ills touch its heart' (Keith, 1922, 400). Wharton's view is that Virgil intended ambiguities in the verse, and as such it is open to multiple interpretations, including those which are aware of indirect communication and intended inferences, and those meant by Virgil which lie beyond the knowledge of Aeneas.
7. IV.449.
8. Montaigne suggests that empty tears flow from Aeneas whose mind, nevertheless, remains unmoved (*Essays*, 2003a, I.12, 49). He is taking this from *City of God* IX. IV. p. 348 (in this edition the translator, David Knowles, says the tears are Dido's).
9. The various elements composing the statue represent those of the ages of humankind found in Ovid's *Metamorphosis* (Ovid, 1986, I.161).
10. Or Be!ing; see below, Chapter 8, pp. 165 and 180n.
11. *Philebus* 21c.
12. *Philebus* 26c.
13. *Philebus* 66e.
14. However, see Phaedo 60B, and above p. 117.
15. For a fuller account of the appearances of Heraclitus and Democritus see Gomez (1984).
16. Reported in Stobaeus III. 20–53. On the 'cynic' Democritus and the 'stoic' Heraclitus see Stewart (1958).
17. Lüthy notes that, through to the 20th century Democritus 'served not only as a defender of the enlightenment against all kinds of superstitions but betrayed a particular proclivity for social reforms and revolutions, particularly during the French revolution' (Lüthy, 2000, 460).
18. See Gomez (1984, 54–6).
19. Much later, from Burton's *Anatomy of Melancholy* (1800) comes this version: 'Well may you weep Heraclitus, for that befits our wretched age; you see nothing but what is shameful, nothing but what is bitter. Go and laugh, Democritus, laugh as much as you please; you see nothing but inanity, nothing but stupidity—now we need (Alas the whole world is quite mad) a thousand men like Heraclitus, a thousand men like Democritus' (Lutz, 1954, 309).
20. Cynthia Pyle (1997) suggests that the fresco in the academy may have been based on the description of the two faces which Sidonius Apollinaris records was represented in the gymnasium of the Aeropagus and the Prytanea in Athens, and that it may have been painted by Leonardo da Vinci, whose own interest in Platonism may have included the laughing and weeping philosophers. Art has contributed to the juxtaposition of the laughing and weeping philosophers, depicting them 'as equally farcical and foolish' (Edgar Wind, 1937–8, 181). Nevertheless, as a Stoic, Rubens gives the philosopher's globe to Democritus, not Heraclitus. Ter Brugghen gives Heraclitus a globe of the Earth and Democritus a globe of the

heavens. Wind argues that Cornelius Van Haarlem's picture of Democritus and Heraclitus boldly portrays Democritus as the image of Christ in the style of *Ecce Homo*. Here the artist provokes by suggesting that 'the laughing philosopher, not the crying one, should be made to resemble the "Man of Sorrow"' (Wind, 1937–8, 182). Pyle sees Dürer's *Melancholia* and engraving of *St Jerome in His Study* (1514) as the juxtaposition of Heraclitus and Democritus, or melancholy and euthymia. St Jerome is the book-loving, solitary, good-humored figure of Democritus (in contrast to the more gloomy countenance of St Jerome from 1521). See also Panofsky (2005, 212–13).

21. See also Pyle (1997, 219–20).
22. Fragment 51
23. From G Santayana, *Persons and Places*.
24. *Essays*, I.50.
25. *Essays*, I.38. Petrarch Sonnet 81.
26. *Essays*, II.20.
27. *Phaedo*, 60B.
28. §110.
29. § 530.
30. § 112.
31. § 621.
32. *Philosophy of Right*, §187z.
33. Hegel adds that 'still more of an alleviation is the expression of one's inner state in words, pictures, sounds and shapes' (1998, 49). But is not a logic of tears as least as powerful as these representations of inner states?
34. §530.
35. §187z.
36. Knox says here that Hegel's pathos is not the English 'pāthos' with its long ā. It is not just a strong passion, for example, love or hate: it is a 'passionate absorption in fulfilling a one-sided ethical purpose' (Hegel, 1998, 232n, from Mure, 1965, 192). Knox has put the term pathos in inverted commas in his book, but I have not.
37. This resistance and acceptance is an example of the aporia that negation and preservation, or the logic of education, plays out. Kierkegaard famously said, marry or don't marry (accept marriage or resist it); you'll regret it either way. A poignant example occurred for me a few days ago. My neighbor, Mike Harcourt Brown, was diagnosed with a grade 4 brain tumour at Christmas 2014. He was told he might have 6 months to live without treatment and possibly 18 months with treatment. Speaking with Jo, his wife, after Mike died, she said that although he had chosen the treatment, it had made him so ill, and his quality of life so poor, that the extra six months it perhaps offered him were not a six months he would have wanted to have. Choose to have chemotherapy or not to have chemotherapy; it is possible you will regret it either way. When we attended Mike's funeral a few days later, we were reminded not just that he had to accept and resist cancer, and did so with tears and laughter, but also of the logic of our tears and laughter regarding our own acceptance of and resistance to death. Our tears are for Mike, and through his life we are invited, or reminded, to understand that our crying and laughing have universal significance. We may cry the same tears for Mike, but differently, when we learn again of death. To understand our tears here is not to stem them; it is to sustain them in ever deeper ways, to find their spiritual significance, to weep not for one death but for death itself and its appearances in life—to cry not to overcome death, but to know its truth in our tears. If I now call this the logic of tears, will our abstract understanding of truth kick in and tell us that logic and tears are incompatible? Will it seduce us to the stereotype of logic as impersonally objective, cold, hard, unfeeling, and

of tears as the opposite, as mere sentimentality? I think not. Instead, in educative truth, logic and tears are the one truth. The logic of tears is the necessity of tears, and the necessity of tears is that they carry educative logic, the logic in which knowing is not overcoming, but sustained in acceptance and resistance of what is being learned; and what is being learned is the significance of the difficulty. The logic of our tears for Mike is this education.

38. *Vernünftigkeit*, Hegel (1970, 311).
39. Originally a speech at Munich University in 1918, and first published in 1919.
40. Fascism, he notes, claims a notion of authenticity by removing it from its religious pathos and from mediation in relation to God.

8   The Dreadful Religious Teacher

If only among us there were to be found teachers.

(Kierkegaard, 1968, 549)

Johannes Climacus is Kierkegaard's philosophical pseudonym. Climacus is in love with thinking and with dialectical thinking in particular. What fascinates him is the way that thoughts connect to one another, especially when such connections appear to lead to ever higher thoughts. From such heights, he would then try to descend back through the chain of thoughts to their origin. But this does not always turn out as he hopes. The steps back are not a replica of those taken in the ascent. The journey to understanding is changed by the understanding it makes possible.

Climacus learns this dialectical process from his father. In arguments with his guests, his father acted as the Socratic gadfly, letting his opponents outline their positions before striking with his own dialectical ripostes. 'In an instant, everything was turned upside down; the explicable was made inexplicable, the certain doubtful, the opposite was made obvious' (Kierkegaard, 1985, 122). In such an atmosphere, Climacus's 'whole life was thinking' (1985, 123).

A little like Rousseau's Emile, Climacus is not influenced by the status of great books or names. He has read the classics (unlike Emile), but they have not influenced his inner dialectical activities. When he came across recent philosophical works, he read them, but most often 'felt dissatisfied and discouraged' (1985, 129). Titles of books rarely delivered what they advertised. The text would spend too much time correcting the views of others, who had themselves corrected the views of others, establishing something of a house of cards. What he did not find was the wonders and the puzzlement of dialectics.

It seemed from such books that one thesis was agreed upon: that *everything* must be doubted, and that this defined the work of the true philosopher. But one difficulty especially unsettled this thesis. If philosophy in particular, or thought more generally, tries to begin with doubt then the eternal and the historical become confused. Either a beginning is made on the (historical) occasion of doubt, or the beginning is subsumed into an eternally existing doubt. If the former, then there is a beginning before doubt, which is not itself doubted; if the latter there is no moment of doubt that can doubt its own eternity. While authors and teachers alike seemed to glide over such fundamental puzzles, for Climacus, as for Kierkegaard, they were compelling. 'All I have is my life, which I promptly stake every time a difficulty appears' (1985, 8). It was *because* of these difficulties that Climacus could not abandon the thesis. Indeed, it was as if 'a mysterious power held him to it, as if something were whispering to him: Something is hiding behind this misunderstanding' (1985, 139). Nevertheless, the truth of the thesis remained 'an impossibility' (1985, 143).

The thesis also contained profound significance for the teacher/student relation. How might one teach the truth that everything must be doubted? Can the thesis only be taught by someone who has its truth as his or her authority? As Christ suffered for all, so is there a teacher who has doubted for all? If so, can one accept the thesis through this teacher, yet not believe it on one's own account, freely as it were? This would undermine the thesis, for everything would be doubted except the teacher of the thesis. Or should the student honor the veracity of the teacher by doubting the teacher of doubt? Is this new element of doubt needed for the truth of the thesis? If so, the teacher 'is obliged to become a sacrifice to his teaching' (1985, 155).

Let us approach the same thesis through the eyes of another pseudonymous student, Phipa Cuttlebone. His pre-university education had overthrown ignorance and innocence, but, as with Faust, it had been a 'fearful dance/Through a maze of error and ignorance . . . [where] All this misery goes to show/There's nothing can ever be known' (Goethe, 2007, 14).[1] So, he makes a Faustian-type pact with higher education. He will offer his soul to those who can show him something meaningful, something true, in the confusion and despair of education in which everything must be doubted.

Like Climacus, he finds philosophy dry and tedious. Like Climacus he asks if there is some almighty force that pushes beyond what is retrievable, or which cannot be returned to in the shape in which one departed from it. Moreover, as Kierkegaard says of Socrates, so Cuttlebone asks of his teachers, did they simply give their own confusion and despair to their students, with little hope, or perhaps without the intention of ever resolving the contradictions that doubt creates? Did the tutors shape the students in their own image out of some need for company in their lonely negative worlds, only to cast them off when they turned to their new students? Are they, unlike Nietzsche's Zarathustra, unable to give life to themselves? In the end, does the pact made with education only reveal, with Keats, that 'to think is to be full of sorrow'?[2]

It is to students like Climacus and Cuttlebone, and to their tutors, that the following thoughts are offered, in attempting to describe the dreadful religious teacher. Three challenges lie before us: to learn how the modern metaphysical logic of education comes into the world by the fact that it is presupposed; to find the educational logic of KT that negates and preserves itself in the work of the dreadful religious teacher; and for teachers and students, to learn how to exist in what we understand. We explore such matters briefly now in the educational logic of the teacher in Rousseau, Hegel, and Nietzsche, before working with Kierkegaard in more detail. What we are looking for is the 'dreadful' teacher who dissembles education by using the logic of presupposition as a seduction into self-awareness; the 'religious' teacher who arrogates to himself the authority of education by presupposing this authority without dread; and the dreadful religious teacher who expresses the logic of education by negating and preserving the dilemma of educational authority. In so doing, we are also rehearsing education and within it the teacher/student relationship, as the modern metaphysical first principle.

Rousseau, Hegel, and Nietzsche

Rousseau

We saw in Part 1 Rousseau's view of religious education expressed through the Savoyard priest. But the project of his *Emile* rehearses an educational philosophy whose goals and pedagogy, ends and means, are for Emile to KT, an education that preserves itself in a negation of and a resistance to social relations determined by private property. Emile's education is to be grounded in self-preservation or self-love, modified by reason and compassion. Individuals are to be educated to recognize real needs, mediated always by their ability to achieve them without needing to become slaves to others, or make others their slaves, and to develop no dependence upon needs which are artificially created by the false values of civil society. Happiness, he says, 'consists in decreasing the difference between our desires and our powers, in establishing a perfect equilibrium between the power and the will' (Rousseau, 1993, 52).

Rousseau's social and political aims for this education are that the child will grow up with his own natural instincts and desires, and not with the influences that civil society demands: politeness, decorum, and disingenuousness. This natural education is to be the basis for a new conception of the social contract in which 'each alone, while uniting himself with all, may still obey himself alone and remain as free as before' (Rousseau, 1973, 191).[3]

But there is intrigue and dissemblance in what has become known as Rousseau's natural or experiential or child-centred pedagogy. Emile is free to learn by running around in fields and climbing trees, but these events are carefully managed by his tutor. The appearance of the child being able to learn from a teacher who teaches 'without doing anything at all' (1993, 99), and who prevents others from doing anything to interfere with this, is a deception. Despite the claims that the child is 'nature's pupil' (1993, 99), in fact the teacher, like everything else in civil society, wears a mask and is not at all as he seems. Rousseau reminds this teacher that such artifice 'consists in controlling events' (1993, 251) in such a way that this control is hidden.

'Let him [the student] always think he is master while you are really master' (1993, 100). The social and political insight that grounds so much of Rousseau's thinking is that 'the mask is not the man' (1993, 237). Yet the teacher must wear a mask to prevent Emile learning to wear one. Of this art of pedagogical dissimulation Rousseau says of himself, as a tutor of a young child, 'I succeeded during the short time I was with him in getting him to do everything I wanted' (1993, 105). The danger here is that the tutor does all the negating on behalf of the student, and the student is preserved only in the tutor's image. This will not fulfil the logic of KT.

But what of Cuttlebone's concerns that at the end of this dissimulation, the tutor casts the students away, leaving them to fend for themselves? Rousseau notes that there will come a time in early adulthood when the tutor will show Emile all that he has done for him and how he is 'made for me' (1993, 344). Moreover,

> I will kindle in his young heart all the sentiments of affection, generosity and gratitude which I have called into being . . . I will say to him: 'You are my wealth, my child, my handiwork; my happiness is bound up in yours: if you frustrate my hopes you rob me of twenty years of my life.' (1993, 344)

Rousseau does not cast his student out, as Cuttlebone suggests of his own teachers, but instead here the tutor seeks to become Emile's confidant. An aporia of authority characterizes this relationship too. Emile, of his own free will, asks his tutor to continue to have power over him, to 'compel me to be my own master' (1993, 347). The tutor agrees, and understands that 'when my authority is firmly established, my first care will be to avoid the necessity of using it' (1993, 348). What this contradiction replicates is the *social contract* where one freely accepts a form of association in which one obeys yet remains free.

Hegel

While Hegel was the rector of the Nuremberg *Gymnasium* (1808–16), he rehearsed this same aporetic logic of authority within the teacher/student relation. He has to teach philosophical content that is only true if and when the students think this content for themselves. Truth is not 'a minted coin that can be given and pocketed ready-made' (Hegel, 1977, 22), because 'no man can think for another any more than he can eat or drink for him' (Hegel, 1975, 36). Nevertheless, in teaching this content, Hegel is the one turning truth into a minted coin, or abstracting it prior to the students' experience of it, granting to himself the authority of one who already possesses this truth, or this treasure, while the students, whose understanding of truth is as yet 'opinion, half-truth, distortion, and indeterminateness' (Hegel, 1984, 280), have yet to think this truth themselves.

Hegel faces the same dilemma that intrigued Climacus. To think for themselves, students must doubt that which is received as given, and consider it for themselves. But with Rousseau, and now with Hegel, the need to teach for students' independence while at the same time demanding dependence upon the teacher is experienced by both parties as a contradiction. The ends do not justify the means because the means contradict the ends, at least as contradiction is understood within the logic of mastery. As we will come to see, if the teacher here doubts his authority too much, he will be dreadful, practicing a paradox without its own meaning and educative significance. If the teacher doubts his authority too little, he will be religious, giving a gift that he believes is not changed in the giving. Hegel's pedagogy here is dreadful and religious. It is Socratic and dreadful in doubting everything—the students must 'die to sight and hearing, be torn away from concrete representation' (Hegel, 1984, 280)—and it is religious—truth is found in this death as freedom and God.

We will explore this more fully with Kierkegaard in a moment. But in anticipation of Kierkegaard's notion of indirect communication, we note Hegel's observation on indirect teaching. Just as the negative, as Hegel says, works 'behind the back of consciousness' (Hegel, 1977, 56), so too teaching for a negative or dialectical experience is best done not directly, but through 'the deficiency of this or that determination' (Hegel, 1984, 264), including the deficiency inherent in the positing of the teacher's authority by the authority of the teacher. For such a teacher, the logic of KT means knowing the teacher as an educational authority in-itself, *and* the negation of that authority, *and* the preservation of this educational logic in the aporia of authority that has to be risked in education, as education, in the teacher/student relationship.

In addition, also like Kierkegaard, Hegel understands that the teacher represents the beginning of an education for freedom, and that any beginning 'precisely because it is the beginning, is imperfect' (1984, 293). Just as Rousseau's tutor has to deceive with regard to his abstract authority over nature and Emile, so Hegel has to be the abstract authority of the students' own dialectical experiences. Both teachers here, and indeed all teachers in modern social relations, carry such abstract authority into their teaching. It is because of the imperfections of the 'beginning' that the teacher/student relation can never be mutual. How teachers choose to mediate this abstraction distinguishes those for whom abstraction, identity, and power are fixed and nonnegotiable from those for whom they are negated and preserved in the educational logic of the teacher/student relation, or in the logic of KT.

Nietzsche (1844–1900)

Is there an educational logic in Nietzsche's account of Zarathustra, and if there is, to what extent is Zarathustra's teaching dreadful and religious? Zarathustra teaches that God is dead and that the overman is coming. In a rich seam of KT, Zarathustra says that this education requires man to have contempt for himself, to learn with disgust his being the same as everyone else in the herd, and to learn of chaos within.

The three metamorphoses that lead to the overman are a journey of KT. The camel is the pious and sanctimonious bearer of other people's sins. This deep *ressentiment* rides into the desert to become the lion, brave enough to know this resentful self, and to replace hypocritical servitude with the truth of the mastery that underpins it. No more 'thou shalt'; now only 'I will'. But even this self-knowing is not the creation of new values. For that, a new beginning is required, a self-education in which the lion becomes the child, 'innocence and forgetting . . . a first movement' (Nietzsche, 1982, 139), a new value of the overman as a first principle, a self-propelling wheel, and 'a sacred "Yes"' (1982, 139). But as the story of Zarathustra shows, forgetting is not the new beginning. Any positing of beginning, new or otherwise, returns eternally to remind Zarathustra that even the overman is only the old value of mastery.

On his journey Zarathustra will teach KT as the education that the one God, like all gods, is 'man-made and madness' (1982, 143). KT here requires a new will, a Yes-saying will, the will-to-power. In a reversal of values KT here means that the healthy despise the soul, and revel in the war of self against illusions of its divinity. KT means that man 'is something that must be overcome' (1982, 149). But throughout the account of Zarathustra, Nietzsche relates how man fails to live up to this new kind of self-knowing, and how Zarathustra negotiates knowing himself as the teacher.

From the teacher of the overman the people receive this education as both dreadful in the self-awareness that accompanies the death of God, and religious in that the dread is issued 'as a command' (1982, 160). As Zarathustra learns painfully, those who learn dread and who need this command do not therein experience a new kind of self-knowing, but only a strong desire to worship and idolize the teacher and commander. The will-to-power of the teacher of the overman has just as strong a hold over the herd as did religion. Zarathustra laments that 'They do not understand me; I am not the mouth for these ears' (1982, 128). His problem is that the power of his own teaching is counterproductive; it opposes itself by attracting followers rather than being the stimulus to a new form of KT. He fails many times, and many times he commands his followers to go away and to learn to 'resist Zarathustra! And even better: be ashamed of him. Perhaps he deceived you' (1982, 190).

But Zarathustra has to face his own aporia of the teacher. He learns first that will-to-power is the life-force, and that this force, in seeking always to overcome itself, has to learn this, and to accept this, as the new value of itself as KT. Pity for this teacher is overcome, and therein the teaching can begin again. The teacher of the overman, now, in KT, is the teacher of will-to-power. This redefines the very idea of a teacher, for teachers and scholars and educated men are 'trained to pursue knowledge as if it were nutcracking' (1982, 237). Nevertheless, to his teaching of will-to-power as the creative value of a new beginning 'his disciples barely listened' (1982, 245).

Zarathustra's next melancholic note of failure is in learning that the event is a recollection of knowledge that eternally returns as the same. Nothing is; everything has been. Now Zarathustra is faced with an even greater challenge of self-knowing. Can he learn to will even this melancholic state of affairs, to say Yes to this eternal return of the same? If he can, then will-to-power will have a new value, its own value, and resentment at the inability to change the past will become a joyous 'Yes' to all that has happened, and all that will happen again. Where before he chastised himself as being one who has the power and yet does 'not want to rule' (1982, 258), now, in the KT of eternal return, peak, and abyss are joined together, and KT is now able to speak of itself as the whole of life affirming itself: 'Was that life? Well then! Once more!' (1982, 269). Now he is the teacher only of saying Yes to himself, and for this he needs no ears to hear him, just his animals on his mountain. His teaching failed not because of the message, but because of the audience. 'Disguised I sat among them, ready to mistake myself that I might endure them' (1982, 297). But this was being untrue to himself. So, KT as the Yes-saying Zarathustra returns to his mountain and at last 'my nose is delivered from the smell of everything human' (1982, 298).

But in returning to the sanctuary of the mountain at the end of Book 3, this Yes-sayer has still said No to the eternal return of the dreadful teacher of the death of God. At the beginning and end of Book 4 Zarathustra asks, what of the happiness of this Yes-sayer? 'I have long ceased to be concerned with my happiness; now I am concerned with my work' (1982, 349). This work requires students; 'what would your happiness be had you not those for whom you shine?' (1982, 121) Now Zarathustra must try to say Yes to the eternal return of Zarathustra the dreadful teacher, only this time he will wait for students to come to him on his mountain. The aporia of his authority as a teacher is now willed as eternal return. This is Zarathustra's attempt to take the Yes-saying of KT to its final moral value, that of self-pity for the suffering teacher plagued by inadequate students.

Seven forms of the higher man make their way to his mountain. Each represents a desire for KT that will overcome a lack of virtue. They are the deceivers, the conscientious, the ascetic, the pious last pope, the murderer of God who also witnessed the depths of the ugliest man, the voluntary beggar who gave all his money to the poor, and finally Zarathustra's own shadow. But each of these higher men still seek the answers to their problems in someone other than themselves. Zarathustra tells them, 'If you would go high, use your own legs. Do not let yourself be carried up; do not sit on the backs and heads of others' (1982, 402). The teacher teaches them laughter at their failure, but these men soon fall to their knees worshiping an ass that accompanied them up the mountain. The pope speaks for them when he says 'Better to adore a God in this form than in no form at all' (1982, 426).

On the mountain, then, in the company of the higher men, God returns because the teacher of the overman is never overcome by those who hear him. The more powerful the teacher, the more the followers worship him.

Unable to do the work of KT as will-to-power, the followers demand the teacher continue to do the work for them. But if God returns in the failure of the will-to-power of the followers to KT, he returns also in the failure of the dreadful teacher to become the religious teacher who wills the eternal return of this failure. But Zarathustra *does* yield to saying Yes to the dreadful and religious teacher when he says Yes to the work of this failure of teaching at the end of Book 4. He returns down the mountain again, this time for the 'first time' as the dreadful teacher in whose work God is not overcome. This 'first time' of the eternal return of the dreadful religious teacher carries in the logic of KT what makes him dreadful and religious.

This reading of Zarathustra as a dreadful religious teacher is not one that falls in line with Deleuzian-inspired interpretations.[4] Nevertheless, there is a second way to illustrate the modern metaphysical educational logic here in its relation to the ancient logic of mastery and identity. Several times the Yes-sayer is described according to the logic of the unchangeable first principle of NN. In the Preface the logic of the unchangeable, unmediated by recollection, is innocence and forgetting, the first movement, the self-creation. At the end of each Book the logic of the unchangeable is the solitude of the mountains offering sanctuary from its mediation by followers. This is especially the case at the end of Book 3 when the logic of the unchangeable is the song of the Yes-sayer and amen. 'How should I not lust after eternity and after the nuptial ring of rings, the ring of recurrence?' (1982, 341).

The ring of rings is the logic of thought thinking itself. The logic of this version of eternal return, and of the Yes to this eternal return, is the logic of its identity with itself, a 'religious' identity that is unmediated by the dreadful. It is this logic of the unchangeable that becomes the new value of the Yes-sayer who also holds a No that is hidden, and is the more dreadful for that. Zarathustra at the end of Book 3 says Yes to the unchangeable as the eternal return of the same, *unchanged*. But the final Yes-saying at the end of Book 4 says Yes to the collapse of this version of eternal return, and Yes to the dreadful work that this failure again requires. This final Yes-saying says Yes to the inability to will backward, and in doing so retrieves the educational truth of the dreadful, that is, not an unknowable God but God known in his mediation by the work of KT. In this sense Zarathustra is a dreadful religious teacher, again, only this time able to preserve the educational truth of the negation of the same, preserved in the KT of the teacher, and ready to be dreadful and religious in teaching KT to others.

Kierkegaard (1813–1855)

The remainder of our study of the dreadful religious teacher is spent with Kierkegaard, specifically with *Concept of Dread* and *Philosophical Fragments* which were published within four days of each other in 1844. We find here an educational logic attending the subjective individual's task 'to understand himself in existence' (Kierkegaard, 1992, 351) and of 'existing in what one understands' (1992, 274). For Kierkegaard this is an inwardness which 'is truth' (1992, 278) and occurs not in the logic of mastery but in the absurdity of a logic of presupposition, which negates and preserves itself in a leap of qualitative educational substance. In the work of the dreadful religious teacher, the difficulty of learning about God and man 'is invested with a new form and thus *actually made difficult*' (1992, 276n).[5]

Concept of Dread[6]

Logic of Logic

In contrast to the logic of mastery, Kierkegaard works with a contingent logic. The logic of this logic is that logic came into the world in such a way that 'by the fact that it is, it is presupposed' (Kierkegaard, 1967, 29). 'To employ something which is nowhere explained is in effect to presuppose it' (1967, 73), and logic does not explain itself. Not explanation then, but the contradiction of presupposition, is 'the only dialectically consistent statement' (1967, 30). The logic of ancient mastery abstracts itself from this difficulty and proceeds as if the logic of logic were not a question at all. It judges everything according to the consistency or inconsistency of the in-itself, conveniently forgetting that this criterion can boast of no such consistency for itself.

Contingency upon presupposition is the logic of logic here. It is grounded in a leap into actuality from a beginning that is known only as lost or missing. If this leap *is* logic and is the logic of logic, then what is logical here is presupposition, and not the explaining away of presupposition by the logic of mastery. This means there is no logic in-itself, there is only a logic of logic that is contingent upon its own presupposition but which, to reiterate, comes into the world such that, by the fact that it is, it is presupposed.[7] If presupposition is the template of logic, how is one to exist in this understanding? If one can only live by going forward, and only understand by looking backward,[8] what is it to live understanding? Kierkegaard's answer is, by means of the absurd template of being that is repetition and recollection.

Repetition and Recollection

Whilst engaged to Regine Olsen between 1840–1, Kierkegaard tries to exist in what he understands. The ancient logic of being offered him the opposition between spontaneous, immediate love and its reduction to a contract in marriage, mediated therein as an object of reflection. Kierkegaard struggles here to exist in the understanding that contradiction, not explanation or resolution, is the only true consistency. Rejecting what he understands Hegelian mediation to be, namely an immediacy somehow known to itself in a logic of mastery, Kierkegaard expresses the consistency of the logic of contradiction as living in recollection and repetition.[9]

In the logic of mastery love as repetition is in-itself only as immediacy. Love lost to thought is love recollected in thought, an immediacy lost to mediation. The 'blissful security of the moment' (Kierkegaard, 1983, 132) cannot be protected from its recollection, and love, again, is not lived spontaneously, but as an object of reflection. Kierkegaard's relation to Regine is the struggle to exist in this understanding, to exist in the love that is posited as lost as soon as it is known. Here the logic of positing retrieves for love the logic of KT, in being repetition and recollection. It makes love more difficult, but also, in the difficulty, makes it knowable and liveable. Placed alongside the Hegelian template of being, that is, of immediacy and mediation, the contradiction of repetition and recollection becomes *living understanding*. What immediacy repeats forward, or lives, is recollection, and what mediation recollects backward, or understands, is repetition. Together they are the living understanding of the logic and being of presupposition, or of the imperfection of beginnings. They are the collapse of the logic of mastery into the logic of education. They are love knowing and living its truth in learning that love so comes into the world that by the fact that it is, it is presupposed. In Chapter 6 above this expressed itself educationally in the logic of tears. Here it will express itself educationally in the logic of the dreadful religious teacher.

In the *Concluding Unscientific Postscript* mediation, when seen merely as resolution, is the resort of the individual who 'can no longer endure to understand existence' (1968, 355) and as such is only 'the miserable invention of a man who became false to himself' (1968, 355). Kierkegaard therefore offers repetition as clarifying 'what has mistakenly been called mediation'[10] (Kierkegaard, 1983, 148). 'The dialectic of repetition is easy, for that which is repeated has been—otherwise it could not be repeated—but the very fact that it has been makes the repetition into something new' (1983, 149).

The idea of the 'new' as a relation between repetition and recollection, or between possibility and actuality, is explored by Kierkegaard as the question not just of continuity, but also of educational transition. It is the kind of continuity that makes a difference to that which it preserves. He rehearses this in the examples of sin, innocence, dread, and faith.

Sin

Whereas mediation (again here, meaning Kierkegaard's version of Hegelian mediation) explains the first sin only by presupposing 'explanation' based on resolution of the absurd, repetition explains that 'sin came into the world by a sin' (1967, 29), presupposing only the sin of presupposition. This is a transition from the quantification of the first sin (the beginning or first moment) to the quality of sinfulness. This transition is a leap from the logic of mastery to the educational logic of presupposition. As such, the first appears only 'with the leap, with the suddenness of the enigmatic' (1967, 28). Such a positing 'is a stumbling block to the understanding' (1967, 29).

The understanding can cope with quantitative leaps where something that already is moves, progresses, or develops 'by quantitative increments' (1967, 47), i.e., increases in amount and frequency. But the understanding struggles to deal with the logic of positing, which finds truth in a difficulty that the understanding registers only as something needing to be mastered.

Faced with positing, all the understanding can do is assert that a qualitative leap is a superstition, and it 'composes poetically a myth which denies the leap, construes the circle as a straight line, and then everything goes on as a matter of course' (1967, 29). All that ancient logic can do is to explain away the absurdity of beginning with recollection and repetition by positing the state of man before the Fall. This is how logic resolves the absurdity of all beginning, by removing the beginning from its own repetition and from its own inherent difficulty. This logic of mastery employs presupposition to solve the problems endemic to presupposition. Therefore it does not master these problems; it only repeats them, and it is not keen to recollect that this is the case. Thus, says Kierkegaard, the account of first sin in Genesis 'is the only dialectically consistent account' (1967, 29), expressing 'profound consistency in representing that sin presupposes itself, that it so came into the world that by the fact that it is, it is presupposed' (1967, 29). The first sin is actual, not potential, or as Kierkegaard puts it: we should not say that 'by Adam's sin sin came into the world' (1967, 30) but rather 'that by the first sin sinfulness came into Adam' (1967, 30), reminding us of Plotinus, who said that the soul is not in the body but rather the body is in the soul.[11] In this way sin knows itself educationally.

Innocence and Dread

The same case is made for innocence. Innocence cannot be known only in the recollection of its loss for then innocence would never exist. In the logic of presupposition, and in repetition, the transition known as the Fall is a quality of 'ignorance' (1967, 34) and the quality of ignorance is 'the qualitative leap of the individual' (1967, 34). How then can innocence be lost but also endure within the absurd logic of presupposition, rather than be unknowable within the logic of explanation and resolution?

Kierkegaard's answer is that 'the profound secret of innocence [is] that it is dread' (1967, 38).[12] This is not fear of something definite; it is 'freedom's reality as possibility for possibility' (1967, 38). It is not a temptation for anything quantitative. He likens dread to the 'sweetest feeling of apprehension' (1967, 38) of a child who seeks adventure in pursuit of the mysterious. It is spirit in a state of immediacy, related to itself as dread. It is the 'immense nothing of ignorance' (1967, 40). It is the relation between innocence and sin, Adam and the generations, eternal and temporal, ignorance and knowledge, and potentiality and actuality. As a 'middle term' (1967, 68) dread 'rescues' (1967, 68) ambiguity, even absurdity, in the transition that turns presupposition into its own logic of non-resolution, its own educational logic.

Here, Kierkegaard pits the ancient logic of the philosophers against themselves. In the account of the Fall in Genesis, one cannot assume that Adam understands the nature of the choice that the prohibition on eating from the tree of knowledge offers him. He cannot know the freedom of choice, or a desire to exercise freedom, since these will be the result of the action, not its cause. So in what condition is Adam on hearing the prohibition? The prohibition induces dread in Adam, awakening the possibility of freedom. It awakens the 'alarming possibility of *being able*' (1967, 40) but what he is able to do, 'of that he has no conception' (1967, 40) because as yet he has no conception of good and evil, for good and evil are only intelligible to freedom.

This possibility of being able, but having no knowledge or understanding of it, is 'a higher form of ignorance, as a heightened expression of dread' (1967, 40), enjoying and at the same time fearing its possibility. For Kierkegaard this is a logic that is beginning to make itself known, a logic of positing as an immanence of motion, a logic that has the 'profound consistency' (1967, 29) of that which can only begin in presupposition. Innocence, dread, and ignorance are in the motion, in the logic, where, like sin, each 'presupposes itself, that it so came into the world that by the fact that it is, it is presupposed' (1967, 29). In this logic, dread is 'the reflex of freedom within itself at the thought of its possibility' (1967, 50). If the spirit is not present in innocence as dread then innocence, when lost, cannot endure, and was always lost. Dread, therefore, is the possibility of its being possible. Or bluntly, dread is freedom's own positing; it is (the ambiguity that constitutes) presupposition, and it is the intermediate between possibility—I can—and actuality—I did (again). Dread here is not a logical explanation of how sin came into the world. Dread is a freedom not yet free for-itself. It no longer makes sense to speak of innocence as something lost, but instead of innocence as the nothing of ignorance that knows itself as the question, demonstrating that ignorance was never nothing, but always something knowing itself.

Faith

Faith carries this same educative significance of transition in this logic of positing. In his Introduction to *CD* Kierkegaard notes that if faith is immediate, then faith has no actuality. It is cleansed of its own history, where history here means relation to its beginning. Instead, faith shares with sin the logic of presupposition. Faith is the repetition of what is lost in its being known. Indeed, faith is the logic of presupposition, and it is the presupposition of this logic. It is absurd, because the logic of presupposition is absurd, and it is actual because it presupposes itself as its own educational work.

What then of faith as a logic of education, or as *faith: KT*? Faith is not a club one joins. It is not a quantity. It is a presupposition in which one learns of one's inwardness. It is an education that preserves its negativity. Johannes de Silentio is right to say that he will not master faith by choosing a leap into faith.[13] Faith is not a choice. It is a learning, including the learning that it is not a choice. One can only recollect the leap as its repetition; and faith is repetition and recollection as an educational vocation. One does not choose the logic of presupposition. It chooses us, claims us, when we are ready to question its 'explanation' of the question. This is to live the transition as existing in what one understands, that is, when this new necessity of the logic of presupposition is ready to choose us. Faith is not a new immediacy. It has its own historical presuppositions, or else it is nothing at all, a faithless faith. This is a very different understanding of what and who God is; God is not 'explained'; god is the illogic of its presupposition.

In terms of learning to exist in what one understands, sin, innocence, dread, and faith enter the world in the individual 'as the individual' (1967, 45). Although there have been lived countless millions of 'selves',

> no science can state what the self is, without stating it in perfectly general terms. And this is the wonderful thing about life, that every man who gives heed to himself knows what no science knows, since he knows what he himself is; and this is the profundity of the Greeks saying, γνῶθι σεαυτόν (know thyself). (1967, 70)

Kierkegaard says that the time has come to no longer think about KT in the German way, as a pure self-consciousness, but rather as 'the qualitative leap' (1967, 71). Sin has a 'reflective' identity not only as paganism, which has no historical point of departure at all, but also as spiritlessness in which he includes paganism within Christianity. The latter is worse than paganism, for whereas paganism is 'the absence of spirit' (1967, 85), paganism in Christianity 'has a relation to spirit which proves not to be a relation' (1967, 84). Spiritlessness can repeat all the words of a relation, can speak dread, but does not live it. 'There is only one attestation of spirit, and that is the attestation of spirit within oneself' (1967, 85).

His reference here to KT is a repetition and recollection of a journal entry nine years earlier. Seeking an idea for which 'I can live and die' (Kierkegaard, 1938, 15) he notes that if he finds a deeper truth it must 'be taken up into my life' (138, 15). To find this idea will be to find himself. Immediacy will not suffice. He has tasted the pleasure of knowledge, but it was fleeting, it 'did not outlast the moment of understanding and left no profound mark upon me' (1938, 17). As such, he declares 'One must know oneself before knowing anything else (γνῶθι σεαυτόν)' (1938, 17). This is an early expression in Kierkegaard of the educational task to understand oneself in existence, and to exist in what one understands.[14]

Philosophical Fragments[15]

As CD began with the question of the presupposition of logic, so PF begins with the presupposition of the question 'Can the truth be learned?' and encompasses too the question of whether the truth can taught. Kierkegaard is clear on the nature of this posited beginning: 'The question is asked by one who in his ignorance does not even know what provided the occasion for his questioning in this way' (Kierkegaard, 1985, 9). Here the beginning is not his own.

Even to be able to explore this question, Kierkegaard states that he will need to create space in the minds of those who think that the understanding of Christianity is completed. This he will do by means of difficulties contained in 'new dialectical combinations' (Kierkegaard, 1992, 276n), including the logic of absolute paradox, and of 'a new kind of contradiction' (Kierkegaard, 1985, 80). Again the difficulty for Kierkegaard is to learn to exist in what he understands, requiring an inwardness for which the quantitative continuity between ideas, or teaching and learning as direct communication, fails to be the qualitative leap or educational transition in which truth can be taught and learned. As ever for Kierkegaard such truth is 'subjectivity [or] inwardness' (Kierkegaard, 1992, 278).

In CD an eternal consciousness was its own possibility as dread within the relation between innocence and guilt. In PF now the starting place (the presupposition) is altogether different. PF asks, can the eternal consciousness have a beginning in the recollective or historical mind? Can a historical point of departure ever be more than or different from recollection, or of more than historical interest? Can an eternal happiness be built on historical knowledge? At stake again is the struggle to exist in what one understands.

As in CD, the question of the transition from beginning to contingency, or from immediacy to mediation, is addressed as a question of education, and now, as a *decisive* education. Kierkegaard asks, how can the Socratic occasion of discovery in recollection that I 'have known the truth from eternity without knowing it' (Kierkegaard, 1985, 13) become a moment of decisive significance, one that moves the learner from learning historically to learning eternally? In *Repetition*, Kierkegaard speaks of this change, this decisive moment, as a sense of well-being.

> My body had lost its terrestrial gravity; it was as if I had no body simply because every function enjoyed total satisfaction, every nerve delighted in itself and in the whole, while every heartbeat, the restlessness of the living being, only memorialized and declared the pleasure of the moment. My walk was a floating . . . My being was transparent . . . Every mood rested in my soul with melodic resonance . . . All existence seemed to have fallen in love with me, and everything quivered in fateful rapport with my being. Everything was prescient in me, and everything was enigmatically transfigured in my microcosmic bliss. (Kierkegaard, 1983, 173)

But Kierkegaard mocks this rather Plotinian description of the decisive moment for being unable to withstand a mote of dust which, irritating his eye, sees him in that same instant 'plunged down almost into the abyss of despair' (1983, 173). The mote of dust, or perhaps an eyelash, is the triumph of the historical bringing the reverie of the eternal crashing down.[16]

Where then is one to look for an eternal education that can preserve itself even in its negation by the historical reflective eyelash? The Socratic here is not enough. Socrates can be the occasion of reminding the learner of the untruth of the mediation of all certainty by doubt. But if the Socratic teacher already knows his ignorance, this education is merely quantitative, more or less ignorance. It is not, also, a qualitative transition from untruth to truth—the same charge laid against Socrates by Kierkegaard in his master's thesis. Kierkegaard suggests that if the transition is not found in the Socratic teacher, or in the student who learns of his own ignorance, it might instead be found in that which the seeker seeks, in the *unknown*. 'Let us call this unknown the god. It is only a name we give to it' (Kierkegaard, 1985, 39).

Learning Untruth

Kierkegaard rehearses the educative logic of recollection and repetition in the language of untruth and sin. As recollection has repetition as the condition of the possibility of recollection knowing itself, so untruth has sin (the fault of the individual) as the condition of the possibility of untruth knowing itself. This is educational logic added to negative Socratic logic to give a decisive and religious transition or education. The Socratic teacher must learn that he cannot give the learner 'what is essential' (1985, 18). What gives substance to this subjective education is that its condition of possibility lies in the individual learning of its own untruth *as* this condition of possibility. Again, this is the logic of presupposition. Untruth must be the fault of the individual, and therefore be sin, for without it untruth remains factual and quantitative. 'I know how much I don't know' is very different from 'I know that the necessity of my untruth is what makes decisive education possible.' The non-seeker of the truth of untruth forfeits the condition of the possibility of transition.

What are we to call the condition of the possibility of decisive transition that is its own presupposition, or its own fault? For Kierkegaard, we can call it the logic and truth of the unknown, for it is of a different logic to that of identity and mastery, or we can call it the god. The god gives the condition of understanding, while the learner learns of the condition as his own fault.

Kierkegaard explains the decisiveness of this moment by likening it to a child who, in choosing to buy one toy from among others, therein destroys the freedom to buy a different one because the first toy has lost its monetary value; and to a knight, who, invited by two competing armies to join them, chooses one, and is then captured by the other. Seeking now to change sides, as was available before the choice, he finds that the cost of the choice was the surrender of the choice.

Such a moment of decisive significance passes by quickly, but it is filled with the eternal and will not be forgotten by the learner. As both a human being and as untruth, the gift of education means not that one becomes a human being for the first time, but that one becomes 'a different person . . . a person of a different quality . . . a *new* person' (1985, 18).

Socrates, then, was the occasion but not the condition for others to learn something. The integrity of Socrates is rare says Kierkegaard, in that he promises nothing he cannot deliver, offers no salvation of souls, 'seducing no one, not even the one who [in idolising the teacher] employs all the arts of seduction to be seduced!' (1985, 24).

Absolute Paradox

This logic of education makes no sense in the ancient logic. But for Kierkegaard it is a new kind of contradiction, one whose uncertainty corresponds not to the ancient logic, but to the educational logic of positing, or to 'the uncertainty of coming into existence' (1985, 86n). This experience of education as its own presupposition—that it comes into the world in such a way that, by the fact that it is, it is presupposed—for the ancient logic is only a *paradox*. Ancient logic eschews any educational logic or truth in this paradox. For it, the paradox demonstrates that thought 'wants to discover something that thought itself cannot think' (1985, 37). Greek philosophy turns to skepticism, where Sextus Empiricus stands ready 'to make the transition implied in "to learn" not merely difficult but impossible' (1985, 38). The paradoxical passion of the understanding, to discover the unknown that thought cannot think, wills this collision and therein 'wills its own downfall' (1985, 39). In the face of the paradox the unknown or the absolute is explained away by reason, which therein avoids the implication that God is in the paradox. Ordinary logic is the escape route here. If God does not exist, there is nothing to prove. If he does exist, then one demonstrates not his existence *per se*, but rather 'the definition of a concept' (1985, 40). Knowing God requires a different logic, a logic of *absolute* paradox, something one only does justice to by being the living understanding of this absolute paradox.

The logic of absolute paradox is the logic of qualitative change, or education. It is where a difference is made, as illustrated above by the child's toy and the knight's capture. For Kierkegaard, the understanding that arises in and of a paradox is a game-changer. It doesn't just move from one landscape to another; it changes what any and all landscapes mean. Meaning here cannot be overlooked. The qualitative leap for the child, the knight, and the person seeking to exist in what one understands, changes the meaning of *what it is to understand*. When one refuses the ordinary logic, 'when I let go of the demonstrative' (1985, 43) there is God existing in the leap, existing in what one (now) understands about understanding. It is the logic of positing and is suffered as the logic in which the understanding collides with the passion for the unknown, and brings about its own downfall, the downfall of its understanding of itself and of this kind of understanding *per se*. It learns that in the downfall of the understanding there is a qualitative change, a change of meaning about understanding.

The logic of the absolute paradox of positing in CD was that the understanding is faced with the profound consistency of the logic of positing, or the profound consistency in representing that sin presupposes itself, that it so came into the world that by the fact that it is, it is presupposed. This profound consistency in PF is the absolute paradox, and one can say of its logic that this is now the challenge of existing in what one understands, namely, to exist in the absolute paradox, in the logic of positing, and in the way that it changes the meaning of understanding, and the understanding of meaning. The logic of absolute paradox, and the logic of presupposition, or educational logic, is described by Kierkegaard here in a way that alludes to the sequel of PF.[17] 'The whole process of demonstration continually becomes something entirely different, becomes an expanded concluding development of what I conclude from having presupposed that the object of investigation exists' (1985, 40). Where skepticism, and all quantitative thinking, make the transition implied in 'to learn' impossible, the logic of absolute paradox enacts what learning is and what learning means, and makes a qualitative difference in doing so, precisely, the difference that is the educational relation between God and man.

Soul

Kierkegaard offers the soul as a further example of this logic of positing. There is an absolute paradox in the idea that one might try to gain one's soul. If one already has a soul then there is no need to gain it, and if one is born without a soul, then it is impossible to gain it, for the soul is not something lying around externally, which can be picked up and made one's own. This logical paradox defines what the soul is: 'The soul is a self-contradiction between the external and the internal, the temporal and the eternal. It is a self-contradiction, because wanting to express the contradiction within itself is precisely what makes it what it is' (Kierkegaard, 1990, 166). Furthermore, this logic changes the meaning of the question of how to gain one's soul. One begins by reflecting on one's immediacy with the world, the reflection in which there is a resistance to such immediacy. This resistance is the soul, and

> if he wants to gain his soul, he must let this resistance become more and more pronounced and in doing so gain his soul, for his soul was this very difference: it was the infinity in the life of the world in its difference from itself. (1990, 165)

Here is how the soul 'is to be possessed and gained at the same time' (1990, 166). The contradiction of the soul is that it is a possession to be gained; and Kierkegaard says here that the way to live this paradox, the way to live with this understanding, is by means of *patience*. As one grows patient, so one gains one's soul. Patience, he says, is 'joy and sorrow' (1990, 189).

The resistance that is the soul can, however, also resist itself. This is the wellspring of those who take offence at the religious, where the meeting between the paradox and the understanding is an unhappy one. The resistance is felt as a suffering; the cause of the suffering is the positing of God. So the ordinary understanding grants itself arbitrary and capricious power to kill the source of the problem and liberate itself from the suffering. The offended judge the paradox comic and absurd, and grant this judgement the status of 'an objection' (Kierkegaard, 1985, 52). What they miss is that resistance to the resistance is the same suffering they were offended at. What they miss is that everything said by them about the paradox has been 'learned from the paradox' (1985, 53). This is again the logic of presupposition. What offends the offended is what Kierkegaard calls 'the happy passion which we call faith, the object of which is the paradox . . . [that] is the eternalizing of the historical and the historicizing of the eternal' (1985, 61).

Teacher

In the remainder of PF Kierkegaard addresses a number of questions raised by not remaining with the Socratic teacher. The Socratic teacher can be the occasion for doubt but does not have the decisive moment ready as his own gift to give to the learner. The teacher who *can* be the decisive moment has appeared on Earth, the god in human form. The descent, the resistance, changes the meaning of the unknown and brings the paradox to all people. His work is to be this education, to be this change of meaning. Thus this god walks around the city:

> to proclaim his teaching is for him the one and only necessity of his life, is for him his food and drink. To teach people is his work, and to be concerned about the learners is for him relaxation from his work. He has no friends and no relatives, but to him the learner is brother and sister. (1985, 57)

But this decisive moment is not factual; it is not dependent upon being an eyewitness to these events. There is a historical point of departure for the eternal and for the decisive learning, but it is not empirical. The follower 'at second-hand' (1985, 58) is no worse off than the eye witness, for the historical event interests the eye witness 'otherwise than merely historically' (1985, 58). Indeed, the historical is really inconsequential, for even if the historical event is demolished, 'if only the moment still remains as the point of departure for the eternal, the paradox is still present' (1985, 59). Put differently, the historical is only recollection, not repetition. Even the thesis of the death of God must be claimed to be empirical, for if it is eternal—as in Nietzsche— then the eternity of the death speaks of the logic of presupposition, of the paradox, and requires, or is, faith. Kierkegaard, and Nietzsche as Zarathustra, are together in that, what knowledge cannot have, but what faith and education can have as the object, is 'this absurdity that the eternal is historical' (1985, 62). In education as faith, as in education as the eternal return of will-to-power, the teacher, as also the learner, is 'eternally occupied with the historical existence' (1985, 62). The name of the unknown is God, but the naming of the condition of the naming is God and man, or is education.

The Dreadful Religious Teacher

We saw above that Climacus and Cuttlebone remain unconvinced that their tutors had learned to live in and with the doubts they taught to others, or that they understood themselves in existence, or existed in what they understood. If this is the case, then the teacher here is dreadful, or religious, but not both.

The Dreadful Teacher

Of the awareness that we have been reflecting on—as dread, as absurdity, or as the new contradiction—'whether one is offended [by them] or whether one believes [in them], the advantage is to become aware' (1985, 93). If one becomes aware only Socratically, one remains only with the Socratic. This is seen to be only a mourning of education carried in the recollection of truth as past and lost. But if one becomes aware of the Socratic as the logic of KT, as an inward truth of subjectivity, then this begins an education regarding the mourning of education and an awareness of learning as a moment of decisive significance. To those offended by more than the Socratic, or by more than the negative, such talk is dismissed as irrational, mystical, supernatural. But as Kierkegaard points out, and as we saw above, the offense owes its own existence to this same awareness of the absolute paradox. Everything it has learned about the paradox it has learned from the paradox. Here offense is the stance of the dreadful teacher who is not religious, who negates but is not also able to preserve the negation as education in its own right. Without preservation, the dread of this dreadful teacher is unaccountable. It is that kind of Socratic teacher who undermines and then leaves, enjoying the thrill of the chase but not staying around to see how to exist in what one understands. In Kierkegaard's world, such a dreadful teacher is the aesthete, the seducer.

Perhaps there is also another example of this dreadful teacher, one who signs a pact with dread, enabling the teacher to teach for dread, for anxiety, and to be the dreadful teacher discharged from any responsibility for the mediation of possibility in the actuality of social and political relations, and able to posit dread as one's *ownmost* being without its contingency within ownership *per se*. Here, pure possibility, or pure being, is seen as pure dread and is granted immunity from mediation in or contingency upon the 'event' that is recollection and repetition, or from living according to what one learns and understands of one's own educative actuality. When dread is relieved of the educational logic by which it comes into existence as the fault of the mind that knows it, then dread is left free to claim itself as its own(most) future. This dreadful teacher is not just negative without preservation; he is also possibility without mediation, and that means that dread is free to become its own present, justified only by the tautological claim that it is also its own future, that it is both being and time.

Another criticism of Socratic recollection is that it rules out the new and looks weak against a theory of being that is its ownmost future of possibility. But Kierkegaard's logic of positing does have a notion of the future and of the new, in which neither are immune from their truth in learning. The future is an *educational* truth, because, against all appearances to the contrary, it is grounded in a logic of presupposition. The future has its own historical point of departure, and as such is presupposed in order for it to be claimed as the possibility of not being knowable in advance. It is recollected to be repeatable as its own possibility.[18] Here, the logic of education redefines the concept of the new. Every repetition of recollection is new, or else learning makes no difference. This is not just dreadful, it is also religious, for when learning makes a difference, it is the difference, the new, that is found in the awareness that the new so comes into the world that by the fact that it is, it is presupposed. Redefined within the logic of positing, the challenge for the new is to KT.

It is the case then that the dreadful teacher who is not also religious is the teacher who refuses a logic of education in the Socratic paradox, or differently, who refuses even Socratic significance to pure being and pure time. Both chase the instant, both lay claim to what is perceived as lying nearest, and both, in different ways, fall back on pure dread for the authenticity and legitimacy of their teaching. Both suppress the religious, but for Kierkegaard this is a religious repression of religion because what one has learned about the paradox one has learned from the paradox. In this way, the dreadful teacher who is not religious is also the dreadful teacher who is religious in being offended by religion.

The Religious Teacher

As the logic of KT draws religion out of the dreadful teacher, so too it draws the dreadful out of the religious teacher. What characterizes the religious teacher and religious education that are not also dreadful is that they are not Socratic enough, not sufficiently committed to the dread of freedom, or to the angst of self-consciousness. The religious teacher believes he has the gift of truth and that this truth can be given to the student, and received by the student, often provided that the conditions for giving and receiving are sufficiently severe to brook no resistance (missing the fact that the resistance is seldom overcome, just displaced to less visible arenas). This religious teacher takes for granted the commensurability of the gift and its mode of communication. But Kierkegaard stresses their incommensurability. In thinking, one thinks the universal, but in learning to live in what one understands, one 'becomes more and more subjectively isolated' (Kierkegaard, 1968, 68). This is the 'double reflection' (1968, 68) that is ignored or suppressed by the religious teacher who is not also dreadful. If the religious teacher teaches truth directly as an ordinary communication between teacher and student, then this teacher does not see that this 'may be the grossest kind of misunderstanding' (1968, 69) of truth and of the teaching of truth.

What this religious teacher does not see is that truth is accompanied by resistance, and that the subjective life is one's trying to live in what one understands of this truth and resistance. Therefore, existing in what one understands cannot be directly communicated. If it is, it not only misunderstands truth, it is 'an attempt to defraud God . . . [and] an attempt to defraud the recipient of the communication' (1968, 69). In short, 'the negative factor in the communication is not reflected upon' (1968, 70) by the religious teacher who is not also dreadful, leaving open the severity of an education that deems itself objective, with all the accompanying abuses that it therein justifies to itself. As such, the direct communication of the religious teacher who is not also dreadful, *is* dreadful.

The Dreadful Religious Teacher

How then does the dreadful religious teacher understand herself in existence and exist in what she understands? How is this teacher *education: KT*?

She exists in the template of educational logic by understanding the downfall of communication in-itself or direct communication, and the downfall of this understanding when it is seen as explanation and resolution. She is the living understanding of the template of educational being, lived as the absolute paradox of the recollection and repetition of the teacher. This dreadful religious teacher, in the absolute paradox of educational logic, of the logic of positing, and of the logic of KT, knows that education is not dread presupposing itself, but that dread is education presupposing itself; and knows too that education is not religion presupposing itself but that religion is education presupposing itself. She knows that education, presupposing itself, and by the fact that it is repeated, is a new recollection of presupposition. She knows this to be the logic of *learning*. This teacher is different even from those teachers who deceive by appearing to reject the logic of explanation and resolution. These teachers merely employ this logic to resolve the aporetic logic of the beginning. In deferring the actual, they are not existing in the understanding of the aporia. It is the dreadful religious teacher who understands how to exist as a teacher in what she understands about the logic of presupposition. She is accountable to the absurdity of this logic and her dread is never pure.

Kierkegaard addresses this directly. Sin conquers and 'dread throws itself despairingly into the arms of remorse' (Kierkegaard, 1967, 103). To avoid this despair one can reject the religious, reject the logic of presupposition, and retreat to the fantasy of pure possibility that is unsullied by the logic of presupposition. But this is merely a dreadful resignation appearing as hope and optimism and potential. Against this,

> The one and only thing which is able to disarm the sophistry of remorse is faith, courage to believe that the state of sin is itself a new sin, courage to renounce dread without any dread, which only faith is capable of— not that it annihilates dread, but remaining ever young, it is continually developing itself out of the death throe of dread. Only faith is capable of doing this, for only in faith is the synthesis eternally and every instant possible. (1967, 104)

This is faith in education and is the teacher existing in what she understands.

As such, the self-consciousness of the dreadful religious teacher 'is a deed, and this deed in turn is inwardness' (1967, 128). KT here is the leap of NN into subjectivity, into KT as the logic of its own presupposition. Repetition 'is the seriousness of existence' (1967, 133n). The object of this seriousness is the individual itself. The individual has to take itself seriously because if 'inwardness is lacking, the spirit is finitized. Inwardness is therefore eternity, or the determinant of the eternal in a man' (1967, 134).

The dreadful religious teacher exists in what she understands. What she understands is that the logic of presupposition, of recollection and repetition, is dreadful. It is dreadful because dread is the present condition of the qualitative leap into a different logic. This logic turns the logic of recollection into the logic of sin, such that recollection is now known in the profound consistency of recollecting presupposing (repeating) itself, that it so came into the world that by the fact that it is presupposed. Recollection learns that this presupposition is its own fault. This is the decisive moment of eternity in history, of the qualitative leap, of the education that makes the transition from ordinary logic to the logic of presupposition. It is where secular reason makes its qualitative rational leap into reason, as spirit. But it *is* rational because it is what reason does to itself. It is its only truly rational act. All the rest is just mastery.

What is the practice of this dreadful religious teacher? The practice is Socratic, for doubt is the work of resistance; thereafter the practice is absurd, for absurdity is the logic of the paradox that does not remain with the Socratic. What, then, of Climacus's and Cuttlebone's suspicions regarding the logic and existence of their teachers? Let us suppose that their tutors knew of the Socratic and of the decisive moment. Would they not appear to be exactly as Climacus and Cuttlebone have presented them? Would they not look directly Socratic, or directly dialectical, and indirectly nothing else? Would not the indirect communication look like non-communication, and would that not look like the betrayal, which, to the ordinary logic, precisely is a betrayal? Did the tutors ever care for their students and for their futures? Perhaps that was always what they cared about most.

Remember too that Climacus had intimated what the decisive moment of learning might mean for the students and their teachers. For the thesis that everything must be doubted to have decisive significance, the teacher too must be doubted, negated, sacrificed, by the student. The tutors must expect this. If they become a target for the sin that is the student's own fault, then so be it. They cannot complain at that. But they can be patient, while the decisive moment learns of itself, of its own work, learns to KT, and learns that the teacher cannot give the answers that the students demand, and demand more urgently the more decisive is the moment of self-retrieval in dread.

Such is the educational logic and truth of the dreadful religious teacher. This logic suggests that philosophy can no more teach truth directly than religion can teach God directly. It suggests that perhaps only the dreadful religious teacher can teach truth and god, because truth and God are the logic of education, expressed in the qualitative leap, and in the moment, the recollection and repetition, of decisive significance. Without this education, the educator is only dreadful, using dread directly and expecting dread to be its own education; or the educator is only religious, using truth objectively and expecting the student to understand this objectivity as discipline and obedience. Dread and religion are truths that speak of and within the logic of presupposition. Faith is the repetition of this logic. The work of the dreadful religious teacher concerns the understanding of the knowing of the unknown, and teaching this as *living understanding*. As Kierkegaard says, we call the unknown 'god', and as Cuttlebone says, to leave this unattended is merely confusion and despair.

Notes

1. *Faust* I. 361–5.
2. Keats, *Ode to a Nightingale*.
3. And of course, Rousseau's pupil is male; his female companion arrives in the final book, and her education is the opposite to Emile's.
4. See Tubbs (2005, Chapter 11).
5. Italics added.
6. Written under the pseudonym of Vigilius Haufniensis, the Watchman of Copenhagen (Rose, 1992, 89). Hereafter shortened to CD.
7. At the beginning of his Introduction, Haufniensis says that if Hegel's logic ends with 'actuality' then this is neither logical nor actual. If it is logical it cannot contain contingency, and if it does not contain contingency, it is not actual. In fact, Hegel's logic ends as it begins, with the logic of presupposition.
8. See Kierkegaard (1938, 127) and below n10.
9. I am not discussing Kierkegaard's reading of Hegel here. Indeed, one biographer has noted that 'his knowledge of Hegel remained superficial . . . [reading only] some of Hegel's Danish and German disciples and . . . a series of second-rank speculative theists' (Thompson, 1974, 57). If their Hegelianism is as Kierkegaard describes, then it is little surprise that Kierkegaard's critical comments on Hegel can be read to be as supportive of Hegel as they are critical of Hegelianism. Specifically, perhaps, Kierkegaard criticizes the idea that the system is complete, or will be 'by next Sunday' (Kierkegaard, 1968, 97) or

that 'the age of distinctions is past and gone, the system has overcome it' (front quotation, *The Concept Of Dread*), a completion that might be claimed by Hegelians but not by Hegel himself (see Stewart, 2003, for the 'standard view' of Kierkegaard's relation to Hegel. Stewart's own review of there being three stages of Kierkegaard's relation to Hegel is summarised in his book on pp. 33–4). In *Concluding Unscientific Postscript* Climacus reads Hegel and logical systems according to a logic of mastery, and refuses Hegel a logic of education by stating that 'logic cannot explain movement' (Kierkegaard, 1992, 110). However, when he says in *Christian Discourses* that 'There is only one who completely knows himself . . . —that is God' (Kierkegaard, 1997, 40), 'completely' here includes the self-knowing of those lowly Christians who are in themselves by being before and for God.

10. Again, as Kierkegaard understands Hegelian mediation.
11. See above, Chapter 1, p. 28 note 67.
12. Dread is Lowrie's translation of the Danish *Angest*. Rheidar Thomte translates it as 'anxiety' (Kierkegaard, 1980).
13. Kierkegaard (1983, 34).
14. See also *Either/Or II* where Kierkegaard, as Judge William, offers 'choose oneself' over KT (Kierkegaard, 1987, 258).
15. Hereafter PF, written under the pseudonym Johannes Climacus.
16. Kierkegaard writes of a similar experience during his trip to Gilleleie in August 1835 where the screech of gulls dissolves his reverie (Kierkegaard, 1938, 12).
17. *Concluding Unscientific Postscript.*
18. In his journal entry of September 10, 1839, Kierkegaard says that it only by facing the past that one can see what lies ahead (Kierkegaard, 1938, 80).

9 The Educational Concept of Monotheism

'If you try to be the lone wolf, all the packs will unite against you.'
—Nathan the Wise

Can there be an educational concept of monotheism? Can there be a logic of education within the experience of the mastery of the One? If there can, then might this educational logic be the modern metaphysical rationality of each of the three Abrahamic faiths, and a rationality that they share? In our selected examples now, *eternity* in Judaism, *history* or the *historical event* in Christianity, and the *angel of revelation* or *intuition* in Islam, will be seen to carry this rationality. In Part 1 above we have presented KT in the three religions historically, but in this final chapter, we present them conceptually. This is not to impose thought, but rather to expose its work. It is to put Islam, Judaism, and Christianity together at the same time as holding them apart.

As we have seen throughout our study, the rationality of the logic of mastery collapses into its internal crisis of authority, unable to solve the aporias that are unavoidably generated when mastery has to defend its presupposition of itself. Each of the three religions shares the logic of mastery, and each therefore shares the internal contradictions that are created in positing its own authority. The rationality of mastery is used as the solution to these contradictions, seeking mastery over the contradictions of mastery. The stakes are high, for the credibility of the religions is seen to rest on the ability to overcome these perceived weaknesses. Wars are fought in the name of such credibility and in defending different cultural shapes of the rationality and mastery of the One.

In the following chapter, we will explore the aporia of mastery in Judaism through Franz Rosenzweig, in Christianity through Hegel, and in Islam through a combination of Henry Corbin's version of Oriental philosophy and Mohammed al-Jabri's notion of Islamic historicism.[1] In looking at how the collapse of the logic of mastery into aporia is negotiated by these philosophers, we see the form of rationality that works as the logic of education. Just as the logic of mastery is shared by the three religions, so too is the logic of education. The challenge to each of them is the challenge of KT, and not just in the aporia of their own mastery, but also in relation to the same aporias in the other monotheistic faiths.

In the work now undertaken in this chapter, we will see how, in Christianity, in Hegel, reason as mastery collapses into the logic of education as *necessity*, and that this necessity re-forms both history and recollection within the logic of KT; how in Islam, in Corbin and al-Jabri, reason as mastery collapses into education as a *historicist phenomenology* and re-forms revelation within the logic of KT; and how in Rosenzweig, reason as mastery collapses into education as the *life and the way*, and re-forms eternity within the logic of KT. None of these thinkers extend educational relations to both of the other two faiths. But we will do so, suggesting that this shared rationality is the *educational* concept of monotheism found within the aporias of the logic of mastery upon which monotheism is grounded. This rationality is the educational vocation of *monotheism: KT*. But above all, and perhaps most controversially, the work of educational reason is only comprehensively stated in the educational concept of monotheism when all three religions are also found in each other, for example, as Christian Islamic Judaism, or Islamic Judaic Christianity, etc.

Christianity as History

Hegel will be our representative of modern educational reason in the European tradition in general, and in the Christian tradition of the West in particular. No doubt Hegel looks to be a controversial choice. In his philosophy of history, the Eastern religions are deemed to have remained immersed in nature while the Greek spirit emerged into the freedom of thinking and self-consciousness. Judaism, at least in his early essays on Christianity, is seen as a 'mechanical slavery' (Hegel, 1992, 69). In turn, Henry Corbin believes Hegel opens up the catastrophe of agnosticism with a form of reason that closes down routes to the beyond; and Rosenzweig sees in Hegel the final resolution of the debate between knowledge and faith, in favor of the former. But it is a different Hegel that we will work with, specifically from the 1829 lectures on the proofs concerning the existence of God. These are mature reflections in which Hegel is able to work with important aspects of the philosophy he developed over the previous forty years. Specifically we will see that his notion of reason is not merely secular and that he is able to negate and preserve an educational relation between knowing God rationally and the immediacy of faith and the beyond of eternity.

Recollection

Alongside the proofs of God, Hegel unfolds Western Christianity within the philosophy of history, and in particular regarding the central role played by recollection. This is often seen as Hegel's most conservative element.

Philosophy, he says, always comes on the scene too late to tell the world what it ought to do. The owl of Minerva, perhaps at the end of history, flies at dusk to recollect the philosophy of history, or its overall and comprehensive meaning. Knowledge here is always after the event, and the event never knows itself more fully than in the standpoint from which it is recollected. This comprehensive view comes from historical distance and not from immediate involvement. As such, in the educational concept of monotheism, Hegel represents Western Christian rationality and truth as history or recollection.

However, we will see in a moment that God, as the recollected event of his own self-consciousness, is seen by Hegel as containing formative ambiguities pertaining to self-mediation that deny a view of history as providing either a static event or a fixed and final knowledge of that event. Recollection is an activity that has its truth in the educational logic of positing or presupposition. Moreover, in knowing itself as the event of such knowing, recollection recollects itself. For ancient logic this opens up the chaos of infinite regression of recollection of recollection of recollection . . . For the educational logic of modern metaphysics, this has truth in the repetition of recollection, or in the self-negating and self-preserving of recollection as *repetition*.[2] Here the logic of positing is its own education, its own KT. Recollection so came into the world that by the fact that it is, it is presupposed.[3] This positing is its repetition and is already a condition of the possibility of recollection. That this is the fault of thought is thought's education about its own logic of positing being also its own truth, its KT. Recollection cannot be a simple reproduction of history or knowledge because it is already its own repetition, preserved as changed, and changed as preserved. There is no privileged standpoint for recollection such that it could survey history, or itself as knowledge, free from the logic of its own negation and preservation, or as we will come to see, its own immediacy and mediation. Nevertheless, Hegel understood that the domination of abstraction in Western Christianity meant that this logic would be understood one-sidedly as just another domination. It is for modern metaphysics to herald the aporetic experiences of abstraction and mediation as self-mediation in and through otherness, just as Hegel's proofs of the existence of God try to do.

The Warm Feeling of Religion

Unlike pantheism or the philosophies of substantiality,[4] Hegel's proof of God is specifically in the form of NN: KT. He argues that the knowledge humanity has of God, and that God has of humanity, 'is God's self-consciousness' (2011, 126) or God's knowing of himself in otherness. NN here becomes the KT of humanity and God, a 'unity' which has its truth precisely where one might least expect it—in the difference within unity. Where Plotinus says that God absolutely cannot have self-consciousness, for that would imply division and change, Hegel argues for God as contingent upon the necessity of self-knowing.

When faith and knowledge, representing immediacy and mediation, diverge and become separated from each other, this bequeaths the 'warm feeling of religion' (2011, 38), unknowable in thought and unprovable in reason. This abstraction sets thinking on one side and truth on the other. Subjectivity posits itself by positing thought as *error*. This is a modern version of keeping NN free from merely human KT. Facing the aporia of the immediacy of NN and the mediation of KT, subjectivity turns to feeling, to inwardness, as a way of feeling (knowing) the unknowability of God. This is why such feeling calls for faith.

Hegel takes a radically different approach here, one which he calls *speculative* and which yields a different (modern metaphysical) notion of unity. 'There is no knowledge, any more than there is any sensation, representation, and volition, or any activity, property, or condition pertaining to spirit that is not mediating and mediated' (2011, 53).[5] Faith both accepts this universality of mediation and posits it as error in relation to truth. Hegel holds this universality and the error to be truth in relation to itself. In his speculative notion of philosophy truth 'is such a power that it is present even in what is false' (2011, 115).

Mediation does not simply overcome or eradicate immediacy or faith. Immediacy is that 'through which mediation is at once posited' (2011, 54). Immediacy is being, or being able to say that something is. But this is to say very little about it. Everything that *is* has being attached to it, but this immediate certainty is not the truth of the existent. In lacking externality, it has no way of being true in the world, and ultimately is unsatisfactory for the religious self. This dissatisfaction can take shape as the beautiful soul, a yearning, a narrowness of heart, and a hollowness of sorrow, suffering, and despair. The need for truth to have external as well as internal truth requires such subjectivity to surrender itself to the very world that the beautiful soul rejects. But as this immediacy yields to mediation in and by otherness, so too mediation is reminded of its dependence upon what is posited as immediate.

Necessity

This same relation of immediacy and mediation is rehearsed by Hegel as contingency and necessity, and as finite and infinite. The contingent is finite, having no necessity within itself that could make it essential to anything else. As such, its being or not-being is indifferent to the truth of anything or anyone else. This indifference to the other is the bourgeois notion of freedom and independence. But it is an illusory indifference. The independence of finite contingency is already compromised by its presupposition as a social relation, and therefore by its already posited relation to the universal. The necessity of the collision of the in-itself and for-another is the actuality of presupposition as the social relation. As such, independence and mediation 'belong to the one necessity' (2011, 106).[6]

But what kind of necessity is it in which two things contradict each other and fall apart from each other, yet remain in a 'unity'? For Hegel, just as the necessity of truth is found in what is false, so truth is found in this necessity of self-opposition. This is the logic of the speculative in Hegel, where truth is preserved in its negative relation to itself because, as its own necessity, it is a 'mediation with another *within itself*' (2011, 106). This process is sublation or *Aufheben*. To the abstract understanding, this is an illegitimate boast by the speculative to be the whole of what is happening. It looks like an imperialism over and against its others. But otherness to or (in)difference from truth is part of the necessity by which independence—including imperialism—is already compromised. Otherness is as much an independence from, as it is a relation to, its other. Necessity here is the whole of this relation, for necessity is this self-relating by means of otherness. Necessity is (its immediate being) in the mediating of itself as its own truth. Here is the speculative rather than the abstract notion of unity. 'In the mediation with the *other* it relates itself to itself' (2011, 106). Speculative unity is abstraction and return; 'neither of the determinate qualities [alone] is sufficient for necessity. Rather, both are required' (2011, 106). As this modern metaphysical process is education, so *learning* is the truth—the logic of negation and preservation, or of KT—of this experience of necessity.

Proof of God's Existence

Hegel proceeds to demonstrate this necessity as the logic and metaphysics of the modern proof of God's existence. It is here we see that his idea of reason is not merely secular, but able to hold revelation and eternity within it. Very often says Hegel, 'absolute' means 'nothing more than abstract' (2011, 107). But necessity has the abstract as one of its necessary elements. This abstraction of itself from itself, or what might be taken as its external aspect,

> is contained in itself in such a way that this very dependence on itself, the identity or reference to self that constitutes the isolation of things in virtue of which they are *contingent*, is an independence that is really a lack of independence. (2011, 107)

Here, 'identity is characterized as what it truly is, as a need' (2011, 108). Spirit enacts this necessity in thought, which elevates thought to both the being and the thinking of God, the proof *that* God is and the knowledge of *what* God is. There is a sadness here, but it is a logic of tears, for sadness is necessity become its own truth. Its tears are the 'empty solitude of self-consciousness with itself' (2011, 110) learning to KT as determinate content, as freedom's own necessity.

Necessity, as *Aufheben*, is self-mediation in an other, and is the 'religious path of the elevation in humanity to God' (2011, 111). The significance is not that a double world is represented here, but rather 'the value attached to such a representation' (2011, 115). On the one side is the world of illusory being (*Schein*) and on the other the eternal world. But for the religious mind, finding the whole to be the logic of KT, and knowing illusory being to be a necessary positing of this necessity, this is the logic of God knowing himself. This is how Hegel is able to argue that this self-mediating necessity is 'God's self-consciousness' (2011, 126) or God's spirit. '[H]umanity knows God only insofar as God knows godself in humanity' (2011, 126). In modern metaphysics as we have conceived it, this logic of self-mediation is the logic of education, in which learning is the truth that is negated and preserved. God and man are the educational necessity of NN: KT.

Christianity

The educational logic of Christianity displayed by Hegel here sees him preserve revelation even as it is negated by mediation, or is known and recollected as the historical event of Jesus. Revelation is the immediacy of being that seeks content, or seeks to understand what it is a revelation of. This immediacy or this beginning is necessity posited as the *question* of the beginning. The question is not just the question of the content. It is also the question as the form of the beginning, or of immediacy forming itself in its own mediation. To the logic of mastery there is no mastery here, and so attempts are made to resolve this problem by imposing identity and ineffability. But in the logic of education the otherness to itself of revelation in mediation is the truth in the false.

This is true also of the eternal and the finite. For the abstract consciousness beholden to the logic of mastery, the finite is on one side and the infinite on the other, and the two remain incompatible (ignoring the way in which truth is present even in the false). Here 'the infinite is thought of as the true, the *only* affirmative . . . [and the] finite, *in order to be*, must keep away from the infinite, must flee from it' (2011, 122). However, as we saw above, the speculative notion of self-mediation occupies itself with the finite in a true way 'insofar as the finite is not taken for itself but is known, recognized, and engaged in *its connection to the infinite*, the infinite within it' (2011, 123). The finite cannot be known without 'the quality of non-being that resides in passing away' (2011, 125). Even to say that the finite *is, now*, shows that by putting it into words 'it no longer exists but is something other' (2011, 125). In the logic of mastery, the negation of the 'now' is recollection or historical knowledge. But in the speculative, or in the educating logic of self and other, the finite endures 'precisely as the negation of this "now", as the negation of the finite, and thus as infinite, as universal' (2011, 125), or as God's self-consciousness.

In sum, in the educational concept of monotheism, Hegel represents Christianity as the loss and preservation of revelation and the eternal to their being known in and by a reason that is not merely secular and a logic that is not merely mastery. Reason, or thinking spirit, holds revelation and eternity while knowing them mediately and finitely. The passing of the now of revelation, or the beyond of eternity, into knowledge or into history, is not their eradication or their being overcome. It is their preservation. In the repetition and recollection of revelation and history, of God and man, the educational truth of Christianity is in the educational logic of KT.

Islam as the Angel of Revelation/Intuition

In the modern metaphysics of educational logic Islam can be presented as bearing the angel of revelation, or intuition, in its relation to God as eternal and to man as the strangeness of matter. This contestation is the logic of KT within Islam, as it is of the relation of Islam to Christianity and Judaism in the educational concept of monotheism as a whole.

Immediate mediation and mediated immediacy—and the contradictions here are both deliberate and formative of KT overall—will be explored in Henry Corbin's interpretation of Oriental philosophy through hermeneutics and comparative philosophy, and in Mohammed al-Jabri's historicist and rational Islam. It is important to bear in mind here that within the educational concept of monotheism, Islam is another rational culture of the ancient logic of harmony and mastery, and that as such its aporetic experiences are of the same logic of monotheism as Christianity and Judaism. In this sense a notion such as emanation need not be judged simply as irrational, for as we saw in Part 1, it too had its rationality within the logic of the One and its aporetic relation to the many.

Corbin and Oriental Philosophy

For Corbin the Neoplatonism of Islamic philosophy made it receptive to the theosophy of ancient pre-Islamic Persia. This plays its part in defining the relation between God and man in conceptions of immediate mediation, such as intuition, illumination, radiation, and emanation, which do not pass through the senses and do not separate subject and object.

In al-Farabi's cosmos, the divine essences become distinctive intelligences. For Avicenna these are angels. The angel closest to man is the active intelligence. It is called the lover of forms because 'it radiates forms into matter, and radiates into the human potential intellect the knowledge of these forms' (Corbin, 2006, 162). The reception of the knowledge of forms is achieved through 'intuition and illumination' (2006, 162) with no need for an intermediary. Herein lies the path for prophetic inspiration. Key to this immediacy is the imagination, for as Corbin says, 'Shi'ite prophetic philosophy gave rise to an entire theory of the Imagination, which vindicated imaginative knowledge and the world perceived by such knowledge' (2006, 164). Against al-Ghazali's later suspicions that such angels are not those found in the Qur'an, Corbin holds that the active intelligence here is identified with the Muhammadan archangel Gabriel, the Holy Spirit.

Avicenna designated his own Neoplatonic Aristotelianism as Oriental philosophy, and Corbin finds here the development of 'a phenomenology of angelic awareness or consciousness' (2006, 171). The motions of the spheres are produced by the desire of each intelligence for that intelligence which is their origin, a desire that is never assuaged. This is the Oriental version, the immediately mediated version, of the beginning being known as the question of beginning, but as we will see, in this version of the rationality of mastery, there is no intention to separate the whole into subject and object. The tenth intelligence is the active intelligence in whom emanation is exhausted and from whom human souls emanate, and to whom it projects forms of knowledge if those souls are turned toward it and are ready to receive. The moments where the Western rationality of mastery would insist on separation of subject and object are dealt with here in an Oriental rationality of mastery as different shades of a continuity. Mediation of light is shadow, and not therefore 'other'. The desire to return to the archangel is at first an exile known as darkness. The material universe is not the creation of something other to it, but is exhaustion. The darkness is also a sadness, but sadness is a character of the continuity of emanation as intellect learns of itself moving further away from its source.

Corbin also rehearses the nature of immediacy in the theophanic against dialectical mediation, and in his own notion of speculative theology. Both concern the question of how to gain access to God. In the theophanic, it is not the isolated I or ego-self that has access. 'God is never an object; he can be known only through himself as an absolute Subject, absolved of all false objectivity' (2006, 257). This is the logical version of *NN:KT* in the esoteric rationality of mastery. 'The divine Subject is in fact the active subject of all knowledge of God. It is God who thinks himself in the thought that the human intellect has of him' (2006, 257). The immediacy of this 'relation' is therefore not dialectical but imperative—the imperative of God to KT as NN in that which thinks him. The rationality of the One in this logic of mastery tries to hold that the Angel enacts mediation, even if what it mediates are not 'separate'. This 'spontaneity' of angelic 'mediation' is speculative according to the idea of speculum or mirror within esotericism. The mirror reflects God but as epiphany, not incarnation. The mirror is the inner man wherein the theophany takes place, i.e., the face of God revealed to man, and the face that man displays to God. This speculative imperative—*NN:KT*—is the immediacy and spontaneity of God knowing himself in man knowing God. It is the esoteric rationality of the logic of mastery here that protects the One from rational inconsistency.

There is a nuance here within Corbin's esoteric version of the logic of mastery. He records that it was Heideggerian hermeneutics that opened up for him the vision of Iranian Shi'ite metaphysics against the Western canon of individual rational self-consciousness.[7] But Heideggerian philosophy is another version of the logic of mastery, one that perhaps contributes to Corbin not seeking a different logic in the educational themes he pursues.

What draws Corbin to Heidegger is the immediacy of Being enjoying mastery over mediation by thinking.[8] In his commitment to a 'spiritual communion between the three branches of the Abrahamic community' (2006, 255), Corbin states that all three religions have practised hermeneutics as 'a spontaneous exegesis' (Corbin, 1976).[9] This involves the unveiling or revelation of that 'which is happening within us' (1976). This spontaneity is *esto*, or the imperative 'Be!' (or Be!ing.[10]) Like Islamic *ta'wil* hermeneutics is an act of presence, or presencing, linking past, present, and future and is the space called the Orient, the dawning light that reveals all presence but is not found in maps and needs no intermediary of representation. This is in contrast to the owl of Minerva in Hegel, who flies at dusk, as history, representing the Occident, which is only decline, the setting of the sun, and an exile from the light of presence (and which includes Heidegger, who, says Corbin, does not herald a beyond). This is a pagan world in relation to the rationality of the logic of mastery in esotericism, holding to a vision of the One with everything, and to the universe of the angels which is 'an eternal universe of the existent' (1976).

In positing this form of the rationality of the mastery of the One against the form of mastery that Corbin found in Hegel, he believes that the moment for reconciliation between East and West, or between the *Ahl al-Kitab*, the people of the 'community of the Book' (Corbin, 1981, 29) is lost. There was a moment, he says, for example in the 12th century, 'when Avicenna was translated into Latin, in Toledo, a moment when our cultures in East and West corresponded to the same type, a moment when the concept of science was inseparable from its spiritual content' (1981, 26–7). In this spirit Corbin unfolds his conception of comparative philosophy, which opposes secularization in the West and Westernization in the East. This comparative philosophy retrieves 'the intuitive perception of an essence' (1981, 4) through the phenomenology in which the invisible beneath the visible is revealed.

He is clear that this is not Hegelian phenomenology or philosophy. Hegel, he says, bequeathed an historicism without hope.[11] Right-wing Hegelianism held to the speculative, but it did not prevail. Instead, in absolute spirit the mission of history has been accomplished. History continues, of course, but now with no orientation; it no longer knows what it is doing. It has become mad. Instead, contrast the absolute spirit with the 'figure of the Holy Spirit whom our traditional philosophers identify with their Active Intelligence and who is the Angel of Humanity, at once the Angel of Understanding and the Angel of Revelation' (1981, 8). The angel stands against the historicism of Hegel, just as the Oriental stands opposed to geography, and internal consciousness stands distinguished from external events.

> The acts of understanding, the bringing forth of the cognitive forms of the active power by this Holy Spirit Angel, have also as their seat this humanity whose Angel he is. But this Holy Spirit is not the Absolute Spirit in Hegel's sense. (1981, 8)

This rift between East and West, says Corbin, is a 'catastrophe' (1981, 9), for not only does Western thinking intoxicate humanity with regard to its own status in the universe, it also leaves humanity without hope, without the possibility of reorienting itself back to the 'simultaneous inspiration' (1981, 9) of both philosophers and prophets ready to receive the angel of revelation. This is a loss of the sense of the eschatological, no longer able to 'open the gates onto a future that flows out beyond this world' (1981, 9), knowing at the same time that 'it is we ourselves who have closed these gates against ourselves' (1981, 9).

Al-Jabri (1935–2010) and Historicism

This logic of mastery in Oriental philosophy has been challenged by a different form of the logic of mastery in Islam, a different kind of rationality, but one still trying to negotiate between the immediacy of intuition and the historicism of hermeneutics. Corbin believes that the immediacy of angelic intellectual substance sealed the fate of Avicennism in the West, denying as it did the need for the earthly Magisterium as mediator between God and man. The West preferred a Latin Averroism, which argued for forms being potential in matter and not therefore placed in matter by the angel. In rejecting the hierarchical procession of emanation Averroes more or less destroyed the *nus poietikos*, the active intellect. In the East, however, Avicennism spelled the end of Aristotelianism, replaced by Orientalism; a theophanic esotericism, gnostic, Shi'ite and Ismaili, 'which was to dominate the universe of Islamic thought down to the present day' (Corbin, 2006, 253).

Against Corbin, Mohammed al-Jabri has argued that the future of Arab-Islamic culture can only be Averroist. This is because the future needs a different past than that which dominates present Arab-Islamic culture. Or to put it another way, one requires to understand how fundamentalism permeates 'the whole of contemporary Arab thinking' (al-Jabri, 1999, 17). This fundamentalism is sometimes a defensive position adopted in response to the challenges of the modern Western world. It invites the vision that a once-great authentic and true Islamic civilization can be retrieved. This impels Al-Jabri to seek a modern Arab Renaissance, which will go beyond this understanding of tradition to establish a contemporary understanding of tradition. To this end, Al-Jabri rethinks the concept of history in Arab-Islamic culture. Time in the latter, he says, lacks development or progression, unlike European culture, which has progression built into it. Where Arab-Islamic time is static, European time is historicist, making it impossible for the past to replace the present, as happens in fundamentalism. This historicism reads the future through the past placed in the context of the present. In Arab-Islamic culture the present and the future are anachronistic to the past. The urgent task is 'rewriting Arab history and restoring its historicity' (al-Jabri, 2011, 46) in the cause of an Arab-Islamic single cultural time, which will sacrifice static time for a contemporary future.

This Renaissance cannot come from within the universalism of European modernity. Even while Arab culture draws inspiration from European modernity regarding the rationale and foundation of its own discourse, this European modernity can only 'engage Arab culture from the outside' (al-Jabri, 1999, 2), thus creating further withdrawal and confinement. The Arab Renaissance requires a modern Arab-Islamic method and 'a modern vision of tradition' (1999, 2), able to embody 'rationality and democracy' (1999, 4) against the medieval irrationality of the governor-governed relationships that reduce the latter to a herd living 'under the shepherd's staff' (1999, 6). This rationality, as we will see, tries to negotiate the authority and the mastery of the One by rejecting esotericism as irrational, preferring an Aristotelianism in which thought or reason can think about itself. This self-knowing is 'a supreme level of rational cognition' (al-Jabri, 2011, 11).

Al-Jabri discerns three versions of the logic of mastery in Islam: *bayan, irfan,* and *barhan. Bayan* is the logic of mastery as language, as the indigenous Arab-Islamic legacy of rhetorical explication and indication. It raises the question of whether the logic of a language, its expression of truth, is common to all languages and means the same, or whether all meanings are different because all utterances are different.[12] Within this question, *bayan* holds religiously sanctioned rationality in the science of syntax, jurisprudence, theology, and rhetoric, which all ground themselves in the Arabic language, and which work on 'analogising the unseen on the basis of what is in evidence' (2011, 415). When the unknown is the future, it is determined by the past by means of analogy, for example, the past taken as the known greatness of a civilization. However, analogy also enabled jurists to judge new cases on the basis of old cases. In turn these new cases became the ground of the next generation of cases, which simply accumulated analogies in an unending, infinite regression of polemics, an infinite regression of legitimizing the legitimizers. This procedure became purely mechanical as the lack of objectivity grew like a giant snowball.[13] The result is a timeless, static practice of the analogy of analogy,[14] 'never able to offer from tradition anything but a fundamentalist reading that treats the past as transcendental and sacral while seeking to extract from it ready-made solutions to the problems of the present and the future' (al-Jabri, 1999, 21).

Al-Jabri sees *irfan* as the irrationality of Sufi, Oriental, esoteric, gnostic, and illuminationist thinking, including Shi'ite thought, Ismaili philosophy, and esoteric exegesis of the Qur'an. He refers to it as reason resigning from ever knowing the truth, abandoned in favor of revelation through disclosure and communion through purification. In part, it was a response to the unsatisfactory mechanical nature of *bayan*. The most important influence here is Avicenna. His philosophy, says al-Jabri, was self-destructive because it held for reason only the ambition to resign in pursuit of truth. Al-Ghazali also adopted this resigned reason, leaving *bayan* only for the masses and claiming *irfan* for an elite, leaving a deep wound within Arab reason 'which is still bleeding' (al-Jabri, 2011, 361).

Both *bayan* and *irfan* reveal the respective forms of their rationality collapsing into the self-contradiction of the logic of their mastery; *bayan* collapses into a mastery that is mechanical (the religious reasonable), and *irfan* collapses into a mastery that is mystical (resigned reason). The contradiction within each is expressed by the opposition of the other. *Irfan* becomes elitist measured against the universality of language, while *bayan* sinks into infinite regression without the truth of revelation.

Barhan is a logic of mastery based on Aristotelian rationalism and came to contradict both *bayan* and *irfan*. It is an epistemological system grounded in demonstration, including logic, mathematics, and the various branches of the natural sciences. It invokes a 'methodology of experimental observation and reasonable deduction' (2011, 415) and against both the religious reasonable and resigned reason is 'the reasonable of the reason' (2011, 415). This became particularly strong in Andalusia, especially around Averroes but, says al-Jabri, 'left no trace in Arab culture' (2011, 416) thereafter. Arab science reached its apex at the beginning of the Era of Codification.[15] This closed the door to *ijtihad* or independent reasoning and interpretation. The science of dialectic declined into sophistry. *Barhan* was itself fixed until Averroes shattered its order by activating its internal contradictions, enabling the growth of science in the European Renaissance, while experimental science remained marginalized in Arab culture, leaving it with a renaissance yet to be achieved. Europe fared better because it ousted Gnosticism early on and rested on Greek universal reason. Where Europe flourished in this new rational spirit, it was subordinated in its infancy in the Arab world, resulting in the Age of Decline dominated by the resignation of reason. Arab science facilitated the European Renaissance but failed to find any midwife who could 'deliver it in the experience of Arab civilization' (2011, 435). Logic became formalism, analogy mere mechanism, and reason in general became habit while theology became stagnant. *Irfan* triumphed and this resignation, says al-Jabri, 'is still unabated' (2011, 409).

Against this failure to establish a logic of mastery of the One that is both rational and democratic, al-Jabri tries to establish a new Islamic form of rationality that is still consistent with the logic of the mastery of the One. He calls not for a break from tradition, but rather for a new and different kind of relationship to the beginning, a new form of mastery. If Corbin worked with mastery as immediate mediation, then al-Jabri can be seen to work with a mediated immediacy.

In the absence of historicity, and in static time, subject and object are held closely together in a relationship that cannot be critical of itself. What is required is for the subject and object to separate and rebuild this relationship 'on a new basis' (1999, 24). This is to disjoin (negate) Islamic history structurally, historically, and ideologically, in order to rejoin (preserve) Islamic history differently. The fixed immediacy here is mediated by reason but in such a way as to preserve continuity. This retrieves both objectivity and subjectivity, but not on the European model of the ego-centred I and its objects.

Using the language of textual analysis, al-Jabri argues that as things stand tradition absorbs the reader, depriving one of independence, freedom, and critique. The new relationship will be one that seeks to uncover in the tradition hidden significance and meaning. Here the subject regains a *dynamism* by trying to intuit the object. This intuition therefore does not have a static or fixed relationship to the object. Instead it can relate to an object while still preserving the latter's identity and objectivity. This is not any kind of mystical intuition or resigned reason. Rather, intuition has a hermeneutical and temporal logic that can reconceive the relation of the reader and the tradition. Of this logic al-Jabri says

> the future is what enables reading to imagine the past; what *was supposed to be* that enables reading to imagine what *was*. Hence the positiveness of what *was* blends in with the ideological of what *was supposed to be*, and the future-past to which the reader aspired becomes the future-to-come that the reading-self pursues. Hence, the read-object which is contemporary to itself becomes contemporary to the subject-reader. (1999, 31)

This is a logic of time in which imagination and intuition are integral, and it is a hermeneutical logic of time antithetical to the static Arab time of fundamentalism. The goal of reading Arab-Islamic philosophy, now, from al-Kindi to Averroes, is to become their contemporaries 'on the level of a spirit aware of its historicity' (1999, 32).

Al-Jabri, then, seeks to establish this form of Islamic rationality against mystical *Irfan*. He argues that Islam's original character was never Sufi, which was instead a Persian import. Sufism is absent from the Hadith. 'The Prophet was never a mystic' (1999, 124). 'The discourse of the Koran was one of reason and not one of "Gnosticism" or "illuminism"' (1999, 125). He advocates a 'reasonable rationalism' (1999, 125) of Averroistic realism against resigned reason. For him, it is Averroes who advocated and still makes possible a future for Arab-Islamic culture. The future, the survival of the Arab-Islamic philosophical tradition, 'can only be Averroist' (1999, 124), and against mysticism and revelation sees the renaissance of Arab-Islamic culture to lie in a reformed 'historical consciousness' (1999, 130).

Education Between the Two Logics of Mastery

Two logics of mastery compete here, which have the same aim: to protect the integrity, consistency, and continuity of the One. Corbin's is a logic of immediate mediation in the angelic phenomenology of emanation. Al-Jabri's is a logic of mediated immediacy in the dynamic intuitive disjoining and rejoining of subject and object within an historicism or historical consciousness. Both refuse the Western experience, which they see sacrificing intuitive hermeneutics to the self-determination of consciousness as an externalized principle of freedom, a freedom we have characterized as recollection and historical knowledge. Man's law here replaces God's law. The Orient as a whole does not trust merely secular reason, which laicizes the relation to truth, and the Occident does not trust the intuitive reason, which holds civil society and the state subservient to revelation, intuition, and prophetism. Put more simply, the Occident cannot find the external—a realm of freedom—in the Orient, and the Orient cannot find the internal—a realm of religiosity—in the Occident.

Within immediate mediation and mediated immediacy, the logic of mastery collapses. Each tries to master the collapse of the other for the sake of the One. Yet in trying to resolve the problems caused by the other, each does not see common cause in the educational logic that is within and between them. Immediacy and mediation are negated by each other, as sadness, or as disjoining, but also preserved in the other by return or historical consciousness. Judged only by the logic of mastery, each is incompatible with the other. Judged within the educational logic of learning as negation and preservation, their incompatibility is a shared logic of KT. If Western reason invokes here only its own logic of mastery to remind Islam that immediate mediation and mediated immediacy do not exhibit freedom because they do not separate into autonomous self-consciousness and its rational experience of objects, this is only another attempt to master the aporias for the sake of the coherence of the One, or of truth. Where Occident and Orient meet is in the collapse of the logic of mastery in each of them, commending itself as a shared logic of education taking different cultural forms. Monotheism within the logic of mastery resembles polytheism, for it has competing forms of mastery, of the One, at war with each other. Monotheism within the logic of education has one God shared in the differences by which it has its logic of KT in each of its cultural forms. This is an invitation to the education that lies within a notion of Islamic Christianity and a notion of Christian Islam.

Judaism as the Eternal

The educational logic of negation and preservation is displayed within Islam as it is between Islam and Christianity. But Islamic Christianity and Christian Islam is still an incomplete educational concept of monotheism. The self-mediation within and between these two aporetic religions is also mediated by the presence on earth of the eternal people. It is to the eternity of history and of dynamic intuition, or the angel, that we now turn our attention.

Franz Rosenzweig (1886–1929) is a philosopher of present eternity who, without naming it as such, again works with the educational logic of negation and preservation, and of KT in the recognition that the logic of mastery cannot sustain itself within its own rationality. This is illustrated in many ways. In 1920, for example, he writes of his collapse into the personal from historical forms and objectivity, or into the 'search for myself' (Rosenzweig, 1998, 95), descending into 'the vaults of my being' (1998, 95). By 1922 these vaults embody a degenerative sclerosis affecting the mastery of movement and speech. Nevertheless, his philosophy of present eternity sees him reject possibility and hope in the face of this illness, preferring real, often small experiences, and requiring patience. The eternal, he says, is not realized by simply negating the present, or by returning to the eternal, the Law, by means of one big leap from the present, but by preserving one's life in the present at the same time as negating it. 'In this way, the person who returns maintains throughout the process of return his accustomed—un-Jewish—mode of life, and is able to stay alive' (1998, 135).

The collapse of mastery from historian to philosopher and from objective form to the personal is also a move from idealism to experience. Idealism has invoked the objective, whereas true objectivity comes only from the thinker who works from 'his own subjective situation' (1998, 179). Idealism has disposed of the individual, and of the meaning of individual death, by its presupposed mastery of the whole. It has denied everything that sets the individual apart from the whole. Hegel, above all philosophers, 'silenced the voice which claimed possession, in a revelation, of the source of divine knowledge originating beyond reason' (Rosenzweig, 1971, 6). Hegel concluded the debate between knowledge and faith, and (Christianized) philosophy consummated and mastered the revelatory world-historical event. Thus, 'the old quarrel seems settled, heaven and earth reconciled' (1971, 7).[16]

The New Thinking

From within the collapse of the logic of mastery comes a different logic, which Rosenzweig calls 'the new thinking'. It sees revelation grounded in the living individual, separate from the categories of philosophical mastery, including the prejudice that traced everything back to an essence. A philosophy of experience will instead trace God back to God, man back to man, and the world back to the world. Against essence, Rosenzweig views this as an experience of time. 'At every moment cognition is bound to that very moment and cannot make its past not passed, or its future not coming' (1998, 197). The desire to purchase an object, the moment of buying it, and the feelings of having done so, are related to each other but are not interchangeable. The created world, the experience of revelation, and the future kingdom are also related but not interchangeable. A present deferred to a future simply obstructs the experience of the present, including in regard to Rosenzweig's illness. Reality as a whole, then, is not an essence, but a present, a past, and a future, including an eternal past and an eternal future.

It is in the experiences of these tenses of reality that God, world, and man are known, and in which they act upon one another. 'God, man, and the world reveal themselves only in their relations to one another, that is, in creation, revelation, and redemption' (1998, 198). This constitutes the new thinking of the experience of reality. True belief, says Rosenzweig, requires a relation between creation and revelation that is able to descend to the moment, each moment, eternally. Emanation does not achieve this because it posits a world able to come out from within itself. This is the same misconception found in idealism, where origin is the subjective self that, positing itself, can name everything a thing, a not-I.

The logic of the relation between creation and revelation in true belief involves two revelations. There is the revelation of creation as creation, and there is a second revelation, which 'frees the things from their state of being merely created' (1971, 161). The second revelation negates the first revelation, but preserves the first creation in this act of learning. This is revelation in time, in every moment, the revelation that is the 'vital present' (1971, 161) of creation. The creator could hide behind eternal laws of the first revelation of creation, but instead he is unconcealed in the present, in the second revelation.

When God said that what was created was not just good but 'very good' (Genesis, 1:31), this distinction between good and very good is a comparison of creation within itself, in which creation learns of itself from itself. 'This "very" heralds a supercreation within creation itself, something more than worldly within the worldly' (1971, 155). This second revelation, then, is not the positing of a reflective ego as its own essence or origin, nor is it an emanation of uninterrupted continuity. Instead, this second revelation can be understood within the logic of education as an educational relation of creation with itself, and living as the actuality of its necessary presupposition. Its logic is that creation so came into the world, that by the fact that it is, it is presupposed. We will see shortly that for Rosenzweig the truth of this presupposition, its own truth, is that it must be *for* someone. The 'very good', the KT of creation in and through an educational logic of self-revelation, is love, God's descending, God's self-sacrifice, and it is this relation in which love is formed in every individual in every present. This love is creation individualized, or moment-ized. It is also the great Nay, the learning of the creature that it is not its own origin. Without the Nay, without the second revelation, there is no love, no inner struggle of belief, no inner comprehension, no inwardness, no inner conversion; there is only a resignation to God in deeds of obedience.

The Eternal Present

In life the return and renewal of revelation is always present as the eternal in the present. Judaism and Christianity, says Rosenzweig, share this renewal for they exist in the course of world-time. They share the quest for 'an eternity that *exists*' (1998, 203). Both proceed

> from the external visible forms by whose means they wrest their eternity from time; in Judaism from the fact of the Jewish people, in Christianity from the event on which the Christian community is founded, and only through these do Law and Faith become visible. (1998, 204)

Present eternity means not a recollected actuality but rather that truth holds its moments in the 'and' of God and man and world. In this new grammar of the new thinking there is an 'and' in truth itself, that is, truth 'must be truth for someone' (1998, 206). If this is to be the *one* truth then 'it can be one only for the One, God' (1998, 206). The truth of God, man, and world for the creature 'must of necessity become manifold' (1998, 206), and this is why 'the' truth must become 'our' truth, 'realized in active life' (1998, 206). By 'our' here Rosenzweig means not just Judaism but also other roads of creation. The last words he wrote for publication in October 1929 were,

> We should realize that this "own" which we defiantly defend—though it is the secret centre of the created world—and this way from which we will not deviate—though it is the secret royal road of creation—form only part of the created world whose detours are also intended as roads. (1998, 170)

The eternal present is also in the real lives of the eternal people, who live in contrast to the (historical) nations of the world, yet also share in their ordinary time. The people of the world hold to mastery in land and soil and live for the new, but the soil always outlives its occupants, and therein their mastery collapses. The eternal people, in contrast, are a blood community. The nations separate past and future, but the fire of the *Star* burns incessantly, eternally feeding upon itself. The eternal people are wanderers in ordinary time, holding eternity in time, in custom, and in law. This people is timeless and an eternal anachronism to time itself, 'denied a life in time for the sake of life in eternity' (1971, 304).

This concept of present eternity also has an educational logic of negation and preservation. Eternity still lives in time even though its people have 'long ago been robbed of all the things in which the peoples of the world are rooted' (1971, 305). What then is the nature of revelation when it is eternity being lived in time? In the Germ Cell of the *Star of Redemption*[17] the living individual is the 'I of revelation' (1999, 55) for whom the beginning is creation and the end is redemption. Presupposition, then, 'that which is proper to God, the will of God, the work of God is entrusted to the human being' (1999, 58) so that he might do God's work. From the point of view of this world, this overturns the anticipated hierarchy, for God submits to the I, and in this relation the I makes room for God in himself. The logic of presupposition here negates what it presupposes and preserves what it negates.

Rosenzweig also finds this logic in the relation of the one people to those within whose boundaries it lives. The one people cannot 'close itself off' (Rosenzweig, 1971, 305) by creating a border within the borders of the nations. Instead it must include the former within itself so that the distinction between the one people and the nations is not drawn on a map, but lived, and lived by preserving what is negated. The eternal people must contain 'opposite poles within themselves' (1971, 306) and in doing so live the logic of KT. From outside the tent pegs of the Torah, this still appears to be a closing off of eternity from the temporal, and of the eternal people from the nations. To the logic of mastery, this looks like an exclusivity, a people within a people, outsiders in the inside. It is the challenge of this source of tension and antagonism that the logic of education rises to meet. Not the logic of mastery but the logic of education expresses this relation of eternity to its presence in time as the same logic of KT that is found in the other two Abrahamic faiths.

As noted above, Rosenzweig expresses the invitation to just such an educational logic in the various ways in which the relation of eternity and the present can be lived: in illness, and knowing that hope and the future avoid life and are only an illusory solace to life loved or revealed in the present; in letting life lead to the Torah and not the Torah to life; in Jews returning to the Law but in small steps and staying alive; in the new thinking, grounded in the real life of the people who have no land, no language, and no time of their own; in essence being deposed by a living present; in truth always being for someone; in the two revelations, one of creation and one of the concept of the universal in which creation knows itself to be creative; and in the eternal people embracing the contradictions of the nations within the tent pegs of the wandering community while at 'the same time' living within these same nations. The ambiguities of being a whole within another whole, or of being eternity within time, lies in the contingency of the very root of the eternal people. The nations 'have a face still in the making' (Rosenzweig, 1955, 81),[18] but the Jews alone among peoples 'did not originate from the womb of nature that bears nations, but . . . was led forth "a nation from the midst of another nation"'[19] (1955, 81). Even at the event of its 'beginning' it contained oppositions within itself. To be formed as a people both within and without another people is to be born with borders within itself, commending a different logic of the One alongside that of mastery, which is already compromised in such a beginning.

How then is the logic of education lived in such a way that the whole is internal to the eternal people, but still living in the world that encompasses it? Asking about essences will not do. Instead, one needs to ask about the lived life (the education) of this paradox. 'What in the investigation of essence seemed a maze of paradoxes falls into an orderly pattern in the yearly rings of life' (1971, 308). Liturgy brings eternity into the circle of the year. Listening in common to a prepared programme becomes the basis of living in common. The Sabbath, for example, 'lends reality to the year' (1971, 310) but recreates it week by week in its whole sequence. The eve of the Sabbath commemorates creation with the day of rest, but the Sabbath morning celebrates the revelation of being elect and eternal. The afternoon prayer is the prayer of redemption, the coming of the kingdom. Overall, the cycle of the Jewish year is what conjures 'eternity up into time' (1971, 328).

The Star (1921)

One last way in which Rosenzweig rehearses time and eternity concerns the relation between Judaism and Christianity and the part that both play in the *Star*.[20] If Judaism knows the eternal as life, Christianity knows it as the way. Revelation in Christianity is of the absence of God in the world and requires the turn inward for an inner reality of faith. Christianity then makes 'an epoch of the present' (1971, 338) and seeks revelation in time. The way of Christianity, says Rosenzweig, is always the mid-point between a beginning and an end which it can never unite, whereas the life of Judaism unites beginning and end in lived eternity. The Jew and the Christian cannot meet in shared contradiction because for the Jew contradiction is within God, within the eternal people, and is in 'ceaseless connection precisely with itself' (1971, 349), while in Christianity contradiction is external to God, as His Son.

Yet crucially Rosenzweig also demonstrates how Judaism and Christianity share an education in a logic of incompleteness. The rays of the Star shine out (Christianity) while its inner glow remains in the interior (Judaism). There is a cost for both here. Christianity loses contact with the One, while Judaism never gains contact with the world. But this education in incompleteness is precisely the logic that relates one to the other. Rosenzweig's new thinking of experience is not overcome here by a universal essence divorced from experience. Rather, it is joined to the modern metaphysics of experience by the shared logic of education. The Jew's presence on earth, says Rosenzweig, constantly reminds the Christian that the unity of man and God remains impossible for it. This is 'the profoundest reason for the Christian hatred of the Jew' (1971, 431). Christianity too is a constant reminder for the Jew that he lacks the way to God in history. As such, 'He has set enmity between the two for all time, and without has bound each to each . . . The truth, the whole truth, thus belongs neither to them nor to us' (1971, 415–16). Both Jew and Christian 'have but a part of the whole' (1971, 416). If Jew and Christian 'both labour at the same task' (1971, 415) it is the labour of learning of the aporia of present eternity and history for the Jew, and learning of the aporia of the present history and eternity for the Christian. For both, the logic of groundlessness is the ground of the relation of each to themselves, and of each to the other. In this education they are open to each other when each is open to the necessity of the logic of KT.

This is not a resolution or overcoming of the differences between Jew and Christian, neither for Rosenzweig nor for modern metaphysics. Rosenzweig is clear that while Judaism has paganism on the outside, Christianity has it within. Judaism reminds Christianity 'constantly' (1971, 413) that it is only ever on the way to truth, never attaining it. But the relation that Rosenzweig speaks of here is 'consummation' (1971, 418), a negation and preservation of self and other. In this consummation, redemption is present as revelation in both the eternal life of the eternal people and in the revelation of the historical life of the eternal way. For Rosenzweig eternal life and eternal way 'enter under one sign of the eternal truth' (1971, 421). Thus the 'divine visage' (1971, 418), the Star, the countenance of God, speaks of a different truth to that of reconciliation and overcoming. It speaks of an openness to truth in the experience of difficulty, and an openness to the groundlessness of self-identity, or mastery, expressed as its own truth as learning. When this openness to the groundless self is open to the groundlessness of its relation to the other, the logic of education expresses this relation not as overcoming, or merely as continual opposition, but as the logic of KT.

Judaism, Christianity, Islam: Know Thyself

Lenn E. Goodman, in his Introduction to *Hayy Ibn Yaqzan*, says that thought in religion comes alive when anthropomorphism is seen as idolatry. Such a move creates not a new God, but 'a new concept' (Ibn Tufayl, 2003, 29), one which grows and changes 'with the growth of the human mind' (2003, 29). We noted above in the *Introduction* that modern metaphysics pushes education further than it is usually encouraged to go. This is even more the case in this final chapter, which argues for an educational concept of monotheism, and of God, within the educational logic of modern metaphysics. It risks something that is impossible and unthinkable within the logic of mastery. It risks a concept of monotheism which expresses not just how the mastery underpinning each rationality of the One collapses, but also how this collapse is preserved in such a way as to re-define each faith educationally.

As we have tried to illustrate, it is a characteristic of modern metaphysics that it does not simply express the collapse of mastery or of the in-itself. On the one hand, in logical terms the negation of the in-itself means that truth is no longer in-itself but is for-another. This is the insight underpinning skepticism, relativism and doubt. On the other hand, there is also the collapse of the in-itself in a self-enlightenment where the in-itself becomes for-itself. Modern metaphysics holds all three terms within it. When the logic of the One collapses, the rationality of modern metaphysics expresses this as the in-itself being for-itself when it is for-another. It is here that the One lives in the logic of KT.

As such, modern metaphysics invites each of the three faiths to find its own internal logic of KT, and also to find this logic alive and well not only in the other faiths, but in the relation of the faiths to each other. Becoming for-another creates a relativism for each faith in relation to its others. In also becoming for-itself each faith is challenged to find a truth in the resulting aporia of its authority. What 'itself' refers to here is that which knows itself in this crisis of authority. It is an 'itself' that has been negated and preserved differently in and by what it has learned. What is the same and different here, and what is 'itself', is the concept of monotheism expressing its truth as education. One way of expressing this is in the seemingly illogical and relativistic concepts of *Islamic Judaic Christianity*, of *Judaic Islamic Christianity*, of *Christian Judaic Islam*, and its three other possible compounds.

These conceptual compounds are highly provocative for the logic of mastery. So let us approach this cautiously with a recollection and repetition of the two logics in which the rationality of the One is lost and found. Monotheism is the rational, logical culture of the identity and the mastery of the One. It has as its presupposition the ancient logic of harmony and mastery. In this logic the One has its identity as independent and unchangeable, and as the antidote to infinite regression. Finite thought cannot ground itself because of the dialectic of reason; if reason can know truth, then truth must be changed by this mediation. Since this is a vicious circle endlessly repeated, truth must of necessity be beyond such thought, beyond the compound, and beyond mediation. The One marks the end of this interminable necessity. The logic of the One must be true against the chaos and irrationality of the compound. Monotheism within the logic of mastery has its meaning precisely in this reasoning.

There are three cultural forms of this logic of mastery that fight it out between themselves to see which one resolves its difficulties, its contradictions, and its inconsistencies most convincingly, or to see which one can sustain the most rationally consistent account of itself—including those moments when earthly difficulties are superseded by the ineffable. The logic of mastery demands mastery. However, in the modern metaphysics of educational logic, the collapse of mastery is not just of one fact contradicting another. It is the collapse of the whole of the rationality of its logic. This collapse is for-itself as learning. This learning has its own logic, the logic of the ever-present vulnerability of mastery. The task accompanying this educational logic is not to overcome rival interpretations as errors of inconsistency. Instead, it is to learn of the truth of these errors as an educational necessity within the rationality of mastery, and therefore within even the logic that sustains the identity of the One.

The educational logic of the rationality of the One is experienced here as aporia. We traced the history of this aporia, in the company of Edward Booth among others, above in Part 1. We tried to show how this logic lay suppressed within the traditions, yet was ever present. Such aporia, we argued, had its actual life in the relation between the immediacy of NN and its being known or mediated. The task set by the contradictions here was for the individual to KT in relation to NN. In Part 2 we suggested that this logic of aporia becomes its own modern metaphysics, where logic is metaphysics and metaphysics is logic in the truth that is education and its work of learning. In this final chapter, now we have brought this education to the three religions to express itself as the concept—the modern metaphysics and logic—of these three religions, or of monotheism.

Judaism, Christianity, and Islam negotiate eternity, history, and intuition/revelation respectively in relation to the logic of the One, and they live this negotiation as the respective culture of each religion. The mastery of Christianity is the descent of the word made flesh. The culture of Christianity is the relation of the revelation of the eternal to its historical knowledge. The mastery of Islam as we have presented it is the descent of the One as sadness, or the truth of the One as intuitive rationality. The culture of Islam is the relation of history/tradition and the eternal to revelation. The mastery of Judaism is the descent of the One as Law. The culture of Judaism is the relation of history and historicist hermeneutics to eternity. Learning, here, is the aporia of mastery expressing itself as the culture that is each religion.

As the aporia of mastery, culture is also the presupposition of the beginning known as the question of beginning. To ask how the eternal is present (Judaism), how the One is revealed intuitively (Islam), or how God became man (Christianity) is, in each case, to posit an opposition between God and man, which requires a resolution. But the question also provokes an aporia of God and man, which offends the logic of mastery and identity. In each case, the posited beginning plays itself out as the cultures of the logic of mastery. In Judaism the beginning is form as the question of Law; in Christianity the beginning is form as the question of the historical event; and in Islam the beginning is form as the question of pure revelation. In each case a prophet answers the question in conformity with the logic that each form of question presupposes, and settles the issue of individual knowledge of the One. But this mastery is fragile and vulnerable to the very logic that supports it.

The three faiths do not just share the educational logic of the concept of monotheism. They also partake of its template of being and are living shapes of logic as the negation and preservation, or culture, of immediacy and mediation. In this sense our chosen representatives are all cultural thinkers, risking ambiguities and illogic—or education—where the logic of mastery demands resolutions. Hegel speaks of history as recollection while preserving its negation of the infinite and the eternal in repetition. Corbin speaks of the angel as revelation while preserving its negation of the individual in sadness. Al-Jabri speaks of historicist hermeneutics while preserving its negation of tradition in a dynamic textual intuition. Rosenzweig speaks of present eternity while preserving its negation of history and the nations in life spent in world-time. Each is implicated in the being of immediacy and mediation. Each expresses this ambiguity differently and of course, not to the satisfaction of the logic of mastery in the other faiths, who demand mastery according to the nature of their own presupposition of the beginning, i.e., as the event of Jesus, the revelation of Muhammad, and the Law of Moses.

But in the logic of education, the logic of presupposition is what the three cultures of presupposition have in common. Each religion is a culture of the work or the learning that relates and separates immediacy and mediation. They are all cultures of the One on earth. It is as these cultures that each can KT internally, and in relation to the other faiths, and within the concept of monotheism as a whole. Each is part of the logic and being of *monotheism: KT*. As such, as we said above, this concept can express itself as the compounds of the three faiths: the Law requires to KT in relation to history and the angel; history requires to KT in relation to the angel and eternity; and intuition requires to KT in relation to history and eternity. Monotheism here is an educational concept, negating and preserving what is different as educationally the same. The logic of education does not belong to one of them any more than to the others, nor is it more correctly expressed by one of them. They are all the thinking of the logic of one God.

As must be clear, such compounds are hugely difficult. No religion will enjoy being negated in its relation to its others, and no religion will relish its aporias of authority being preserved in a compound of Judaic Islamic Christianity, or Islamic Judaic Christianity, etc. But the educative power of the concept of monotheism is that it enables us to talk of Christian Islamic Judaism, Judaic Christian Islam, and so on, as cultures of the concept of monotheism, or as the truth of monotheism: KT. Each compound expresses relationships that empirically, geographically, politically, and doctrinally are not apparent. Each compound speaks of relationships which the logic of identity will resist. But the logic of education challenges each religion to deepen its own self-understanding regarding the logic of its masterful assumptions. As we saw in Part 1, the vulnerability of mastery carried in and by the work of KT has always been at the heart of the three religions. We do not need reminding that today this vulnerability still expresses itself in and as various forms of conflict. But perhaps we do need reminding that, as it has always done, this commends the vocation for ever deeper self-understanding. In the aporias of the mastery of each religion lie the discovery that all three religions are cultures of the concept of monotheism.

But perhaps our chosen representatives of the educational concept of monotheism harbored just such comprehensive educational visions: Hegel in an all-inclusive world spirit, Rosenzweig in his final published statement— to know the roads of others in the created world—Corbin in seeking communion between the Abrahamic faiths, and al-Jabri in the shared work of reason able to think itself. As Corbin notes, there was a time in Toledo in the 12th century when the three religions worked together in educational endeavor, and of which Menocal says,

> This was the chapter of Europe's culture when Jews, Christians and Muslims lived side by side and, despite their intractable differences and hostilities, nourished a complex culture of tolerance . . . [This culture] found expression in the often unconscious acceptance that contradictions—within oneself, as within one's culture—could be positive and productive. (Menocal, 2002, 11)

Now, in the global village in which all three again live side by side, modern metaphysics retrieves from within the acceptance of such contradictions a new, rational form of shared religious education.

Notes

1. Any such selection will look arbitrary and somewhat dubious. We have chosen these religious philosophers as representatives because each has a strong educational theme in his thinking which, in turn, lends itself to the work we wish to do with them.

2. Bringing Kierkegaard and Hegel together again here. See Chapter 7 above.
3. This takes recollection to Kierkegaard's expression, which is explored more fully in Chapter 7.
4. For example, Spinoza, who posits the unity of substance as merely 'an eternal night' (Hegel, 2011, 138).
5. Italics removed.
6. Italics removed.
7. See also Chapter 3 above.
8. The logic of mastery in Heidegger, or Heideggerian rationality, replaces the actuality of truth by the imperative continuity of Being which is its own mastery as the historical community, or mastery as being and time.
9. There are no page numbers on this version of the interview.
10. Rebecca Bligh wrote of this as Be!ing in her doctoral dissertation; see Bligh (2012).
11. Interestingly, Booth notes that the young Hegel cites Eckhart, saying 'the eye with which God sees me is the eye with which I see him; my eye and his are one' (Booth, 1989, 34–5).
12. Rosenzweig, speaking about translation, says 'We are able to translate because every language has the potentialities of every other' (Rosenzweig, 1998, 254), adding that included in the oneness of each language is the demand for communication between them.
13. Bassam Tibi, agreeing with al-Jabri that the future of Islam must be Averroist, notes that Weber's notion of disenchantment that accompanies increasing instrumentalism continues to be 'relevant to the world of Islam in the twenty-first century' (Tibi, 2009, 175).
14. On the idea of analogy or the 'as if' in Kant see Tubbs (2004, Chapter 1).
15. This refers to the time when the Days of the People began to be systematically recorded, during the reign of Abbasid Caliph al-Mansur, between AH 138–158 (CE 755–775). See al-Jabri (2011, Chapter 3).
16. It was Kierkegaard, says Rosenzweig, who 'contested the Hegelian integration of revelation into the All' (1971, 7) for he found revelation to be personal and untranslatable into general philosophical terms.
17. A letter to Rudolf Ehrenberg, November 1917.
18. From the essay 'The Builders' written in 1923.
19. Deuteronomy 4:34.
20. I will not explore Rosenzweig's critique of Islam. But in brief it is that Islam prioritizes obedience over love, lacking inner struggle and inner comprehension. Revelation, he says, has no life in the world because the God of Islam, unlike the God of Judaism and Christianity, did not enact his own self-sacrifice and descend to his creation. As such, Islam knows no second revelation, the Nay, and therefore has no concept of the universal in which universal and individual are aporetic, and which opens up the space for revelation as God and Caesar. Against this, I am exploring how Islam does share this aporia of self-mediation, and plays its part in the concept of monotheism, prioritizing immediacy—but not to the exclusion of knowledge and its eternal significance—within the self-mediation or KT of the three religions.

References

Adorno, T.W. 1973. *Negative Dialectics*. Translated by E.B. Ashton. London: RKP.

Adorno, T.W. 1974. *Minima Moralia*. Translated by E.F.N. Jephcott. London: Verso.

Adorno, T.W. and Horkheimer, M. 1979. *Dialectic of Enlightenment*. London: Verso.

Al-Ghazali, A.H.M. 1980. *Deliverance from Error*. Translated by R.J. McCarthy. Louisville: Fons Vitae.

Al-Ghazali, A.H.M. 2005. *Letter to a Disciple*. Translated by T. Mayer. Cambridge: The Islamic Texts Society.

Al-Ghazali, A.H.M. 2008. *The Alchemy of Happiness*. Translated by C. Field. www.forgottenbooks.org

Al-Jabri, M.A. 1999. *Arab-Islamic Philosophy: A Contemporary Critique*. Translated by A. Abbassi. Austin: University of Texas Press.

Al-Jabri, M.A. 2011. *The Formation of Arab Reason*. London: I.B. Tauris.

Altmann, A. 1969. *Studies in Religious Philosophy and Mysticism*. New York: Cornell University Press.

Altmann, A. and Stern, S.M. 2009. *Isaac Israeli*. Chicago: University of Chicago Press.

Aquinas, T. 1922. *Summa Theologica Part I*, volume 4. Translated by the Fathers of the English Dominican Province. London: Burns Oates and Washbourne Ltd.

Aquinas, T. 1953. *Truth (Questiones Disputatae de Veritate)*. Translated by J.V. McGlynn. Chicago: Henry Regnery Company. http://dhspriory.org/thomas/english/QDdeVer.htm

Aquinas, T. 1975a. *Summa Contra Gentiles Book 2*. Translated by J.F. Anderson. Notre Dame: Notre Dame University Press.

Aquinas, T. 1975b. *Summa Contra Gentiles Book 3 Part 1*. Translated by V.J. Bourke. Notre Dame: Notre Dame University Press.

Aristotle. 1984a. *The Complete Works of Aristotle*, volume 1. Princeton: Princeton University Press.

Aristotle. 1984b. *The Complete Works of Aristotle*, volume 2. Princeton: Princeton University Press.

Asin, M. 2008. *Islam and the Divine Comedy*. Translated by H. Sunderland. New Delhi: Goodword Books.

Augustine. 1998. *Confessions*. Translated by H. Chadwick. Oxford: Oxford University Press.

Augustine. 2002. *On the Trinity*. Translated by S. MacKenna. Cambridge: Cambridge University Press.

Avicenna. 2005. *The Metaphysics of the Healing*. Translated by M. Marmura. Provo: Brigham Young University Press.

Bainton, R. 1978. *Here I Stand: Martin Luther*. Oxford: Lion Press.

Baxter, R. 2010 [1662]. 'The Mischiefs of Self-Ignorance and the Benefits of Self-Aquaintance', in *The Practical Works of Richard Baxter: Selected Treatises*. Peabody, MA: Hendrickson Publishing. 755–861.

Bendix, R. 1977. *Max Weber: An Intellectual Portrait*. London: Methuen.

Bligh, R. 2012. 'The Réalité-Humaine of Henry Corbin.' Doctoral thesis, Goldsmiths, University of London. [Thesis]: Goldsmiths Research Online. http://research.gold.ac.uk/7800/

Boethius. 1999. *The Consolation of Philosophy*. Translated by P.G. Walsh. Oxford: Oxford University Press.

Booth, E. 1975. 'St Augustine's *notitia sui* Related to Aristotle, the Early Neo-Platonists and Hegel.' PhD, University of Cambridge. www.repository.cam.ac.uk/handle/1810/244771

Booth, E. 1977. 'St Augustine's "notitia sui" Related to Aristotle and the Early Neo-Platonists', *Augustiniana*, vol. 27, 70–132 & 364–401.

Booth, E. 1983. *Aristotelian Aporetic Ontology in Islamic and Christian Thinkers*. Cambridge: Cambridge University Press.

Booth, E. 1989. *Saint Augustine and the Western Tradition of Self-Knowing*. Villanova: Villanova University Press.

Bottomore, T. and Nisbet, R. 1978. *A History of Sociological Analysis*. London: Heinemann.

Brehier, E. 1958. *The Philosophy of Plotinus*. Translated by J. Thomas. Chicago: University of Chicago Press.

Browne, T. 1965. *Religio Medici and other writings*. London: J.M. Dent and Sons.

Burckhardt, J. 1944. *The Civilization of the Renaissance in Italy*. Oxford: Phaidon Press.

Burke, P. 1999. *The Italian Renaissance*. Cambridge: Polity Press.

Calvin, J. 1989. *Institutes of the Christian Religion*. Translated by H. Beveridge. Grand Rapids, MI: Eerdmans.

Cassirer, E. 2000. *The Individual and the Cosmos in Renaissance Philosophy*. New York: Dover Publications.

Chittick, W.C. 2015. 'The Quran and Sufism', in *The Study Quran*. Edited by Seyyed Hossein Nasr. New York: HarperOne. 1737–1749.

Cicero. 1853. 'De Legibus', in *Treatises of Cicero*. Translated by C.D. Yonge. London: Henry G. Bohn. 389–483.

Cicero. 1913. *De finibus*. Translated by H. Rackham. London: Heinemann.

Clement of Alexandria. 1867. *The Writings of Clement of Alexandria*, volume 1, Stromata I. Translated by W. Wilson. London: Hamilton and Company; Dublin: John Robertson and Company; Edinburgh: T&T Clark.

Clement of Alexandria. 1885. 'The Stromata', in *Ante-Nicene Fathers*, volume 2. Translated by W. Wilson. Buffalo, NY: Christian Literature Publishing Company. 349–469.

Collingwood, R.G. 1960. *The Idea of Nature*. Oxford: Oxford University Press.

Cooper, J.M. and Procopé, J.F. (eds.). 1995. *Seneca, Moral and Political Essays*. Cambridge: Cambridge University Press.

Copleston, F. 1962. *A History of Philosophy*, volume 2, part II. New York: Image Books.

Corbin, H. 1976. 'From Heidegger to Suhravardi: An Interview with Philippe Nemo; Biographical Post-Scriptum to a Philosophical Interview'. Translated anonymously. www.imagomundi.com.br/espiritualidade/corbin_heid_suhr.pdf Accessed 08.01.16.

Corbin, H. 1981. *The Concept of Comparative Philosophy*. Translated by P. Russell. Ipswich: Golgonooza Press.

Corbin, H. 1990. *Avicenna and the Visionary Recital*. Princeton: Princeton University Press.

Corbin, H. 1998. *Alone with the Alone*. Princeton: Princeton University Press.

Corbin, H. 2006. *The History of Islamic Philosophy*. London: Kegan Paul.

Cory, T.S. 2014. *Aquinas on Human Self-Knowledge*. Cambridge: Cambridge University Press.

Cusanus, N. 1962. *Unity and Reform: Selected Writings of Nicholas de Cusa*. Edited by J.P. Dolan. Notre Dame: University of Notre Dame Press.

Cusanus, N. 2007. *Of Learned Ignorance*. Eugene, OR: Wipf and Stock Publishers.

Cyril of Alexandria. *Against Julian*. www.tertullian.org/fathers/cyril_against_julian_02_book2.htm

Davies, J. 1876. *The Complete Poems of Sir John Davies*, volume 1. London: Chatto and Windus.

Descartes, R. 1984. *The Philosophical Writings of Descartes*, volume 2. Translated by J. Cottingham, R. Stoothoff and D. Murdoch. Cambridge: Cambridge University Press.

Descartes, R. 1985. *The Philosophical Writings of Descartes*, volume 1. Translated by J. Cottingham, R. Stoothoff and D. Murdoch. Cambridge: Cambridge University Press.

Doering, B. 2004. '*Lacrimae Rerum*—Tears at the Heart of Things: Jacques Maritain and Georges Rouault', in *Truth Matters: Essays in Honour of Jacques Maritain*. Edited by John Trapani, Jr. Washington, DC: Catholic University of America Press. 205–223.

Elyot, T. 1962. *The Book Named The Governor*. London: Dent.

Emperor, J. 1913. 'IV Oration: To the Uneducated Cynics', in *The Works of the Emperor Julian*, volume 2. Translated by W.C. Wright. Edited by T.E. Page and W.H.D. Rouse. London: Heinemann. 5–71.

Erasmus, D. 1964. *The Essential Erasmus*. Translated by J.P. Dolan. New York: New American Library.

Erasmus, D. 1971. *Praise of Folly*. London: Penguin.

Erasmus, D. 1974. *Collected Works: Correspondence: Letters 1–141 (1484–1500)*. Toronto: University of Toronto Press.

Erasmus, D. 2001. *The Adages of Erasmus*. Toronto: University of Toronto Press.

Eusebius of Caesarea. 1903. *Praeparatio Evangelica* (Preparation for the Gospel). Translated by E.H. Gifford. London: Aeterna Press.

Ficino, M. 1997. *Meditations on the Soul*. Rochester: Inner Traditions.

Gillis, D. 2015. *Reading Maimonides' Mishneh Torah*. Oxford: The Littman Library of Jewish Civilization.

Gilson, E. 2012. *The Spirit of Medieval Philosophy*. Translated by A.H.C. Downes. Notre Dame: University of Notre Dame Press.

Goethe, J.W. 1971. *Conversations with Goethe*. Translated by J.P. Eckermann. London: Dent.

Goethe, J.W. 2007. *Faust*. Translated by J.R. Williams. Ware: Wordsworth Classics of World Literature.

Goldin, J. 1955. *The Fathers According to Rabi Nathan*. New Haven: Yale University Press.

Gomez, A.M.G. 1984. *The Legend of the Laughing Philosopher and its Presence in Spanish Literature (1500–1700)*. Cordoba: Servicio de Publicaciones Universidad de Cordoba.

184 *References*

Halevi. 1964. *The Kuzari*. New York: Schocken Books.

Hamann, J.G. 1967. *Hamann's Socratic Memorabilia*. Translated by J.C. O'Flaherty. Baltimore: Johns Hopkins Press.

Haskins, C.H. 1957. *The Rise of the Universities*. Ithaca: Cornell University Press.

Hegel, G.W.F. 1967. *Philosophy of Right*. Translated by T.M. Knox. Oxford: Oxford University Press.

Hegel, G.W.F. 1969. *Science of Logic*. Translated by A.V. Miller. London: George Allen and Unwin.

Hegel, G.W.F. 1970. *Vorlesungen über die Ästhetik I. Werke 13*. Frankfurt: Suhrkamp Verlag.

Hegel, G.W.F. 1971. *Philosophy of Mind: Part Three of the Encyclopaedia of the Philosophical Sciences*. Translated by W. Wallace and A.V. Miller. Oxford: Oxford University Press.

Hegel, G.W.F. 1975. *Hegel's Logic*. Translated by W. Wallace. Oxford: Clarendon Press.

Hegel, G.W.F. 1977. *Phenomenology of Spirit*. Translated by A.V. Miller. Oxford: Oxford University Press.

Hegel, G.W.F. 1984. *Hegel: The Letters*. Translated by C. Butler and C. Seiler. Bloomington: Indiana University Press.

Hegel, G.W.F. 1985. *Introduction to the Lectures on the History of Philosophy*. Translated by T.M. Knox and A.V. Miller. Oxford: Clarendon Press.

Hegel, G.W.F. 1986. *Vorlesungen uber die Geschichte der Philosophie, I. Werke 18*. Frankfurt am Main: Suhrkamp.

Hegel, G.W.F. 1990. *Lectures on the History of Philosophy*, volume 3. Edited by R.F. Brown. Translated by R.F Brown, J.M. Stewart and H.S. Harris. Berkeley: University of California Press.

Hegel, G.W.F. 1992. *Early Theological Writings*. Translated by T.M. Knox. Philadelphia: University of Pennsylvania Press.

Hegel, G.W.F. 1998. *Hegel's Aesthetics, Lectures on Fine Art*. Translated by T.M. Knox. Oxford: Clarendon Press.

Hegel, G.W.F. 2008. *Hegel on Hamann*. Translated by L.M. Anderson. Evanston: Northwestern University Press.

Hegel, G.W.F. 2011. *Lectures on the Proofs of the Existence of God*. Translated by P.C. Hodgson. Oxford: Clarendon Press.

Hegel, G.W.F. 2013. *Lecture on the Philosophy of Religion*, volume 1. Translated by E.B. Spiers and J.B. Sanderson. New Delhi: Isah Books.

Henderson, D. 2010. 'The Coincidence of Opposites.' *Studies in Spirituality*, vol. 20, 101–13.

Henry, J. 1873. *Aeneidea*, volume 1. London: Williams and Norgate.

Heraclitus. 1987. *Fragments*. Translated by T.M. Robinson. Toronto: University of Toronto Press.

Herwaarden, J. van. 2003. *Between St. James and Erasmus*. Leiden: Brill.

Hobbes, T. 1968. *Leviathan*. London: Penguin.

Hugh of St. Victor. 1991. *The Didascalicon of Hugh of Saint Victor*. Translated by J. Taylor. New York: Columbia University Press.

Hume, D. 1984. *A Treatise of Human Nature*. London: Penguin Classics.

Ibn Arabi, M. 1976. *"Whoso Knoweth Himself . . ."*. Translated by T.H. Weir. London: Beshara Publications.

Ibn Arabi, M. 1980. *The Bezels of Wisdom*. Translated by R.W.J. Austin. Mahwah, NJ: Paulist Press.

Ibn Arabi, M. 2011. *Know Yourself.* Translated by C. Twinch. Cheltenham: Beshara Publications.

Ibn Saddiq, J. 2003. *The Microcosm of Joseph Ibn Saddiq.* Translated by J. Haberman. Madison: Fairleigh Dickinson University Press.

Ibn Tufayl. 2003. *Hayy Ibn Yaqzan.* Chicago: University of Chicago Press.

Jaeger, W. 1962. *Aristotle.* Oxford: Oxford University Press.

Johnson, A.P. 2013. *Religion and Identity in Porphyry of Tyre.* Cambridge: Cambridge University Press.

Johnson, Dr. S. 1825. *The Works of Samuel Johnson,* volume 2. Oxford: Tallboys and Wheeler.

Julian the Apostate. 1913a. 'Orations VII, "To the Cynic Heracleios"', in *The Works of the Emperor Julian,* volume 2. Translated by W.C. Wright. Edited by T.E. Page and W.H.D. Rouse. London: William Heinemann. 73–166.

Julian the Apostate. 1913b. 'Orations IV, "To the Uneducated Cynics"', in *The Works of the Emperor Julian,* volume 2. Translated by W.C. Wright. New York: Macmillan. 5–72.

Kant, I. 1956. *The Critique of Practical Reason.* Translated by L.W. Beck. New York: Macmillan.

Kant, I. 1996. *The Metaphysics of Morals.* Translated by M. Gregor. Cambridge: Cambridge University Press.

Keith, A.L. 1922. 'A Vergilian Line', *The Classical Journal,* vol. 17, no. 7, April, 398–402.

Kierkegaard, S. 1938. *The Journals of Soren Kierkegaard.* Translated by A. Dru. London: Oxford University Press.

Kierkegaard, S. 1954. *Fear and Trembling & the Sickness unto Death.* Translated by W. Lowrie. Princeton: Princeton University Press.

Kierkegaard, S. 1967. *The Concept of Dread.* Translated by W. Lowrie. Princeton: Princeton University Press.

Kierkegaard, S. 1968. *Concluding Unscientific Postscript.* Translated by D.F. Swenson and W. Lowrie. Princeton: Princeton University Press.

Kierkegaard, S. 1980. *The Concept of Anxiety.* Translated by R. Thomte. Princeton: Princeton University Press.

Kierkegaard, S. 1983. *Fear and Trembling/Repetition.* Translated by H.V. Hong and E.H. Hong. Princeton: Princeton University Press.

Kierkegaard, S. 1985. *Philosophical Fragments/Johannes Climacus.* Translated by H.V. Hong and E.H. Hong. Princeton: Princeton University Press.

Kierkegaard, S. 1987. *Either/Or II.* Translated by H.V. Hong and E.H. Hong. Princeton: Princeton University Press.

Kierkegaard, S. 1990. *Eighteen Upbuilding Discourses.* Translated by H.V. Hong and E.H. Hong. Princeton: Princeton University Press.

Kierkegaard, S. 1992. *Concluding Unscientific Postscript.* Translated by H.V. Hong and E.H. Hong. Princeton: Princeton University Press.

Kierkegaard, S. 1997. *Christian Discourses/The Crisis and the Crisis in the Life of an Actress.* Translated by H.V. Hong and E.H Hong. Princeton: Princeton University Press.

Kierkegaard, S. 2003. *The Soul Of Kierkegaard.* Edited by Alexander Dru. Mineola, NY: Dover Publications.

Koran. 2003. Translated by N.J. Dawood. London: Penguin Classics.

Kozicki, H. 1986. 'Tennyson's "Tears, Idle Tears": The Case for Violet', *Victorian Poetry,* vol. 24, no. 2, Summer, 99–113.

Kristeller, P.O. 2015. *Philosophy of Marsilio Ficino.* Translated by V. Conart. Glouces- ter, MA: Peter Smith; New Delhi: Facsimile Publisher.

Lambert, R.T. 2007. *Self Knowledge in Thomas Aquinas.* Bloomington: Author House.

Locke, J. 2004. *An Essay Concerning Human Understanding.* London: Penguin.

Lucian. 1905. *The Works of Lucian Samosata.* Translated by H.W. Fowler and F.G. Fowler. Oxford: Clarendon Press.

Luther, M. 1989. *Martin Luther's Basic Theological Writings.* Edited by T.F. Lull. Minneapolis: Fortress Press.

Luther, M. 2010. *The Sermons of Martin Luther*, volume 2. Grand Rapids, MI: Baker Book House.

Luther, M. (ed.). 1893. *Theologica Germanica.* Translated by S. Winkworth. Cre- ateSpace Independent Publishing.

Lüthy, C. 2000. 'The Fourfold Democritus on the Shape of Early Modern Science', *Isis*, vol. 91, no. 3, 443–79.

Lutz, C.E. 1954. 'Democritus and Heraclitus', *The Classical Journal*, vol. 49, no. 7, 309–14.

Maimonides, M. 1963. *The Guide of the Perplexed*, volume 1. Translated by S. Pines. Chicago: University of Chicago Press.

Maimonides, M. 1981. *The Book of Knowledge.* Translated by H.M. Russell and R.J. Weinberg. Edinburgh: The Royal College of Physicians of Edinburgh.

Maimonides, M. 1983. *Ethical Writings.* Edited and Translated by R.L. Weiss and C. Butterworth. New York: Dover Publications.

Martin, J.J. 2004. 'Myths of Renaissance Individualism', in *A Companion to the Worlds of the Renaissance.* Edited by G. Ruggiero. Oxford: Blackwell. 208–224.

Mason, J. 2012. *A Treatise on Self-Knowledge.* London: Forgotten Books.

Mathews, G. 2005. *Augustine.* Oxford: Wiley-Blackwell.

Mayer, J.P. 1944. *Max Weber and German Politics.* London: Faber and Faber.

Menander. 1921. *Menander, the Principal Fragments.* Translated by F.G. Allinson. https://archive.org/details/menanderprincipa00menauoft

Menocal, M.R. 1987. *The Arabic Role in Medieval Literary History.* Philadelphia: University of Pennsylvania Press.

Menocal, M.R. 2002. *The Ornament of the World.* New York: Little, Brown and Company.

Montaigne, M. de 2003a. *The Complete Essays.* Translated by M.A. Screech. London: Penguin.

Montaigne, M. de 2003b. *Apology for Raymond Sebond.* Translated by R. Ariew and M. Grene. Indianapolis: Hackett Publishing Company.

Mure, G.R.G. 1965. *The Philosophy of Hegel.* Oxford: Oxford University Press.

Nauert, C.G. 2006. *Humanism and the Culture of Renaissance Europe.* Cambridge: Cambridge University Press.

Netton, I.R. 1994. *Allah Transcendent.* Richmond: Curzon Books.

Nietzsche, F. 1982. *The Portable Nietzsche.* New York: Viking Penguin.

Origen. 1979. *Origen.* Translated by R.A. Greer. Mahwah, NJ: Paulist Press.

Ovid, P. 1986. *Metamorphosis.* Translated by A.D. Melville. Oxford: Oxford World Classics.

Panofsky, E. 2005. *The Life and Art of Albrecht Dürer.* Princeton: Princeton Uni- versity Press.

Pascal, B. 1966. *Pensées.* Translated by A.J. Krailsheimer. London: Penguin.

Philo Judaeus. 1993. *The Works of Philo*. Translated by C.D. Yonge. Peabody, MA: Hendrickson Publishers.

Plato. 1966. *Plato in Twelve Volumes*, volume 7. Translated by R.G. Bury. Cambridge, MA: Harvard University Press; London: William Heinemann Ltd. www.perseus. tufts.edu/hopper/text?doc=Perseus%3Atext%3A1999.01.0164%3Aletter%3D2% 3Asection%3D312e

Plato. 1997. *Plato: Complete Works*. Edited by J.M. Cooper. Indianapolis: Hackett Publishing Company.

Plotinus. 1991. *The Enneads*. Translated by S. MacKenna. London: Penguin.

Plutarch. 1898. *Morals: Ethical Essays*. Translated by R.R. Shilleto. London: George Bell and Sons. 153–201.

Pope, A. 1994. *Essay on Man & Other Poems*. New York: Dover Publications.

Porphyry. 1910. *Porphyry the Philosopher to His Wife Marcella*. Translated by A. Zimmern. London: The Priory Press.

Porter, R. 1997. *Rewriting the Self*. London: Routledge.

Proctor, R. 1998. *Defining the Humanities*. Bloomington: Indiana University Press.

Pyle, C. 1997. *Milan and Lombardy in the Renaissance: Essays in Cultural History*. Rome: La Fenice.

Quinn, S. 1999. *Why Virgil? A Collection of Interpretations*. Mundelein, IL: Bolchazy-Carducci.

Richard of Saint Victor. 1979. *The Twelve Patriarchs, the Mystical Ark, Book Three of the Trinity*. Translated by G.A. Zinn. New York: Paulist Press.

Rose, G. 1992. *The Broken Middle*. Oxford: Blackwell.

Rosenzweig, F. 1955. *On Jewish Learning*. Translated by W. Wolf and N.N. Glatzer. New York: Schocken Books.

Rosenzweig, F. 1971. *The Star of Redemption*. Translated by W. Hallo. London: Routledge and Kegan Paul.

Rosenzweig, F. 1998. *Franz Rosenzweig, His Life and Thought*. Edited by N. Glatzer. Indianapolis: Hackett Publishing Company.

Rosenzweig, F. 1999. *Franz Rosenzweig's "The New Thinking"*. Translated by A. Udoff and B.E. Galli. Syracuse: Syracuse University Press.

Rousseau, J.J. 1973. *The Social Contract and Discourses*. Translated by G.D.H. Cole. London: Dent.

Rousseau, J.J. 1979. *The Indispensable Rousseau*. Edited by J.H. Mason. London: Quartet Books.

Rousseau, J.J. 1993. *Emile*. Translated by B. Foxley. London: Dent.

Seneca. 1925. *Moral Epistles*, volume 1. Translated by R.M. Gummere. London: Heinemann.

Seneca. 1961. *Tragedies II*. Translated by F.J. Miller. London: Heinemann. www. theoi.com/Text/SenecaThyestes.html

Seneca. 1968. *The Stoic Philosophy of Seneca*. Translated by M. Hadas. New York: Norton and Company.

Seneca. 2010. *Natural Questions*. Translated by H.M. Hine. Chicago: University of Chicago Press.

Shaftesbury, A.A.C. 1999. *Characteristics of Men, Manners, Opinions, Times*. Edited by L. Klein. Cambridge: Cambridge University Press.

Sterne, L. 1973. *The Sermons of Mr Yorick*. Cheadle: Carcarnet Press.

Stewart, J. 2003. *Kierkegaard's Relations to Hegel Reconsidered*. Cambridge: Cambridge University Press.

Stewart, Z. 1958. 'Democritus and the Cynics', *Harvard Studies in Classical Philosophy*, vol. 63, 179–91.

Swift, J. 1898. *The Prose Works of Jonathan Swift*. London: George Bell and Sons.

Thamaturgus, G. 1920. *Panegyrica, Address to Origen*. Translated by W. Metcalfe. London: Macmillan.

Thompson, J. 1974. *Kierkegaard*. London: Victor Gollancz Ltd.

Tibi, B. 2009. *Islam's Predicament with Modernity*. London: Routledge.

Tubbs, N. 2004. *Philosophy's Higher Education*. Dordrecht: Kluwer.

Tubbs, N. 2005. *Philosophy of the Teacher*. Oxford: Blackwell.

Tubbs, N. 2008. *Education in Hegel*. London: Continuum.

Tubbs, N. 2009. *History of Western Philosophy*. Basingstoke: Palgrave Macmillan.

Tubbs, N. 2014. *Philosophy and Modern Liberal Arts Education*. Basingstoke: PalgraveMacmillan.

Van Gogh, V. 1996. *The Letters of Vincent Van Gogh*. Edited by R. de Leeuw. Translated by A. Pomerans. London: Penguin Books.

Vico, G. 1993. *On Humanistic Education (Six Inaugural Orations 1699–1707)*. Translated by G.A. Pinton and A.W. Shippee. Ithaca: Cornell University Press.

Virgil. 2002. *Aeneid*. Translated by M. Oakley. Oxford: Wordsworth Classics.

Walther, I. 2000. *Van Gogh*. Köln: Taschen.

Weber, M. 1930. *The Protestant Ethic and the Spirit of Capitalism*. Translated by Talcott Parsons. London: George Allen and Unwin.

Weber, M. 1970. *From Max Weber: Essays in Sociology*. Edited by H.H. Gerth and C. Wright Mills. London: RKP.

Weber, M. 1978. *Economy and Society*, volume 1. Edited by G. Roth and C. Wittich. Berkeley: University of California Press.

Wharton, D. 2008. 'Sunt Lacrimae Rerum: An Explanation in Meaning', *The Classical Journal*, vol. 103, no. 3, February–March, 258–79.

Wilkins, E. 2013. *"Know Thyself" in Greek and Latin Literature*. New Delhi: Isher Books.

Wilkins, E. 2014. *Delphic Maxims in Literature*. Whitefish, MT: Kessinger Legacy Reprints.

Wind, E. 1937–8. 'The Christian Democritus', *Journal of the Warburg Institute*, vol. 1, 180–2.

Xenophon. 1897. *The Memorabilia*. Translated by H.G. Dakyns. London: Macmillan and Company.

Xenophon. 2009. *Cyropaedia: The Education of Cyrus*. Translated by H.G. Dakyns. www.gutenberg.org/files/2085/2085-h/2085-h.htm

Zizek, S. 2015. 'Slavoj Zizek: A Modest Rejoinder', *New Statesman*, 27th March.

Index